The Limited Liability Company under German Law (the GmbH)

Dr Alexander Schröder-Frerkes
Dr Armin Göhring

Globe Law and Business
GLP
German Law Publishers

Authors
Dr Alexander Schröder-Frerkes
Dr Armin Göhring

Managing director
Sian O'Neill

The Limited Liability Company under German Law (the GmbH)
is published by

Globe Law and Business Ltd
3 Mylor Close
Horsell
Woking
Surrey GU21 4DD
United Kingdom
Tel: +44 20 3745 4770
www.globelawandbusiness.com

The Limited Liability Company under German Law (the GmbH)

ISBN 9781787423626
EPUB ISBN 9781787423633
Adobe PDF ISBN 9781787423640
Mobi ISBN 9781787423657

Table of contents

Preface

Welcome to *The Limited Liability Company under German Law (the GmbH)*. With over one million entities, by far the most common and, thus, the most important legal company form used in Germany is the limited liability company (the GmbH). The GmbH has a number of advantages: it limits shareholder liability, it can be adapted to the specific needs of shareholders and their business model, and it provides a platform for small businesses as well as for holding companies for international groups and not-for-profit organisations. Given its ample scope, and the fact that it can be very easily established and requires minimal administrative effort, the GmbH is also the most frequent legal form used by foreign investors in Germany.

Against this backdrop, this book explores the most relevant legal issues and topics for investors seeking to establish or acquire a GmbH in Germany and is aimed at readers with a legal background, as well as those without, focusing (where relevant) on the most important legal discussions without losing itself in lengthy academic argument.

In addition to providing an overview of the requirements of the formation process, this book demonstrates the GmbH's inherent flexibility as well as helping legal practitioners (based in Germany and elsewhere) to decide on whether a GmbH is most suitable for their needs.

We would like to address a special thank you note to Lucinda Bowles for her great efforts in proofreading the volume and providing helpful advice in making the book easier to read.

Any comments or proposals are welcome. You may contact the authors via the contact details set out in the 'About the authors' section at the back of the book.

Dr Alexander Schröder-Frerkes
Dr Armin Göhring

I. Introduction

1. Basic concepts underlying the GmbH

The GmbH is a limited liability company (*Gesellschaft mit beschränkter Haftung*) under German law, being a separate legal entity distinct from its shareholders. A GmbH may have one or several shareholders, and shareholders in a GmbH may either be an individual or another legal entity. The total number of shareholders is not limited. As a separate and distinct legal entity, the GmbH itself and not its shareholders holds title to its assets, is bound by agreements it enters into, is the partner acting in legal relationships of any kind, and is the entity which may sue other parties or entities or be sued itself in court.[1] The GmbH is also entitled to acquire ownership of real property and other legal rights in real property.

Regarding its liabilities, only the GmbH itself is liable for the fulfilment of its obligations towards third parties.[2] The shareholders in a GmbH are generally not liable towards third parties for the fulfilment of the obligations of the GmbH. There are, however, some exceptions to this principle within German case law (for details see Section 65 *et seq.* below).

A GmbH under German law is established upon its registration in the commercial register.[3] All GmbHs have two mandatory corporate bodies: (i) the managing directors (*Geschäftsführer*), and (ii) the shareholders' meeting (*Gesellschafterversammlung*). According to statutory law, the shareholders' meeting is the principal corporate body which reaches decisions (passes resolutions) on fundamental corporate matters such as, for example, changes to the articles of association, an increase or decrease in the share capital, the approval of financial statements, and the nomination or removal of the managing directors etc. The GmbH is represented by one or several managing directors who also manage the daily business

---

1 *Gesetz betreffend die Gesellschaft mit beschränkter Haftung* (GmbHG) (Act on Limited Liability Companies) 1892, s13, para. 1 (FRG).

2 *Gesetz betreffend die Gesellschaft mit beschränkter Haftung* (GmbHG) (Act on Limited Liability Companies) 1892, s13, para. 2 (FRG).

3 *Gesetz betreffend die Gesellschaft mit beschränkter Haftung* (GmbHG) (Act on Limited Liability Companies) 1892, s11, para. 1 (FRG).

of the company. In contrast to many other countries, in Germany the managing directors all have an executive function and none of them can take on a supervisory role in overseeing the other managers or the company as a whole. The supervision of the managing directors is the task of the shareholders' meeting or of a supervisory board. Such a supervisory board may be established at any time on a voluntary basis unless a supervisory board is mandatorily required under certain Co-Determination laws.[4] Speaking very generally, the Co-Determination laws prescribe the appointment of a supervisory board if the number of employees of the company or associated group companies goes beyond a certain threshold, in which case, the employees must be mandatorily represented within the supervisory board, either with a quota of one third or 50% (half of the seats on the board).

In order to establish a GmbH a minimum share capital of at least €25,000 is required.[5]

The Act on Limited Liability Companies (GmbHG) sets out the basic rules that apply to a GmbH. Since most of the provisions of the Act on Limited Liability Companies are flexible regulations, to a large extent the shareholders may establish their own (tailor-made) set of rules in the articles of association.

2. Other important legal forms of entities in Germany

Other forms of legal entity which are often used for conducting business in Germany are the stock corporation (*Aktiengesellschaft* – AG), the general partnership (*offene Handelsgesellschaft* – OHG), the limited partnership (*Kommanditgesellschaft* – KG) and limited partnerships with a GmbH as the (sole) general partner (GmbH & Co. KG).

A stock corporation under German law (AG) is a separate legal entity distinct from its shareholders which is itself responsible for the fulfilment of its obligations. In other words, the corporate veil protects the shareholders from personal liability towards third parties as is the case where the GmbH is concerned. An AG has three mandatory corporate bodies: (i) the board of directors (*Vorstand*), (ii) the shareholders' meeting (*Hauptversammlung*), and (iii) the supervisory board (*Aufsichtsrat*). The statutory rules on stock corporations (in particular the German Stock Corporation Act – AktG) are in most

4 For details see Sections 141–156.

5 For the exception with regard to the so-called *Unternehmergesellschaft*, see Section 34.

cases mandatory laws, which makes it more difficult to establish a 'tailor-made' company designed to meet the special requirements of the shareholders. This makes the GmbH the simpler form for doing business. If, however, the company is supposed to be listed on the stock exchange, this is only possible with an AG, as a GmbH does not issue shares to be traded on the stock exchange. To establish a stock corporation, a minimum stated capital of €50,000 is required.

In a general partnership, all shareholders are jointly and severally liable for any and all obligations of the general partnership, even though the general partnership is a separate legal entity in its own right. In other words, a debtor of a general partnership may sue the partnership itself along with any of its shareholders in full for the fulfilment of its obligations. The general partners are accessorily liable for the liabilities of the partnership. This makes this type of company rather uncommon as an investment vehicle for foreign entities in Germany. The same applies to limited partnerships. In these kinds of companies, the liability of at least one shareholder is limited to the contribution he or she has undertaken to pay – as set down in the articles of association and entered in the commercial register (*Kommanditeinlage*).[6] Additionally, a limited partnership requires at least one general partner whose liability towards a third party is unrestricted as is the case in a general partnership. Like the general partnership, the limited partnership is therefore not the preferred vehicle for foreign investments in Germany. Moreover, both kinds of partnerships are associated with tax disadvantages and may give rise to complicated tax compliance issues compared with a corporation such as a GmbH.

In the case of a GmbH & Co. KG, it is possible to combine a limited partnership (KG) with a GmbH. In principle, such a company is a limited partnership. The GmbH is the general partner, which is fully liable towards the debtors of the GmbH & Co. KG. However, since the liability of a GmbH itself is limited to its assets and not the assets of its shareholders, the liability of the general partner in a GmbH & Co. KG is as a matter of fact limited to the assets of the GmbH. Aside from this, the (limited) liability of the limited partner in a KG remains unaffected. There is no minimum amount which the limited partner must undertake to contribute and thus his or her liability in the KG may be as low as just €1.00. A GmbH & Co. KG is a company form which is typically chosen when the founders

6 *Handelsgesetzbuch* (HGB) (German Commercial Code) 1897, s171, para. 1 (FRG).

wish to avoid the applicability of certain Co-Determination laws or if potential company founders wish to attract a large number of investors. The investors typically acquire the status of a limited partner, thus bypassing the strict regulations which apply to a stock corporation (so-called capital investment entities – *Kapitalanlagegesellschaften*).

3. Advantages of the GmbH

A GmbH under German law combines two important advantages: adaptability and limited liability. As for adaptability, the body of regulations applying to a GmbH is much more flexible than in the case of a stock corporation (*Aktiengesellschaft*). The articles of association of a GmbH may be adapted to the particular needs and requirements of the shareholders, especially regarding the division of powers between the shareholders' meeting and the managing directors. The Act on Limited Liability Companies also allows the establishment of additional corporate bodies such as a supervisory or advisory board.

Finally, as a corporation, the GmbH protects its shareholders from being personally liable for the obligations of the corporation. With very few exceptions,[7] creditors may only have recourse to the assets of the GmbH itself as a means of satisfying the company's obligations. In contrast, the partners of a general partnership or a limited partnership may be held personally liable for the obligations of their entities. The GmbH thus combines adaptability to the needs of the shareholders with the protection of a corporate veil. These two elements make the GmbH by far the most successful legal form under German law.

4. Statistics

In the year 2015, the total number of GmbH registrations in Germany amounted to 529,268, compared with approximately 7,862 stock corporations (AG).[8] The second most popular legal form, with numbers far below those recorded for the GmbH, is the limited partnership, with approximately 240,000 registrations. These figures clearly show that the GmbH is by far the most popular legal form for business and non-commercial purposes in Germany.

---

7 For details on these exceptions, see Sections 65–70.

8 *Statistisches Bundesamt für das Jahr* 2015. Approximately 40% of all exisiting companies.

II. Company formation: establishing a new GmbH

5. The regular GmbH and the *Unternehmergesellschaft* in general

Under German law, there are two basic types of limited liability companies. The 'regular' GmbH is a company which has a stated share capital of at least €25,000.[1] In addition, by means of The German Act to Modernise the Law Governing GmbHs and Combat Abuses (*Gesetz zur Modernisierung des GmbH-Rechts und zur Bekämpfung von Missbräuchen* – MoMiG), effective as of 1 November 2008, the so-called *Unternehmergesellschaft (haftungsbeschränkt)* (entrepreneurial company with limited liability) was established as a (sub) form of GmbH. The *Unternehmergesellschaft* is an entity to which all regulations of the Act on Limited Liability Companies apply, with the exception of certain regulations relating to share capital. Further details will be outlined in Section 34.

A. Pre-registration phases

6. General

A GmbH is only effectively established once it is registered in the relevant commercial register.[2] Prior to registration, a distinction can be drawn between two different phases in the company creation process: the phase between the decision of the shareholders to establish a GmbH and the notarisation of the articles of association (pre-formation phase), and the stage between the notarisation of the articles of association and the entry of the GmbH into the commercial register (pre-registration phase).

---

1 *Gesetz betreffend die Gesellschaft mit beschränkter Haftung* (GmbHG) (Act on Limited Liability Companies) 1892, s5, para. 1 (FRG).

2 *Gesetz betreffend die Gesellschaft mit beschränkter Haftung* (GmbHG) (Act on Limited Liability Companies) 1892, s11, para. 1 (FRG).

7. Pre-formation phase (*Vorgründungsgesellschaft*)

In the period prior to the notarisation of the articles of association, the GmbH does not yet exist as a legal entity. At this point in time, the existing entity is a *Vorgründungsgesellschaft*. The *Vorgründungsgesellschaft* either takes the legal form of a civil law association under the German Civil Code (*Gesellschaft bürgerlichen Rechts* – GbR) or of a general partnership, depending on the scope of the activities and the purpose the entity is pursuing (aside from establishing a GmbH). During this phase, neither the representation of the entity nor the liability of the shareholders are governed by the principles pursuant to a GmbH, but by those pertaining to a civil law association or a general partnership. In other words, the shareholders are jointly and severally liable for any and all obligations which arise in the company's name at this point in time. The company is managed and represented jointly by all shareholders, in so far as there is no agreement to the contrary already existing at this point in time. If, at a later point in time, the GmbH is finally registered, the rights and obligations created by the *Vorgründungsgesellschaft* are not transferred automatically by law to the GmbH; the obligations arising during this phase remain unaffected and must be fulfilled by the still existing *Vorgründungsgesellschaft* or its shareholders respectively. However, the liabilities may be transferred to the GmbH with the consent of the creditors. The same applies to the rights created by the *Vorgründungsgesellschaft*, wherein third-party consent may be required here too.

8. Pre-registration phase (*Vor-GmbH*)

The so-called *Vor-GmbH* or *GmbH in Gründung* (iGr) exists as an individual legal entity in the period of time between the notarisation of the articles of association and the registration of the company in the commercial register. The *Vor-GmbH* is already governed by the Act on Limited Liability Companies (GmbHG) and the articles of association in so far as they do not call for a registration of the company. The relationship between the managing directors and the shareholders' meeting is thus determined by the articles of association and, in addition, the Act on Limited Liability Companies. The managing directors are entitled to represent the *Vor-GmbH* *vis-à-vis* third parties. However, their powers of representation are limited to purposes relating to the formation of the company and do not extend beyond these purposes. Typical activities pertaining to the company formation are, for example, the opening of bank accounts, the acquisition of real property, the leasing of office space, etc. If the parties wish to contribute (*einbringen*) a company to the GmbH by way of a contribution in kind, the scope of authority of the managing directors also includes the right to continue to run such a company, since it may not be left unmanaged whilst waiting for the registration of the GmbH to finally be concluded.

The most important difference compared with a fully registered GmbH, however, is in terms of liability towards third parties. Since a *Vor-GmbH* is not yet registered in the commercial register and the GmbH is thus not yet fully founded, liability towards third parties cannot be limited to the assets of the GmbH. According to s11, para. 2 of the Act on Limited Liability Companies, all persons acting on behalf of the GmbH prior to its registration are jointly and severally liable for any obligations resulting therefrom. Such a person is typically the (designated) managing director, but may also be a shareholder or a third person acting in the capacity of a managing director when representing the company externally. Additionally, all shareholders are personally liable without limitation towards the GmbH itself in the event that, at the time of the entry into the commercial register, the value of the assets of the GmbH fails to match the amount of the stated share capital.[3] A use of the assets (*Verkehrsgeschäft*) is, however, permitted, for instance if the cash contributions are used to buy office equipment. In other words, the contributions must exist in terms of their value but the contributions themselves do not have to exist. This shareholder liability continues to apply after the registration, in the event that negative equity is still present.

The GmbH is fully established at the point of its registration in the commercial register. By law, all rights and obligations of the *Vor-GmbH* are transferred to the GmbH. The *Vor-GmbH* and the GmbH are identical legal entities, with the GmbH being the legal successor of the *Vor-GmbH*. In addition, the liability of the persons acting on behalf of the company prior to its registration ceases according to section 11, paragraph 2 of the Act on Limited Liability Companies.

B. Formation by contributions

9. Formation by contributions in cash

Typically, a GmbH is established by way of a contribution of the share capital in cash. In a regular GmbH, the stated share capital

---

3 So called '*Verlustdeckungshaftung*'.

required to establish the company amounts to €25,000. In the case of the *Unternehmergesellschaft*, the stated share capital may be lower, with a minimum stated share capital of €1.00 being required. In both cases, the entry in the commercial register may only be successfully filed if at least one quarter of each subscribed share has been contributed and the total of all contributed shares amounts to a minimum of half of the stated share capital.[4] Since the Act to Modernise the Law Governing GmbHs and Combat Abuses came into force, the same rules apply if the GmbH is only established by one individual shareholder. The provision of collateral is no longer required. If there are any funds outstanding with regard to the stated share capital, the managing director is responsible for demanding that these amounts are paid.

10. Formation by contributions in kind

In the articles of association, the shareholders of a GmbH may also agree to raise the stated share capital not by contributions in cash but by contributions in kind.[5] An *Unternehmergersellschaft*, however, may not be established by contributions in kind. The object of the contribution and the amount of the share capital to be raised by a contribution in kind are to be determined in the articles of association. Furthermore, in a special report (*Sachgründungsbericht*), the shareholders must outline the relevant circumstances which explain why the value of the contribution in kind matches at least the value of the subscribed share capital.[6] If an entire company or enterprise is to be contributed to the GmbH as a contribution in kind, the financial statements for the last two business years must also be submitted.

The contribution in kind may consist of any assets which have a determinable economic value. The assets may be tangible or intangible, movable or immovable. They may also include claims, intellectual property rights and real estate. The mere provision of services by a shareholder, however, is not acceptable as a contribution. The uncertainty surrounding the value of the services in question and the matter of whether or not they are provided is

4 *Gesetz betreffend die Gesellschaft mit beschränkter Haftung* (GmbHG) (Act on Limited Liability Companies) 1892, s7, para. 2, sentence 1 (FRG).

5 *Gesetz betreffend die Gesellschaft mit beschränkter Haftung* (GmbHG) (Act on Limited Liability Companies) 1892, s5, para. 4 (FRG).

6 *Gesetz betreffend die Gesellschaft mit beschränkter Haftung* (GmbHG) (Act on Limited Liability Companies) 1892, s5, para. 4 (FRG).

deemed to disqualify them as an appropriate means of raising the subscribed capital.

Prior to filing of the registration for the GmbH, the contribution in kind must be effected in full and the asset must be transferred to the GmbH.[7]

If the value of the contribution in kind does not amount to the value of the assumed share capital when the GmbH registration is filed, the shareholder must pay the difference in cash. Such a claim on the part of the company will be barred by the statute of limitations after a ten-year period following the entry of the company into the commercial register.[8] Only when all of these requirements are satisfied is the contribution in kind considered duly fulfilled and the respective share capital fully contributed.

11. Combined contributions

Combined contributions to raise the share capital are generally allowed and may take two different forms. A shareholder may effect the contribution in kind by transferring assets to the company whose value exceeds the amount of the share capital he or she has subscribed in the articles of association. In this context, the law refers to a '*gemischte Sacheinlage*' (mixed contribution in kind). The shareholder is entitled to receive compensation for the value of the transferred asset which exceeds the share capital he or she has undertaken to contribute. This compensation may take various forms, for example, the granting of a corresponding loan or the provision of services by the GmbH. Such forms of contribution in kind must also be in compliance with the rules as set out in Section 10.

A combined contribution may also refer to the obligation to contribute the share capital being partly satisfied by a contribution in cash and partly by a contribution in kind. In such cases, the respective requirements regarding contributions in cash and in kind as set out in the previous sections must be satisfied in order for the share capital to be fully and duly contributed. Aside from this, there are no special regulations which must be observed.

---

7 *Gesetz betreffend die Gesellschaft mit beschränkter Haftung* (GmbHG) (Act on Limited Liability Companies), 1892, s7, para. 3 (FRG).

8 *Gesetz betreffend die Gesellschaft mit beschränkter Haftung* (GmbHG) (Act on Limited Liability Companies), 1892, s9, para. 2 (FRG).

C. Articles of association

12. General remark

The Act on Limited Liability Companies stipulates certain mandatory provisions which must be contained in the articles of association. If the articles fail to satisfy these minimum requirements, the company will not be entered into the commercial register. In practice, the notary would refuse to notarise such articles of association and would instead first ensure that they at least satisfy the legally prescribed minimum in terms of their content. We will explain such mandatory provisions in further detail below. In addition, we shall briefly outline some provisions which can typically be found in the articles of a GmbH.

13. Mandatory provisions

The mandatory provisions pertaining to the articles of association as set out under section 3, paragraph 1 GmbH are explained in the following subsections.

14. Mandatory provisions: company name

The name of the company must contain the designation '*Gesellschaft mit beschränkter Haftung*' or a generally understandable abbreviation thereof, such as 'GmbH'.[9] Apart from this restriction, the name of the company may be freely chosen. Names can be entirely fictitious.

However, when selecting the name of the company certain limitations which apply to all trading companies must be observed. First, the name must identify the company appropriately and distinguish it from any other company.[10] Secondly, the name of the company may not contain any element which might mislead people as to the true business situation involved.[11]

Finally, the company name must be distinct from other company names which are already registered in the commercial register of the same community.[12]

---

9 *Gesetz betreffend die Gesellschaft mit beschränkter Haftung* (GmbHG) (Act on Limited Liability Companies) 1892, s4 (FRG).

10 *Handelsgesetzbuch* (HGB) (Commercial Code) 1897, s18, para. 1 (FRG).

11 *Handelsgesetzbuch* (HGB) (Commercial Code) 1897, s18, para. 2 (FRG).

12 *Handelsgesetzbuch* (HGB) (Commercial Code) 1897, s30, para. 1 (FRG).

15. Mandatory provisions: place of business

The articles must state the company's place of business.[13] The company's place of business is the domestic location as indicated in the articles of association.[14] This means that the business address in Germany may be freely chosen, even if the company does not have any production site or administration in this country. Thus, even when it is only active abroad, the GmbH may have its formal place of business in Germany. Before the Act to Modernise the Law Governing GmbHs and Combat Abuses came into force, a German GmbH could only choose as its place of business the location where it either had its administrative headquarters or maintained business premises.

16. Mandatory provisions: business purpose

The articles must furthermore state the purpose of the business.[15] A GmbH may be set up for any legally permissible purpose,[16] whether it be economic, political, religious, athletic or otherwise.

Some business activities may require the prior consent of the authorities, examples here are for instance banking and the activities of other credit institutions, insurance companies, weapons manufacturing and similar enterprises. Apart from these few exceptions, general permission or a licence to establish a GmbH and to conduct its business is not required in Germany. The company only needs to be registered with the trade tax office (*Gewerbesteueramt*) for tax purposes.

17. Mandatory provisions: share capital (*Stammkapital*)

Unless a GmbH is formed as an *Unternehmergesellschaft*, its share capital must amount to at least €25,000, which must be set out in the articles of association.[17]

---

13 *Gesetz betreffend die Gesellschaft mit beschränkter Haftung* (GmbHG) (Act on Limited Liability Companies) 1892, s3, para. 1, no. 1 (FRG).

14 *Gesetz betreffend die Gesellschaft mit beschränkter Haftung* (GmbHG) (Act on Limited Liability Companies) 1892, s4a (FRG).

15 *Gesetz betreffend die Gesellschaft mit beschränkter Haftung* (GmbHG) (Act on Limited Liability Companies) 1892, s3, para. 1, no. 2 (FRG).

16 *Gesetz betreffend die Gesellschaft mit beschränkter Haftung* (GmbHG) (Act on Limited Liability Companies) 1892, s1 (FRG).

17 *Gesetz betreffend die Gesellschaft mit beschränkter Haftung* (GmbHG) (Act on Limited Liability Companies) 1892, s5, para. 1; s3, para. 1, no. 4 (FRG).

18. Mandatory provisions: shares

The articles must state the number and the nominal values of shares held by each shareholder.[18] Before the Act to Modernise the Law Governing GmbHs and Combat Abuses came into force, a shareholder could not subscribe for more than one share in a GmbH at the time of its formation. Now, a shareholder may hold several shares when establishing the GmbH or may acquire these later. The shares held by a shareholder may also have different nominal values. The nominal value of each share must be stated in full in euros (at least €1.00); that is, the creation of 'penny-shares' is not possible.[19] Prior to the Act to Modernise the Law Governing GmbHs and Combat Abuses, the minimum nominal value of each share to be held by a shareholder had to amount to €100. Even if several shares with different nominal amounts are created, the total sum of the nominal amounts of all shares together must be identical to the share capital amount as stated in the articles.[20]

Unlike a stock corporation, a GmbH does not issue tangible shares and its shares may not be traded (directly) on a stock exchange. The ownership of a share in a GmbH is not determined by the ownership of a tangible piece of paper, but by the list of shareholders which is to be recorded in the commercial register at the request of the managing director or a notary (if the latter participated in any changes to the shareholders' structure or their respective shareholding). The list is accompanied by a corresponding notarial deed or documentation issued by the managing directors indicating the distribution of the shares between the founding shareholders and any subsequent notarial deeds pertaining to the transfer of shares in a GmbH to a third person. For further details on changes in the shareholder structure, please refer to Sections 178–193.

19. Mandatory provisions: shareholders

The articles of association must set forth the names of the founding shareholders,[21] wherein a GmbH may have either one or several

---

18 *Gesetz betreffend die Gesellschaft mit beschränkter Haftung* (GmbHG) (Act on Limited Liability Companies) 1892, s3, para. 1, no. 4 (FRG).

19 *Gesetz betreffend die Gesellschaft mit beschränkter Haftung* (GmbHG) (Act on Limited Liability Companies) 1892, s5, para. 2 (FRG).

20 *Gesetz betreffend die Gesellschaft mit beschränkter Haftung* (GmbHG) (Act on Limited Liability Companies) 1892, s5, para. 3 (FRG).

21 *Gesetz betreffend die Gesellschaft mit beschränkter Haftung* (GmbHG) (Act on Limited Liability Companies) 1892, s3, para. 1, no. 4 (FRG).

shareholders.[22] Shareholders in a GmbH may be individuals or legal entities. There are no restrictions and permission is not required with regard to foreign individuals or entities becoming shareholders in a German GmbH.

20. Mandatory provisions: miscellaneous

If the GmbH is only established for a limited period of time or if the shareholders have additional obligations towards the company apart from contributing the part of the share capital they undertook to contribute, these particular items must also be included in the articles of association.[23] Additional obligations of this kind could for instance be the provision of goods and services, the payment of cash outside the subscribed share (eg, a premium or agio) or the provision of other assets necessary for the operation of the business (office space, licences, machinery, etc).

21. Other typical provisions

Apart from the mandatory provisions to be contained in the articles of association as set forth under Sections 13–20, the shareholders are principally free to include other provisions in the articles, and typically do so. The articles may deviate from most of the statutory provisions as provided in the Act on Limited Liability Companies.

22. Other typical provisions: business year

Typically, and if the articles of association do not stipulate otherwise, the business year equals the calendar year. However, the articles may provide for a business year which deviates from the calendar year, as long as it does not exceed a period of 12 months.[24]

23. Other typical provisions: representative powers of the managing directors

According to the Act on Limited Liability Companies, a GmbH under German law is represented jointly by all of its managing directors.[25] If the company has only one managing director, he or she represents

---

22 *Gesetz betreffend die Gesellschaft mit beschränkter Haftung* (GmbHG) (Act on Limited Liability Companies) 1892, s1 (FRG).

23 *Gesetz betreffend die Gesellschaft mit beschränkter Haftung* (GmbHG) (Act on Limited Liability Companies) 1892, s3, para. 2 (FRG).

24 *Handelsgesetzbuch* (HGB) (Commercial Code) 1897, s42, para. 2, sentence 2 (FRG).

25 *Gesetz betreffend die Gesellschaft mit beschränkter Haftung* (GmbHG) (Act on Limited Liability Companies) 1892, s35, para. 2, sentence 2 (FRG).

the company individually. However, the articles of association typically stipulate that a company is either represented by only one managing director, or, in the case of there being several managing directors, by either two managing directors or a managing director together with an authorised signatory (*Prokurist*). Furthermore, the articles often stipulate that the managing directors are exempted from the prohibition of self-dealing in order to be able to enter into agreements between themselves and the GmbH.[26]

24. Other typical provisions: powers of the shareholders' meeting and consent requirements

Very often, the articles of association also contain information regarding the powers of the shareholders' meeting. The responsibilities of the shareholders' meeting of a GmbH are set forth under section 46 of the Act on Limited Liability Companies. However, these powers may to a large extent be amended by the articles of association.

Typically, the articles provide for two different possible amendments of the powers of the shareholders' meeting. First, the articles usually provide for certain types of transactions the managing directors may not enter into without the prior consent of the shareholders' meeting. In this case, the powers of the shareholders' meeting are extended in the articles. Secondly, the articles may also stipulate that powers of the shareholders' meeting are shifted to another corporate body such as a supervisory board or even the managing directors. The articles may thus reduce the powers of the shareholders' meeting.

24a. Other typical provisions: formal requirements for the shareholders' meeting

Very often the articles contain provisions regarding formal procedures and rules pertaining to the calling and holding of a shareholders' meeting.[27] These typically set forth who is responsible for calling a meeting, the notice period for calling regular and extraordinary shareholders' meetings, the means of communication by which the invitation must be extended, the majority which is required to pass a resolution, whether or not a resolution may also

---

26 *Bürgerliches Gesetzbuch* (BGB) (Civil Code) 1900, s181 (FRG).

27 For details see Section 73a *et seq.*

be passed outside a shareholders' meeting and if yes, which means of communications are acceptable to do so (telephone, facsimile, email, etc), what must be contained in the minutes of the meeting and, in some cases, which formal requirements must be observed when objecting to shareholders' resolutions.

25. Other typical provisions: change in the shareholder structure

The articles often contain provisions with respect to a change in the shareholdings in the company. The articles may stipulate that transferring shares in the company requires the prior consent of the GmbH.[28] Furthermore, a typical provision pertains to a pre-emptive right on the part of the other shareholders in the event that a shareholder wishes to sell its share to a third party. This enables the prevention of third-party access to the company, and allows the shareholder structure to remain homogeneous.

25a. Other typical provisions: finances

Provisions regarding the financial situation may also often be found in the articles. They set forth, first, certain formal requirements with regard to the establishment of the financial statements on behalf of the company. Secondly, the articles often contain provisions on the use and distribution of the profits of the GmbH.

26. Sample articles (*Musterprotokoll*)

Since the Act to Modernise the Law Governing GmbHs and Combat Abuses entered into force, the Act on Limited Liability Companies now also provides sample articles of association which may be used as an alternative to individually drafted articles when establishing a GmbH. The sample articles contain all the information mandatorily required according to the Act on Limited Liability Companies.[29] They contain provisions pertaining to the firm and the seat of the company, its purpose, the share capital and the names of the shareholders, the nomination of the managing directors and the list of shareholders (*Gesellschafterliste*). In addition to these mandatory provisions, the sample articles may not contain any other provisions which in any way deviate from the Act on Limited

28 *Gesetz betreffend die Gesellschaft mit beschränkter Haftung* (GmbHG) (Act on Limited Liability Companies) 1892, s15, para. 5 (FRG).

29 *Gesetz betreffend die Gesellschaft mit beschränkter Haftung* (GmbHG) (Act on Limited Liability Companies) 1892, s3, para. 1 (FRG).

Liability Companies.[30] One advantage of using sample provisions is that the notarial fees are lower when a GmbH is established based thereon.[31] Additionally, the process of registration in the commercial registers may be faster for these 'sample GmbHs', even though there is little empirical data to date in this regard.

The sample articles, however, can only be used by those companies which have up to three shareholders and only one managing director.[32] Furthermore, the sample articles may only be used if the share capital is raised in cash and not in the form of contributions in kind.

27. Notarial form requirement

A notarial deed, which must be signed by all shareholders, is required for the articles of association and in order to establish the GmbH.[33] This means that all shareholders, whether they are natural persons or legal entities, have to appear in person before the notary or send a duly authorised agent in their place (for further details on agents see Section 30). In order to draw up the notarial deed, the content of the deed of establishment and the articles of association must be read aloud to the present or represented shareholders in the presence of the notary. After the deed has been read aloud, it must be signed by all shareholders (or their representatives) and the notary.

The notarial form described above is also required if any further changes are made to the articles of association in the form of either the addition or deletion of content.[34]

28. Notarial form requirements: notarisation abroad

Even though they are limited and regulated by statute, notarial fees in Germany can sometimes be rather high compared with other European countries. This sometimes raises the question as to whether a notarisation of certain documents relating to a GmbH – in

---

30 *Gesetz betreffend die Gesellschaft mit beschränkter Haftung* (GmbHG) (Act on Limited Liability Companies) 1892, s2, para. 1a (FRG).

31 *Gerichts-und Notarkostengesetz* (GnotKG) (Court and Notary Cost Act) 2013, s107, para. 1.

32 *Gesetz betreffend die Gesellschaft mit beschränkter Haftung* (GmbHG) (Act on Limited Liability Companies) 1892, s2, para. 1a (FRG).

33 *Gesetz betreffend die Gesellschaft mit beschränkter Haftung* (GmbHG) (Act on Limited Liability Companies) 1892, s2, para. 1 (FRG).

34 *Gesetz betreffend die Gesellschaft mit beschränkter Haftung* (GmbHG) (Act on Limited Liability Companies) 1892, s53, para. 2, sentence 1 (FRG).

particular share transfer agreements – may be undertaken by a foreign notary in order to save costs. Under German law, the recognition of notarial deeds issued in a foreign country is subject to very stringent rules and the issue of whether or not a notarisation meets the requirements under German law in specific cases is often highly disputed amongst scholars and courts. If difficulties associated with the validity of notarial deeds are to be avoided, it is advisable to have any deeds in connection with a GmbH notarised by a notary in Germany. In the event that a notarisation shall be carried out by a foreign notary, in each case the parties should assess whether, in view of the transaction or the amendment of the articles in question, the notarisation by the specific foreign notary would be accepted as equivalent to notarisation performed by a German notary. In connection with a transfer of shares, effected in certain Swiss cantons, courts have recognised the notarisation as being equivalent to a notarisation by a German notary.[35] The issue of potential equivalence usually only bears relevance in this particular context (share transfer), as the notarial fees for the foundation of a GmbH are comparatively low.

29. Notarial form requirements: shareholder signature

As outlined in Section 27, in principle the shareholders must sign the notarial deed of establishment for the GmbH and the articles of association in person. Legal entities are represented by their responsible corporate body, that is, their directors. With regard to foreign legal entities, the notary may request sufficient evidence of the authorisation of the person representing such an entity to sign legal documents on its behalf (eg, a notarised excerpt from the company register certified with an apostille etc). Moreover, the shareholders may also be represented by agents (see Section 30).

30. Notarial form requirements: representation by agents

The shareholders who must sign the notarial deed of establishment for a GmbH may also be represented by agents. In this case, the power of attorney by virtue of which they are acting requires notarisation itself.[36] A simple written power of attorney is not sufficient (unlike

35 For further details on the notarial form requirement in connection with the transfer of shares, see Section 181.

36 *Gesetz betreffend die Gesellschaft mit beschränkter Haftung* (GmbHG) (Act on Limited Liability Companies) 1892, s2, para. 2 (FRG).

in the case of a transfer of shares). The power of attorney may also be notarised by a foreign notary, but must then be further certified by means of an apostille in order for it to be recognised in Germany. There may be an exception in this regard if the country where the power of attorney has been notarised has entered into a treaty with Germany according to which an apostille is not required for the recognition of such foreign documents within Germany (eg, Austria, Belgium, France, Italy, Denmark). In this case, a simple notarisation of the power of attorney is deemed sufficient. A list of countries and the formal requirements for the recognition of documents drawn up in these countries may be found on the website of the German Institute of Notaries (*Deutsches Notarinstitut – DnotI*) under www.dnoti.de.

30a. Amendment of articles of association

Any subsequent amendments to the articles of association (in particular changes with regard to the stated share capital) must be approved by a shareholders' resolution.[37] This authority to amend the articles may not be transferred to another corporate body such as, for example, the supervisory board (see Section 73 for details). The resolution requires a majority of three quarters of the votes cast (not of the total share capital) and must be notarised.[38] The articles may provide for a higher majority and may even require the consent of all shareholders. However, they may not prescribe a lower majority (eg, a simple majority). The articles of association may stipulate additional requirements such as, for example, the consent of a particular shareholder and special formal requirements in connection with the invitation to vote and the passing of the resolution. The consent of a third party outside the company (eg, a bank or the authorities) or of another corporate body to the amendments to the articles is, however, not permissible. The amendments to the articles only become valid once they have been entered into the commercial register.[39]

---

37 *Gesetz betreffend die Gesellschaft mit beschränkter Haftung* (GmbHG) (Act on Limited Liability Companies) 1892, s53, para. 1 (FRG).

38 *Gesetz betreffend die Gesellschaft mit beschränkter Haftung* (GmbHG) (Act on Limited Liability Companies) 1892, s53, para. 2 (FRG).

39 *Gesetz betreffend die Gesellschaft mit beschränkter Haftung* (GmbHG) (Act on Limited Liability Companies) 1892, s54, para. 3 (FRG).

D. Filing for registration

31. Documents to be filed

A GmbH must be registered with the relevant commercial register in order to be fully established.[40] The commercial register in Germany is maintained by the local courts (*Amtsgerichte*). The competent local court is the court in whose district the company has its business seat.[41]

If the stated share capital is raised by contributions in cash, the registration may only be filed if at least one quarter of each share has been contributed and the total contributions paid in for all shares amount to at least half of the stated share capital.[42] In the event that the GmbH is established by way of contributions in kind, these contributions must be paid in in full prior to filing.[43] The applications for entry in the commercial register are to be signed and filed by the managing directors.[44] Furthermore, the signatures of the managing directors must be notarised, that is, the application for registration must be signed before a notary and forwarded to the court for entry in the commercial register accompanied by an electronic signature of a notary.[45] The application letter together with the documents is therefore filed for entry into the commercial register by the notary on behalf of the company.

The application itself must contain the following documents and declarations:[46]

- articles of association and, if applicable, power of attorney of the agents who signed the notarial deed on behalf of the shareholders;
- documents providing evidence for the nomination of the managing directors, if their nomination has not yet been recorded in the articles of association;

---

40 *Gesetz betreffend die Gesellschaft mit beschränkter Haftung* (GmbHG) (Act on Limited Liability Companies) 1892, s7, para. 1; s11, para. 1 (FRG).

41 See Section 15 for details on the place of business of a GmbH.

42 *Gesetz betreffend die Gesellschaft mit beschränkter Haftung* (GmbHG) (Act on Limited Liability Companies) 1892, s7, para. 2, sentences 1 and 2 (FRG).

43 *Gesetz betreffend die Gesellschaft mit beschränkter Haftung* (GmbHG) (Act on Limited Liability Companies) 1892, s7, para. 3 (FRG).

44 *Gesetz betreffend die Gesellschaft mit beschränkter Haftung* (GmbHG) (Act on Limited Liability Companies) 1892, s78 (FRG).

45 *Handelsgesetzbuch* (HGB) (Commercial Code) 1897, s12 (FRG).

46 *Gesetz betreffend die Gesellschaft mit beschränkter Haftung* (GmbHG) (Act on Limited Liability Companies) 1892, s8, para. 1 (FRG).

- list of shareholders including family name, first name, date of birth, domicile (in the case of a legal entity: place of business), subscribed shares, indicating their respective nominal value, the serial number thereof in the list of shareholders and the shareholder who has subscribed for the respective share;
- agreements which are the basis for contributions in kind (if applicable) on the part of the shareholders, in particular the non-cash contribution report (*Sachgründungsbericht*); and
- in the case of a contribution in kind, expert opinion proving that the value of the assets contributed in kind is at least on the level of the nominal capital.

The former stipulation that if a licence is required for the company the respective licence document must also be filed ceased to apply once the Act to Modernise the Law Governing GmbHs and Combat Abuses entered into force. This means that a GmbH may be registered in the commercial register even if the required licence is still missing. However, the licence must be submitted without delay once it has been granted.

To facilitate communication with the GmbH, the new Act on Limited Liability Companies now requires that the company must file a domestic business address for registration.[47] All communication may then be forwarded to this address. Moreover, the company may voluntarily file a domestic address of a third person entitled to receive communication on behalf of the GmbH.[48]

31a. Declarations to be issued

Within the application, the managing directors must issue a declaration to confirm that all contributions towards the stated share capital have been duly made according to the minimum statutory requirement (ie, half of the amount in the case of a cash contribution, the full amount in the case of a foundation on the basis of an in-kind contribution) and that the respective amounts are ultimately at the free disposal of the managing directors.[49] If the court has serious doubts regarding the correctness of these declarations,

47 *Gesetz betreffend die Gesellschaft mit beschränkter Haftung* (GmbHG) (Act on Limited Liability Companies) 1892, s8, para. 4, no. 1 (FRG).

48 *Gesetz betreffend die Gesellschaft mit beschränkter Haftung* (GmbHG) (Act on Limited Liability Companies) 1892, s10, para. 2, sentence 2 (FRG).

49 *Gesetz betreffend die Gesellschaft mit beschränkter Haftung* (GmbHG) (Act on Limited Liability Companies) 1892, s8, para. 2, sentence 1; s7, paras. 2, 3 (FRG).

it may request additional documentation.[50] If a shareholder and the GmbH have agreed that his or her contribution shall be repaid to him or her, this arrangement must also be recorded in the commercial register.[51] For details regarding the conditions for the fulfilment of the shareholder's obligation to contribute towards the stated share capital please refer to Section 162.

In addition, the managing directors must issue a declaration to confirm that they are not prohibited from practising certain professions which are either wholly or partly identical in nature to the business purpose of the GmbH, and that they have not been sentenced either in Germany or abroad under, *inter alia,* certain provisions of the German Criminal Code, the German Commercial Code and the German Law Regulating the Transformation of Companies.[52] The managing directors must also confirm that they have been instructed by the court, a domestic or foreign notary, a person practising a similar legal profession or a consular clerk as to their unlimited disclosure obligation towards the court. Such instruction may also be given in written form.[53]

Finally, the managing directors must indicate the form of their power of representation in the application letter, for example, joint or individual, and any exemptions from section 181 of the German Civil Code,[54] which allows contracts between the managing director him- or herself and the GmbH or between the GmbH and other companies represented by the managing director (self-contracting).

32. Registration and publication

Once all of these documents have been filed, the court responsible for the respective commercial register assesses whether all the requirements for establishing a GmbH have been fulfilled. If the company has not been properly established or the registration has

50 *Gesetz betreffend die Gesellschaft mit beschränkter Haftung* (GmbHG) (Act on Limited Liability Companies) 1892, s8, para. 2, sentence 2 (FRG).

51 *Gesetz betreffend die Gesellschaft mit beschränkter Haftung* (GmbHG) (Act on Limited Liability Companies) 1892, s19, para. 5, sentence 2 (FRG).

52 *Gesetz betreffend die Gesellschaft mit beschränkter Haftung* (GmbHG) (Act on Limited Liability Companies) 1892, s8, para. 3 and s6, para. 2, sentence 2, nos. 2 and 3 (FRG). For details see Section 98.

53 *Gesetz betreffend die Gesellschaft mit beschränkter Haftung* (GmbHG) (Act on Limited Liability Companies) 1892, s8, para. 3, sentence 2 (FRG).

54 *Gesetz betreffend die Gesellschaft mit beschränkter Haftung* (GmbHG) (Act on Limited Liability Companies) 1892, s8, para. 4, no. 2 (FRG).

been incorrectly filed, the court may refuse to register the GmbH.[55] This applies in particular if the contributions in kind have been 'significantly' overvalued. In such a case, however, the court may order that the respective shareholder must match the missing share capital by means of a payment in cash.[56] Typically, the court will notify the filing notary if it believes that the application contains certain errors or the company formation is incorrect in order to give the notary and the shareholders the opportunity to amend the mistakes.

Once all of the documents have been filed correctly, the GmbH is then registered with the commercial register. When registering the company, the court publishes the trade name and the place of business of the company, the purpose of the company, the registered share capital, the day upon which articles of association were signed and the names of the managing directors in the commercial register.[57] Additionally, the powers of representation of the managing directors are also published in the commercial register.

Since the Act to Modernise the Law Governing GmbHs and Combat Abuses came into force, it has also been a requirement that the domestic business address under which documents or other notices may be served to the company is published in the commercial register.[58] If the company has also nominated a person who is entitled to receive declarations of will and documents served upon the company in the company's name, these details must also be published.[59] Such persons are typically legal or tax advisers, and as long as they are registered with the commercial register, they are deemed to be authorised to receive declarations of will and other documents on behalf of the company. The publication of these addresses facilitates communication with the GmbH and it is more difficult for managing directors to avoid receiving documents on behalf of the GmbH. Moreover, if the company cannot be reached

---

55 *Gesetz betreffend die Gesellschaft mit beschränkter Haftung* (GmbHG) (Act on Limited Liability Companies) 1892, s9c, para. 1, sentence 1 (FRG).

56 *Gesetz betreffend die Gesellschaft mit beschränkter Haftung* (GmbHG) (Act on Limited Liability Companies) 1892, s9, para. 1 (FRG).

57 *Gesetz betreffend die Gesellschaft mit beschränkter Haftung* (GmbHG) (Act on Limited Liability Companies) 1892, s10, para. 1 (FRG).

58 *Gesetz betreffend die Gesellschaft mit beschränkter Haftung* (GmbHG) (Act on Limited Liability Companies) 1892, s10, para. 1, sentence 1 (FRG).

59 *Gesetz betreffend die Gesellschaft mit beschränkter Haftung* (GmbHG) (Act on Limited Liability Companies) 1892, s10, para. 2, sentence 2 (FRG).

under its registered address, under the address of the third party or under any other known domestic address, declarations of will and other documents may be served via public notification (*öffentliche Zustellung*).[60] In addition, if the GmbH has no managing director, either in factual or in legal terms (*Führungslosigkeit*), declarations of will and documents may also be served upon the shareholders of the company.[61] Therefore, the possibility of 'burying' a GmbH by avoiding the service of declarations of will and other documents is significantly reduced.

In addition, the information to be registered as outlined above must also be published in the electronic information and communication system prescribed by the administration of justice department for the respective state (*Landesjustizverwaltung*). The publication may thus be effected in different ways depending on the state in which the company is registered. Typically, the information is published under www.handelsregisterbekanntmachungen.de, or in the electronic federal gazette (*elektronischer Bundesanzeiger*; www.bundesanzeiger.de).

33. Legal consequences of registration

Upon registration, the GmbH is fully established as separate legal entity.[62] Any rights and obligations created by the *Vor-GmbH* are transferred automatically by law to the fully established GmbH.

E. *Unternehmergesellschaft (haftungsbeschränkt)*

34. General

When the Act to Modernise the Law Governing GmbHs and Combat Abuses was enforced, a second type of GmbH was created which is referred to as an '*Unternehmergesellschaft (haftungsbeschränkt)*' or '*UG (haftungsbeschränkt)*'. The characterising feature of the *Unternehmergesellschaft* is that its registered share capital is lower than €25,000.[63] It may even be as low as just €1.00.[64] The name

60 *Handelsgesetzbuch* (HGB) (Commercial Code) 1897, s15a (FRG).

61 *Gesetz betreffend die Gesellschaft mit beschränkter Haftung* (GmbHG) (Act on Limited Liability Companies) 1892, s35, para. 1, sentence 2 (FRG).

62 *Gesetz betreffend die Gesellschaft mit beschränkter Haftung* (GmbHG) (Act on Limited Liability Companies) 1892, s11, para. 1 (FRG).

63 *Gesetz betreffend die Gesellschaft mit beschränkter Haftung* (GmbHG) (Act on Limited Liability Companies) 1892, s5a, para. 1 (FRG).

64 *Gesetz betreffend die Gesellschaft mit beschränkter Haftung* (GmbHG) (Act on Limited Liability Companies) 1892, s5, para. 2, sentence 1 (FRG).

of the company must contain the words '*Unternehmergesellschaft (haftungsbeschränkt)*' or '*UG (haftungsbeschränkt)*',[65] by which means it should be clearly distinguishable from an 'ordinary' GmbH, which has a minimum share capital of €25,000.

The *Unternehmergesellschaft* may only be established by way of a contribution in cash, and not by contributions in kind.[66] The contribution must be paid in full prior to the filing of the company for registration.[67]

The Federal Supreme Court has confirmed the prohibition of contributions in kind by stating that the formation of an *Unternehmergesellschaft* by way of the company being split off from an existing entity pursuant to section 123, paragraph 2, no. 2 of the German Law Regulating the Transformation of Companies is not permissible.[68] In another decision of the same year,[69] the court ruled, however, that the prohibition of contributions in kind for an *Unternehmergesellschaft* should not apply to situations in which the share capital of the company is increased by a contribution in kind which results in a share capital for the company of €25,000 or more, that is, the minimum share capital of a (regular) GmbH. By these means, the *Unternehmergesellschaft* would then fulfil the criteria of a regular GmbH upon the registration of the capital increase. The court argued that otherwise the founders of a *Unternehmergesellschaft* would be discriminated against in comparison with the founders of a regular GmbH, where a contribution in kind is possible at any time. However, a capital increase in the case of the *Unternehmergesellschaft* which does not amount to the level of the minimum share capital of a GmbH is still only possible by way of contributions in cash.

Prior to reaching the minimum stated share capital of €25,000, the *Unternehmergesellschaft* is obliged to create capital reserves (*Rücklagen*) in its balance sheet and must increase these reserves by a quarter of its yearly net profits (*Jahresüberschuss*) until the minimum stated share capital amount for a GmbH is reached or exceeded.[70]

---

65 *Gesetz betreffend die Gesellschaft mit beschränkter Haftung* (GmbHG) (Act on Limited Liability Companies) 1892, s5a, para. 1 (FRG).

66 *Gesetz betreffend die Gesellschaft mit beschränkter Haftung* (GmbHG) (Act on Limited Liability Companies) 1892, s5a, para. 2, sentence 2 (FRG).

67 *Gesetz betreffend die Gesellschaft mit beschränkter Haftung* (GmbHG) (Act on Limited Liability Companies) 1892, s5a, para. 2, sentence 1 (FRG).

68 11 April 2011, *Bundesgerichtshof* (German Federal Supreme Court) (II ZB 9/10).

69 19 April 2011, *Bundesgerichtshof* (German Federal Supreme Court) (II ZB 25/10).

70 *Gesetz betreffend die Gesellschaft mit beschränkter Haftung* (GmbHG) (Act on Limited Liability Companies) 1892, s5a, para. 3 (FRG).

The GmbHG also lists cases in which the capital reserve may be used for purposes other than to increase the share capital (eg, to balance yearly losses or loss-carry forwards). In order to appropriately account for the low capital base of the *Unternehmergesellschaft*, a shareholders' meeting must be called not only when half of the stated share capital is lost according to the balance sheet of the company (as is the case in a GmbH), but also as soon as the company is threatened by insolvency (*drohende Zahlungsunfähigkeit*).[71] Once the minimum level for the stated share capital for a GmbH (€25,000) is reached, the *Unternehmergesellschaft* may change its company form and call itself a GmbH, and the restrictions outlined above no longer apply.[72] However, it may also choose to retain the company description '*Unternehmergesellschaft*'.

Aside from these particular regulations, the Act on Limited Liability Companies applies in full to the *Unternehmergesellschaft*.

71 *Gesetz betreffend die Gesellschaft mit beschränkter Haftung* (GmbHG) (Act on Limited Liability Companies) 1892, s5a, para. 4 (FRG).

72 *Gesetz betreffend die Gesellschaft mit beschränkter Haftung* (GmbHG) (Act on Limited Liability Companies) 1892, s5a, para. 5 (FRG).

III. Acquisition of a shelf company

35. **Requirements**

Apart from establishing a company 'from scratch', another possible way of becoming a shareholder in a GmbH is by means of the acquisition of a previously founded shelf company. This is a popular method of obtaining a fully established and registered GmbH which is ready to operate. In order to acquire shares in the GmbH, a notarised share purchase and transfer agreement is required.[1] As well as acquiring the shares in the GmbH, the managing directors of the shelf company must be replaced by new managing directors, and the articles of association must be adapted to the requirements of the acquiring party. The corresponding shareholder resolutions to be passed are usually included within the same notarial deed which pertains to the acquisition of the shares.

36. **Formal requirements and liability**

On 9 December 2002, the German Federal Supreme Court (*Bundesgerichtshof*) ruled that the acquisition of a shelf company is to be considered (in economic terms) as a new foundation, and thus that the rules pertaining to the formation of a GmbH apply accordingly.[2] This means, in particular, that at the point in time at which the amendments to the articles of association or the notification regarding the new managing director(s) are filed for registration with the commercial register, the managing directors must confirm that the stated share capital has been fully contributed and (remains) at their free disposal (for further details see Sections 157–160). They must also declare that they are not prohibited from practising certain professions associated with the business purpose of

1 *Gesetz betreffend die Gesellschaft mit beschränkter Haftung* (GmbHG) (Act on Limited Liability Companies) 1892, s15, para. 3 (FRG).

2 9 December 2002, *Bundesgerichtshof* (German Federal Supreme Court) (II ZB 12/02) – BGHZ 153, 158; confirmed, eg, by decision of 18 January 2010; *Bundesgerichtshof* (German Federal Supreme Court) (II ZR 61/09).

the company and that they have not been sentenced in connection with certain specific criminal offences (for details see Section 32). In other words, at the point in time at which the shelf company is activated and (re-)commences its business activities, it is treated like a newly founded company and, in particular, the share capital must still be present in full. It is therefore advisable that the shelf company to be acquired has not yet participated in or commenced any business activities prior to its acquisition and prior to the filing of the changes with regard to the articles of association and of the managing director(s). In a more recent decision,[3] the German Federal Supreme Court ruled that specific acts relating to the planning and preparation for commencing the business are in themselves sufficient to be considered 'business activities', thus depriving the company of its status as a shelf-company. If a company has forfeited its status as a shelf company in this way, the privileges accorded to new formation in economic terms as outlined in this chapter will not apply. The acquisition of such a GmbH would in this case not be considered equal to the (original) foundation of a GmbH.

Furthermore, besides confirming that the stated share capital remains present in full, the managing directors of a shelf company are obliged to explicitly disclose to the court maintaining the respective commercial register that the activation of the shelf company is a new formation of the company in economic terms (*wirtschaftliche Neugründung*).[4] By these means, the court maintaining the register is able to verify whether the stated share capital is still fully available. If there is a failure to disclose the *wirtschaftliche Neugründung* and to declare that the full stated share capital remains available, the shareholders may be held personally and unlimitedly liable for all obligations of the company (*Unterbilanzhaftung*). The details surrounding this liability have proved to be an issue of dispute amongst academics in the field and the courts. In a recent decision, the Federal Supreme Court ruled that the liability of the shareholders is limited to the difference between the statutory share capital and the actual value of the assets of the company (excluding the costs connected with its foundation which are borne by the company).[5] According to the Federal Supreme Court, this

---

3 18 January 2010, *Bundesgerichtshof* (German Federal Supreme Court) (II ZR 61/09).

4 See, eg, 11 March 2010, *Oberlandesgericht München* (Munich Court of Appeal) (23 U 2814/09).

5 6 March 2012, *Bundesgerichtshof* (German Federal Supreme Court) (II ZR 56/10).

even applies if the *wirtschaftliche Neugründung* is not disclosed to the court maintaining the respective commercial register. However, in practice, it continues to be advisable to undertake the disclosure as outlined to facilitate the registration of changes to the articles of association of the company during the acquisition process. The burden of proof as regards the non-existence of a difference of this nature lies with the shareholders. The Federal Supreme Court ruled that the decisive point in time with regard to proving that the statutory share capital continues to be held by the company is the point in time at which the company files the amendments to its articles for registration or commences its business operations. In particular, it is unclear whether the evidence provided by the shareholders to the effect that the stated share capital was actually available in full when the *wirtschaftliche Neugründung* was registered, or a later disclosure of the existence of a *wirtschaftliche Neugründung*, will release them from personal liability.

IV. Shareholders

A. Shareholder rights

37. General

The rights of the shareholders in a GmbH may be divided into three categories: individual rights, minority rights, and the collective rights of all of the shareholders as a whole. The most important rights represented within these groups shall be briefly described in the following sections.

38. Individual rights

Each shareholder has certain individual rights, ranging from the right to participate in shareholders' meetings and information rights to rights on profits, to name some of the most important of these here. The following subsections describe specific individual rights.

39. Individual rights: the right to participate in shareholders' meetings

Every shareholder in a GmbH is entitled to actively and passively participate in each shareholders' meeting. The active participation right comprises the right to speak and to vote at the shareholders' meeting (see Section 40). The passive participation rights comprise the right to appear at the shareholders' meeting and to receive all the information provided at or prior to the shareholders' meeting. The participation right is generally an irrevocable right. A (partial) exclusion of a shareholder from participation in the shareholders' meeting is only possible under very rare and exceptional circumstances, that is, when the participation of a shareholder at a shareholders' meeting is unacceptable to the other shareholders. This may be the case if a participating shareholder might use the information he or she receives in the course of the shareholders' meeting for his or her own purposes or against the company (for instance a competitor who has managed to become a shareholder of the GmbH).

A shareholder does not necessarily have to appear at a shareholders' meeting in person. Unless the articles of association stipulate otherwise, shareholders may send a proxy or an agent to represent them at the shareholders' meeting. In such cases, a written power of attorney is required and deemed sufficient.[1] The articles may, however, set out further requirements regarding the representative and allow only certain persons, for example, other shareholders or persons practising certain professions (lawyers, tax advisers etc) to act as proxies.

40. Individual rights: the right to vote and restrictions upon the right to vote

Generally, all shareholders in a GmbH are entitled to exercise their voting rights during the shareholders' meeting at their sole discretion. Some restrictions on the right to exercise voting rights, however, apply by virtue of the duty of loyalty towards the company and the other shareholders. This duty may sometimes result in the shareholders being obliged to vote in a certain way in order not to harm the interests of the company or the other shareholders (for details on the duty of loyalty see Section 64).

According to statutory law, each euro of a share grants the right to cast one vote at the shareholders' meeting.[2] The articles of association may, however, contain provisions which amend this rule entirely at the discretion of the shareholders. The articles may, for example, stipulate that the voting rights of certain shareholders are excluded, that the voting rights of a shareholder are limited to a certain number of votes (*Höchststimmrecht*) or may increase the number of votes of a shareholder to a level beyond the nominal amount for his or her share (*Mehrfachstimmrecht*). Since these regulations affect the voting rights of the other shareholders, they may only be granted with the consent of the affected shareholders.

The right to vote is exercised by the shareholder him- or herself, but may also be exercised by proxies based on a power of attorney. This power of attorney must be submitted in writing. The articles of association may set out further requirements for exercising the right to vote on behalf of a shareholder. These requirements may be

---

1 *Gesetz betreffend die Gesellschaft mit beschränkter Haftung* (GmbHG) (Act on Limited Liability Companies) 1892, s47, para. 3 (FRG).

2 *Gesetz betreffend die Gesellschaft mit beschränkter Haftung* (GmbHG) (Act on Limited Liability Companies) 1892, s47, para. 2 (FRG).

of a formal nature (eg, the agent must be nominated sufficiently in advance) or of a material nature (eg, only certain qualified persons are acceptable as agents, like lawyers, tax advisers etc). The right to vote at a shareholders' meeting cannot be legally separated from the share it relates to. A permanent transfer of the voting rights is only possible if the share itself is transferred. This also applies to any other administrative rights (such as information rights) in the company. Nevertheless, shareholders may enter into agreements either with their fellow shareholders or with third parties which oblige them to exercise their voting rights in a certain way (*Stimmbindungsvertrag*). Several or more shareholders may agree to exercise their voting rights collectively and in a certain way by creating a voting pool (*Stimmrechtskonsortium*). The scope of such voting arrangements is prescribed by accepted principles of morality (*gute Sitten*)[3] and statutory prohibitions (*gesetzliche Verbote*).[4] Also, the voting rights may of course not be exercised contrary to the fiduciary duties of a shareholder towards the company.

Finally, shareholders are excluded by law from exercising their voting rights if by so doing they end up adjuducating over their own affairs. Cases such as these constitute an evident conflict of interests between the shareholder and the company. Conflicts of this nature would occur if the shareholder were to be disencumbered in some way by the resolution or discharged from an obligation, if the company were to resolve on entering into an agreement with the shareholder, or if the company were to resolve on initiating or settling a legal dispute with a shareholder.[5]

41. Individual rights: information rights

At the request of a shareholder, the managing directors must: (i) provide information on the company's business affairs; and (ii) allow the shareholder to inspect the books and records of the company, in each case without undue delay.[6] As opposed to the case where a stock corporation is concerned, such a right to information may be exercised at any time and not only in or in connection with a shareholders' meeting.[7] The 'affairs of the company' constitute

3 *Bürgerliches Gesetzbuch* (BGB) (Civil Code) 1900, s138 (FRG).
4 *Bürgerliches Gesetzbuch* (BGB) (Civil Code) 1900, s134 (FRG).
5 *Gesetz betreffend die Gesellschaft mit beschränkter Haftung* (GmbHG) (Act on Limited Liability Companies) 1892, s47, para. 4 (FRG). For details see Section 86.
6 *Gesetz betreffend die Gesellschaft mit beschränkter Haftung* (GmbHG) (Act on Limited Liability Companies) 1892, s51a, para. 1 (FRG).
7 For details see *Aktiengesetz* (AktG) (Stock Corporation Act) 1965, ss131, 132 (FRG).

the subject matter of the information rights. This term is to be interpreted broadly. In basic terms, there should not be any secrets between the company and its shareholders. The affairs of the company encompass all facts relating to the assets, the management, the business strategy and the calculation and distribution of profits, as well as all other legal and economic relationships within the company or towards third parties. The right to information also extends to the affairs of subsidiaries and affiliated companies. If necessary, the management of the GmbH must collect the information relating to the subsidiary or affiliated company. The right to information allows the shareholders to be fully informed with regard to their investment and provides them with the factual foundation on which to base the exercising of their voting rights. The shareholder is entitled to commission a qualified professional to review the books and records of the company. It is highly disputed whether or not the articles may stipulate that the right to inspect the books and records may only be exercised by a qualified professional nominated by the shareholder. This position is rather difficult to uphold in a GmbH with just a few shareholders.

The managing directors may, however, refuse to provide information and to agree to the inspection of the books if they suspect that the shareholder will use the information provided for purposes which are not related or detrimental to the company (in particular pursue competition), thereby giving rise to a disadvantage for the company or an affiliated company. The refusal requires a shareholders' resolution to this effect.[8] Therefore, if the managing directors are of the opinion that a shareholder is not entitled to access information of the GmbH, they must request that a resolution be passed by the shareholders. If the shareholders' meeting denies such a right to information, the shareholder requesting the information in question may seek a decision from a competent court as to whether his or her information right exists.[9] Since the right to information is mandatory by law, the shareholders may not exclude such a right from the articles of association. However, the shareholders are entitled to set out certain formal requirements with regard to the exercising of the right to information (eg, solely

8 *Gesetz betreffend die Gesellschaft mit beschränkter Haftung* (GmbHG) (Act on Limited Liability Companies) 1892, s51a, para. 2 (FRG).

9 *Gesetz betreffend die Gesellschaft mit beschränkter Haftung* (GmbHG) (Act on Limited Liability Companies) 1892, s51b (FRG).

by written request, the dates and times when the books may be inspected, such as during normal business hours, etc) as long as the right to information remains unaffected in terms of its essential core.

42. Individual rights: right to profits

According to statutory law, the shareholders are entitled to receive the annual profits plus any profit carried forward minus any losses carried forward, unless the articles of association or a shareholders' resolution stipulate otherwise.[10] The profits are distributed among the shareholders according to their shareholdings in the company. However, the articles of association may stipulate another arrangement for the distribution of the profits.[11] The articles may also stipulate, or the shareholders may resolve, that the company shall not make or distribute any profits at all. This is usually the case in non-profit or profitless companies. Profitless companies are typically those which only provide services for other (group) companies or their member companies and thus are only compensated for their 'out-of-pocket' expenses (subject to observance of the arm's-length principle). In companies which make profit and have minority shareholders, a resolution not to distribute any profits at all but to keep them within the company may stand in conflict with the duty of loyalty of the majority shareholder.

43. Individual rights: subscription right in the event of a capital increase

Although the Act on Limited Liability Companies does not provide an explicit provision in this regard, it is generally recognised that in the event of an increase in the share capital of a GmbH, all shareholders are entitled to receive the newly created shares in relation to their current shareholding in the company. Thus the shareholders may maintain the respective voting and profit share entitlements in the company to which they were entitled prior to the capital increase. These principles have been established by the courts in line with German stock corporation law.[12] In certain circumstances, however, the subscription right of one or even all

10 *Gesetz betreffend die Gesellschaft mit beschränkter Haftung* (GmbHG) (Act on Limited Liability Companies) 1892, s29, para. 1, sentence 1 (FRG).

11 *Gesetz betreffend die Gesellschaft mit beschränkter Haftung* (GmbHG) (Act on Limited Liability Companies), 1892, s29, para. 3 (FRG).

12 *Aktiengesetz* (AktG) (Stock Corporation Act) 1965, s186 (FRG).

shareholders may be excluded if there is a predominant interest on the part of the company to the effect that a new shareholder joining the company should receive the new shares. A predominant interest of this kind may for instance exist when a contribution in kind is necessary for the company and neither the company nor the shareholders are able to provide this (eg, a company or business as a whole). An exclusion of shareholders has also been found to be legitimate if the GmbH needs to cooperate with an external partner or if the company is in need of new funds which cannot be raised by the current shareholders.

44. Individual rights: the right to challenge shareholders' resolutions

Each shareholder is entitled to challenge a shareholders' resolution before an arbitration court by filing a claim either that the resolution is null and void or that it is contestable. With regard to the right to contest a shareholders' resolution, it is not necessary that the shareholder claiming the invalidity of the resolution has participated in the shareholders' meeting. The claim must be directed against the company itself and not the other shareholders.

A shareholders' resolution may first be challenged by an action for nullity (*Nichtigkeitsklage*) if the resolution entails a severe violation of applicable law. Potential grounds which may constitute a severe violation of this nature could include the fact that the shareholders' meeting has not been properly convened, a resolution has not been notarised although this is required by law, a resolution has been passed which does not comply with the nature of a GmbH, a resolution has been passed which violates provisions which exclusively or predominantly aim to protect the debtors of the company or are otherwise in the interests of the general public, or that a shareholders' resolution is in direct violation of moral standards. In this regard, the conditions as outlined in the Stock Corporation Act under which a resolution of the shareholders is deemed to be rendered void, apply accordingly.[13] There is no statutory time limit within which an action for nullity regarding a resolution passed within a GmbH must be filed with a court. However, since, if it goes unchallenged, a null and void resolution will become valid three years after its registration in the commercial register or the passing of the resolution respectively, the claim must be filed within this

---

13 *Aktiengesetz* (AktG) (Stock Corporation Act) 1965, s241 (FRG).

time frame at the latest.[14] Before that point in time, the right to challenge a resolution may, however, also be forfeit according to general principles of law.

Aside from these specific reasons which may lead to a shareholders' resolution being found null and void, a shareholders' resolution may generally be challenged on the basis of a violation of applicable statutory law or the articles of association.[15] Since any violation of the law or the articles of association gives rise to a right to challenge the respective shareholders' resolution in question, a violation will only result in a successful challenge of the resolution if the violation of the law or the articles bore relevance where the passed resolution was concerned. Whether or not a violation was 'relevant' depends on the intention of the violated rule to protect the interest of each shareholder in adequately participating in the decision-making process of the company. Each case must be considered individually, taking into account the specific rule in question. A relatively substantial body of case law has been developed by the courts and legal scholars in this regard. The burden of proof as regards this lack of relevance lies with the company, wherein the shareholder filing the claim must specify the violation of the provision in question to the extent reasonably possible. This depends largely upon whether he or she had insight into the reasons for the violation of the provision.

The respective action of opposition (*Anfechtungsklage*) must be filed with the court within an appropriate period of time after the resolution has been passed. The Federal Supreme Court considers a period of four weeks to be appropriate, but this may also be extended if particular grounds to justify an extension are demonstrated.

The outcome of both actions (for nullity and of opposition) is that the respective shareholders' resolution is declared null and void. The decision is binding on all shareholders, managing directors, the supervisory board (if applicable) and the company itself.[16]

45. Individual rights: actions on behalf of the company

It is the obligation of the managing directors or of the responsible corporate body as stipulated in the articles of association to assert claims against the shareholders based on their (corporate)

---

14 *Aktiengesetz* (AktG) (Stock Corporation Act) 1965, s242, para. 2 (FRG) accordingly.

15 *Aktiengesetz* (AktG) (Stock Corporation Act) 1965, s243, para. 1 (FRG) accordingly.

16 *Aktiengesetz* (AktG) (Stock Corporation Act) 1965, ss248, 249 (FRG) accordingly. For details on the challenging of shareholders' resolutions see also Section 92 *et seq*.

relationship towards the company. In particular, this includes payment obligations, such as paying in the contribution to the share capital. Under particular conditions, however, a shareholder may be entitled to assert such a claim him- or herself on behalf of the company and request payment or the fulfilment of the obligation of the other shareholder towards the company (*actio pro socio*). In other words, the shareholder pursuing an *actio pro socio* may not require that the obligation is fulfilled towards himself, but only towards the company. An *actio pro socio* is a subsidiary remedy and may only be pursued if all other remedies fail. Prior to pursuing such a claim him- or herself, the shareholder must request the managing directors or any other competent corporate body to assert the claim against the other shareholder(s). If the respective corporate body refuses to pursue such a claim, the shareholder must then try to obtain a shareholders' resolution instructing the managing director to require that the non-performing shareholder provide payment or fulfil his or her obligation. In the case of a negative shareholders' resolution, the shareholder must challenge the shareholders' resolution itself prior to acting on behalf of the company. The right to pursue an *actio pro socio* is mandatorily prescribed by law and may not be excluded by the articles of association.

46. Individual rights: the right to withdraw for cause

Even though this right is not explicitly regulated by statutory law, a shareholder may withdraw from the company for cause (*wichtiger Grund*). The shareholder must issue a declaration *vis-à-vis* the company that he or she wishes to surrender his or her shareholding. For further details regarding withdrawal, see Section 190.

47. Individual rights: action for the nullity of the company

A shareholder may file an action for the nullity of the company (*Nichtigkeitsklage*) as a whole with the commercial register if the articles of association do not contain regulations regarding the amount of the share capital and of the purpose of the company.[17] The motion must be filed against the company and, in the event of success, the company is declared null and void. It will then be deleted from the commercial register. According to prevailing opinion, the motion is not subject to any time limits with regard to its submission. If,

17 *Gesetz betreffend die Gesellschaft mit beschränkter Haftung* (GmbHG) (Act on Limited Liability Companies) 1892, s75 (FRG).

however, the time period between the knowledge of the defect present in the articles and the filing of the motion is too long, the right to file the motion may be forfeited. Aside from the shareholders, managing directors and members of the supervisory board, if applicable, are also entitled to file a motion for nullity.

48. Individual rights: the right to liquidation profits

In the event that a GmbH is liquidated, each shareholder is entitled to proportionately participate in the liquidation profits according to his or her shareholding. The articles of association may, however, set forth other regulations for the distribution of the liquidation profits.[18] For further details on the rights of a shareholder in connection with the liquidation process, see Section 263.

49. Minority rights

Minority shareholders also have specific individual rights, such as the right to call a shareholders' meeting and to initiate other specific actions explained in the following sections.

50. Minority rights: the right to call a shareholders' meeting

Usually, the shareholders' meeting is convened by the managing director(s).[19] Furthermore, shareholders holding at least 10% of the share capital are entitled to request the calling of a shareholders' meeting, stating the purpose of and the reasons for the meeting.[20] If their request is denied, the shareholders may call the meeting themselves.[21] Additionally, shareholders holding at least 10% of the share capital always have the right to demand that certain items be put on the agenda of the shareholders' meeting.[22] For further details see Section 73a *et seq*.

---

18 *Gesetz betreffend die Gesellschaft mit beschränkter Haftung* (GmbHG) (Act on Limited Liability Companies) 1892, s72 (FRG).

19 *Gesetz betreffend die Gesellschaft mit beschränkter Haftung* (GmbHG) (Act on Limited Liability Companies) 1892, s49, para. 1 (FRG).

20 *Gesetz betreffend die Gesellschaft mit beschränkter Haftung* (GmbHG) (Act on Limited Liability Companies) 1892, s50, para. 1 (FRG).

21 *Gesetz betreffend die Gesellschaft mit beschränkter Haftung* (GmbHG) (Act on Limited Liability Companies) 1892, s50, para. 3 (FRG).

22 *Gesetz betreffend die Gesellschaft mit beschränkter Haftung* (GmbHG) (Act on Limited Liability Companies) 1892, s50, para. 2 (FRG).

51. Minority rights: action for the dissolution of the company

A GmbH may be dissolved by court decision if the purpose of the company can no longer be achieved or on other important grounds relating to the situation of the company.[23] In the latter case, the shareholders must agree that it is unacceptable for them to continue operating the company. The claim for dissolution may be filed by shareholders who hold at least 10% of the share capital.[24] The claim must be filed against the company itself.[25] It is the last resort (*ultima ratio*) as a means of solving problems within the company and may only be filed if all other solutions for solving the problems between the shareholders and within the company (eg, exclusion of a shareholder) prove unsuccessful.

52. Minority rights: the right to nominate and revoke liquidators

Once a resolution to liquidate the company has been passed or a court has issued an order to this effect, the liquidation (or winding up) process begins. The liquidation process is pursued by the liquidators of the company, these being, in the absence of any provisions to the contrary, its managing directors/managing director.[26] However, based on a request submitted by shareholders holding at least 10% of the share capital, the court may appoint another person as a liquidator if there is cause for the removal of the designated liquidator and the nomination of a new one.[27]

A liquidator may be removed by the court in the same way.[28] For further details on the liquidation procedure, see Section 263 *et seq.*

53. Rights to be exercised collectively by the shareholders as a whole

Certain rights require the collective action of the shareholders as a whole, such as rights involving the shareholders' directives for

23 *Gesetz betreffend die Gesellschaft mit beschränkter Haftung* (GmbHG) (Act on Limited Liability Companies) 1892, s60, para. 1, no. 3, 61; para. 1 (FRG).

24 *Gesetz betreffend die Gesellschaft mit beschränkter Haftung* (GmbHG) (Act on Limited Liability Companies) 1892, s61, para. 2, sentence 2 (FRG).

25 *Gesetz betreffend die Gesellschaft mit beschränkter Haftung* (GmbHG) (Act on Limited Liability Companies) 1892, s61, para. 2, sentence 1 (FRG).

26 *Gesetz betreffend die Gesellschaft mit beschränkter Haftung* (GmbHG) (Act on Limited Liability Companies) 1892, s66, para. 1 (FRG).

27 *Gesetz betreffend die Gesellschaft mit beschränkter Haftung* (GmbHG) (Act on Limited Liability Companies) 1892, s66, para. 2 (FRG).

28 *Gesetz betreffend die Gesellschaft mit beschränkter Haftung* (GmbHG) (Act on Limited Liability Companies) 1892, s66, para. 3 (FRG).

and relationship with the management, as will be discussed in the following sections.

54. Rights to be exercised collectively by the shareholders as a whole: instructing the managing directors

The shareholders may give instructions to the managing directors regarding how to run the company.[29] Such instructions may be of a general nature (guidelines) relating to certain types of business or may be issued specifically in connection with a particular measure. Instructions of a general nature may typically be found in the articles, by-laws or in the service agreement pertaining to the managing directors. Individual instructions for specific operational situations are usually based on a shareholders' resolution. In practice, the articles often stipulate a range of measures for which the prior consent of the shareholders' meeting is required. At the shareholders' meeting, the majority requirements as prescribed by law or within the articles is sufficient in this regard. The shareholders thus maintain control over the activities of the managing directors and the general business decisions of the company. The managing directors must respect these guidelines and instructions when managing and running the company. If, however, the guidelines and instructions constitute a clear violation of applicable law and/or may expose the directors to personal liability, the directors have the right to object to them.

In exception to the foregoing, it is also possible to grant instruction rights to an individual or certain shareholders or a supervisory/advisory board within the articles of association.

55. Rights to be exercised collectively by the shareholders as a whole: the right to supervise the management

The shareholders of a GmbH are entitled to establish rules for the supervision of the managing directors.[30] Aside from stipulating a range of operational procedures for which the prior consent of the shareholders is required as outlined in the previous section, the shareholders' meeting as the supreme corporate body has an all-encompassing right of supervision *vis-à-vis* the managing directors.

---

29 *Gesetz betreffend die Gesellschaft mit beschränkter Haftung* (GmbHG) (Act on Limited Liability Companies) 1892, s37, para. 1 (FRG).

30 *Gesetz betreffend die Gesellschaft mit beschränkter Haftung* (GmbHG) (Act on Limited Liability Companies) 1892, s46, no. 6 (FRG).

In other words, the shareholders may establish any mechanisms which are not disproportionate or contrary to the spirit of the GmbHG in order to supervise the managing directors in fulfilling their tasks. Typical measures in this respect would be the establishment of regular reporting obligations on the part of the managing directors towards the shareholders. In this regard the shareholders can also engage a third-party adviser to examine the books and records of the company. The supervision of the managing directors may also be transferred to another corporate body, such as, for example, the supervisory board or a shareholders' committee, which may be created for this purpose.

56. Rights to be exercised collectively by the shareholders as a whole: the right to claim damages

The shareholders of a GmbH are entitled to issue decisions on the enforcement of claims of the company against the managing directors and certain shareholders relating to the formation or the management of the GmbH.[31] Usually, the managing directors are entitled to pursue and enforce any claims the company may have. In the aforementioned cases, however, there is a danger that internal information of the company may be revealed in a process connected herewith or that the corresponding claims will be detrimental to relations between the shareholders and towards the managing directors. Therefore, since such claims may have these kinds of far-reaching effects on the company as a whole, the shareholders' meeting, as the superior corporate body, shall reach a resolution as to whether such claims should be enforced or not. Without a resolution to this effect, the enforcement of a claim of the company against the managing director or against a shareholder would be invalid. The defendant may claim in court that a resolution to this effect has not been passed, in which case, the court would dismiss the claim on the merits, solely on the grounds of a failure to satisfy this procedural requirement. Shareholders against whom a claim is to be enforced are not entitled to vote in the shareholders' resolution regarding the enforcement of the claim.[32]

---

31 *Gesetz betreffend die Gesellschaft mit beschränkter Haftung* (GmbHG) (Act on Limited Liability Companies) 1892, s46, no. 8 or, alternatively, 1 (FRG).

32 *Gesetz betreffend die Gesellschaft mit beschränkter Haftung* (GmbHG) (Act on Limited Liability Companies) 1892, s47, para. 4, sentence 2 (FRG).

The term 'claims' in this context must be interpreted broadly and comprises any and all damage claims on whichever legal grounds due to the violation of duties either on the part of the managing directors or the shareholders.

The enforcement of such a claim not only comprises the initiation of court proceedings (which is the usual case), but also extrajudicial measures such as payment reminders, set-offs or waivers and settlement of the claim.

The aforementioned regulation may, however, be freely amended by the shareholders in the articles of association and may even be entirely excluded.

57. Rights to be exercised collectively by the shareholders as a whole: the right to represent the GmbH against managing directors in court proceedings

The shareholders are not only entitled to decide whether claims shall be enforced against the managing directors but are also responsible for deciding who will represent the company in proceedings against its managing directors.[33] Since the shareholders decide upon the enforcement of the claim *per se*, it makes sense that the shareholders should also decide who is to represent the company, as it is not always guaranteed that the other managing directors of the company will pursue the interests of the company with the necessary vigour. In addition, a decision to this effect on the part of the shareholders is in any case required if the GmbH only has one managing director. If a managing director is also a shareholder in the company, he or she is excluded from voting on a corresponding resolution in which the shareholders decide who will represent the company in the proceedings.[34] Persons entitled to represent the company in proceedings against the managing director may be one or several shareholders, members of the supervisory board, or third parties (typically legal or tax advisers). The person appointed by the shareholders acquires the status of a legal representative of the company (like a managing director) and is bound by the instructions given by the shareholders, just as a managing director would be.

---

33 *Gesetz betreffend die Gesellschaft mit beschränkter Haftung* (GmbHG) (Act on Limited Liability Companies) 1892, s46, no. 8, Alt. 2 (FRG).

34 *Gesetz betreffend die Gesellschaft mit beschränkter Haftung* (GmbHG) (Act on Limited Liability Companies) 1892, s47, para. 4, sentence 2 (FRG).

Again, this provision is subject to any amendments or specifications in this regard in the articles of association of the company.

A different situation arises in a GmbH which is subject to one of the Co-Determination laws. In this case, the mandatory provisions of the Co-Determination laws replace the regulations of the Act on Limited Liability Companies.[35] According to these provisions, in cases where the company is engaged in proceedings against a managing director, the company is mandatorily represented by the supervisory board.[36]

58. Exclusive rights of individual shareholders

Apart from the rights of the shareholders based on statutory law and case law, a shareholder may also be granted exclusive rights in the articles of association. The shareholders may draft the articles of association according to the particular requirements of their business and thus create a personalised GmbH. The articles may thereby grant a shareholder exclusive administrative or financial rights such as, for example, multiple voting rights, veto or approval rights, the right to appoint or remove managing directors or members of the supervisory board (if applicable), preferred dividends etc. The only restrictions upon the granting of such exclusive rights are those prescribed by the mandatory regulations of the Act on Limited Liability Companies or by general civil law (eg, standards of morality and good faith). These exclusive rights may already be contained in the articles of association at the point in time of the formation of the company or they may be introduced at a later date. Amendments to this effect require the consent of all other shareholders affected by such exclusive rights. If there is a failure to obtain this consent, the resolution is challengeable. The exclusive rights may only be revoked with the respective consent of the privileged shareholder and by way of an amendment of the articles of association. An increasing number of legal scholars are of the opinion that exclusive rights may also be revoked for cause. Cause is in particular given if, upon weighing all of the respective interests,

35 *Gesetz über die Mitbestimmung der Arbeitnehmer* (*MitbestG*) (Co-Determination Act) 1976, s25 (FRG); *Gesetz über die Drittelbeteiligung der Arbeitnehmer im Aufsichtsrat* (Drittelbeteiligungsgesetz – DrittelbG) (One Third Employee Participation Act) 2004, s1, para. 1, no. 3 (FRG); *Aktiengesetz* (AktG) (Stock Corporation Act) 1965, s112 (FRG). For details on the application and consequences of the various Co-Determination Acts, see Sections 141–156.

36 For further details on the Co-Determination Acts, see Sections 141–156.

the continued existence of the exclusive right of the shareholder is felt to be unacceptable to the company or the other shareholders.

Additionally, as well as granting such exclusive rights based on the membership of the GmbH, the articles of association may also grant certain rights which are not based on membership, but only confer upon the respective shareholder an ordinary contractual (*schuldrechtlich*) position. A right based on a contractual obligation on the part of the company, for example the use of certain company facilities or the right for a person to avail themselves of certain other company benefits, may be terminated not by amendment of the articles of association, but by the means of the ordinary applicable contractual and legal rules. The distinction between whether a right granted to a shareholder in the articles is based on his or her membership or is a mere contractual right must be drawn on the basis of the intention of the company and the shareholders.

B. Shareholder obligations

59. Obligation to pay in contributions

The most important obligation of the shareholders in a GmbH is the obligation to make the contribution as set down in the articles of association.[37] As outlined above, the obligation to pay in the share capital may either take the form of a contribution in cash or a contribution in kind.[38] The contribution must actually be paid in, that is, the stated share capital must really be raised.[39]

60. Additional contributions

The articles of association may stipulate that the shareholders may resolve to call for additional contributions from the shareholders beyond the contributions they agreed to pay when founding the company.[40] The additional contributions may either be limited or unlimited in terms of their amount.[41] The purpose of such additional contributions is to enable the company to call for additional

---

37 *Gesetz betreffend die Gesellschaft mit beschränkter Haftung* (GmbHG) (Act on Limited Liability Companies) 1892, s19, para. 1 (FRG).

38 For details, see Sections 9–10.

39 For details, see Section 157 *et seq.*

40 *Gesetz betreffend die Gesellschaft mit beschränkter Haftung* (GmbHG) (Act on Limited Liability Companies) 1892, s26, para. 1 (FRG).

41 *Gesetz betreffend die Gesellschaft mit beschränkter Haftung* (GmbHG) (Act on Limited Liability Companies) 1892, ss27, 28 (FRG).

funds in case they are needed without the necessity of collecting the money from third parties.

In the event that the amount of the additional contributions is not limited, a shareholder who is not willing or able to pay this additional contribution in whose regard a resolution has been reached by the majority shareholders has the right to free him or herself from such an obligation by placing his or her share at the disposal of the GmbH.[42] This step must occur within a period of one month after the company has requested the shareholder to pay in his additional contribution. If the shareholder fails to respond to the request of the company (either by paying in the contribution or by placing the share at the disposal of the company), the GmbH may declare towards the shareholders via registered letter that it considers his or her share to be placed at the disposal of the company. Once the share is at the disposal of the company, the GmbH is entitled to sell the share by way of public auction within a period of one month after it was placed at the GmbH's disposal or, with the consent of the shareholder, in any other way the company deems appropriate. If the company generates a surplus when selling the share, the shareholder abandoning the share is entitled to receive the surplus. If the price achieved when selling the share is not sufficient to cover the outstanding additional contribution, the share falls to the GmbH.[43] The other shareholders are not liable for the payment of any outstanding additional contribution if a shareholder fails to pay in the contribution or if the sale of the share does not yield sufficient funds to cover the additional contribution.

If the additional contributions are limited to a certain amount and the shareholder does not pay in his or her contribution in due course, the share may be forfeited and the company may sell it by way of auction to collect the outstanding amount.[44] Remaining shareholders may not be held liable for any unpaid additional contributions owed by one of the shareholders.

---

42 *Gesetz betreffend die Gesellschaft mit beschränkter Haftung* (GmbHG) (Act on Limited Liability Companies) 1892, s27, para. 1 (FRG).

43 *Gesetz betreffend die Gesellschaft mit beschränkter Haftung* (GmbHG) (Act on Limited Liability Companies) 1892, s27, para. 3 (FRG).

44 *Gesetz betreffend die Gesellschaft mit beschränkter Haftung* (GmbHG) (Act on Limited Liability Companies) 1892, s28 (FRG). For details on the forfeiture of the shares see Section 185.

61. Obligation to refrain from competition

The Act on Limited Liability Companies does not contain an explicit provision regarding the prohibition to compete with the company – neither for managing directors nor for shareholders – whereas for instance the stock cooperation law[45] (members of the board of directors) or the law on general partnerships[46] (shareholders) do.

In practice, the articles of association or the service agreements of the managing directors often contain wording to this effect. If neither the articles nor the service agreement provide a corresponding regulation, it is generally recognised under German case law that a managing director of a GmbH, whether or not he or she is a shareholder, must refrain from any kind of competition with the company unless explicitly entitled to do so. An entitlement of this kind may be based on a shareholders' resolution to this effect if the articles of association stipulate that such an exemption may be granted.

Shareholders who are not managing directors are also subject to an obligation to refrain from competition if they hold the majority of the shares in the company or in any other way exercise a dominant influence within the company.[47]

Irrespective of a dominant influence, shareholders are subject to an obligation to refrain from competition if they become aware of certain business opportunities in their capacity as a company shareholder and the business is either important for the company or falls within the scope of its business purpose. The shareholder must then refrain from pursuing the business opportunity and must inform the company of the said opportunity. The shareholder may only pursue the transaction when the company does not seize the opportunity itself.

In its decision of 11 November 2010,[48] the Munich Court of Appeal (*Oberlandesgericht München*) had to issue a ruling on a non-compete clause contained in the articles of association of a GmbH. The clause was directed towards the shareholders and towards the managing directors of the company alike. In particular, it prohibited any kind of activities, whether independent or under employment, direct or indirect, in the party's own name or in the name of a third

---

45 *Aktiengesetz* (AktG) (Stock Corporation Act) 1965, s88 (FRG).

46 *Handelsgesetzbuch* (HGB) (Commercial Code) 1897, s112 (FRG).

47 Decision as of 5 December 1983, *Bundesgerichtshof* (German Federal Supreme Court) – BGHZ 89, 162 *et seq.*

48 File no. U K 2143/10.

party, for its own account or for the account of a third party, in an enterprise having a business similar to the business of the GmbH, or any of its subsidiaries or affiliates, which: (i) competed or could compete with these entities, or (ii) entertained a significant business relationship with any of these entities. The shareholders and the managing directors were also not allowed to hold any stakes in such entities. In the event of violation, a contractual penalty in the amount of €50,000 was due for each violation. The shareholders' meeting could grant an exemption from the non-compete clause by way of a shareholders' resolution. The Court of Appeal came to the conclusion that the clause was invalid and that it constituted a violation of moral standards[49] and of the Act against Restraints of Competition.[50] When considering any non-compete clause, the courts must weigh the valid business interests of the company against the professional aspirations of the shareholder/managing director in continuing to work in the business segment he or she was active in.[51] A non-compete clause may not be used to exclude competition from the market. In this context, a provision prescribing that, irrespective of their business purpose and also encompassing their (currently unknown) future business purposes, any and all subsidiaries constitute a barrier for competitive activities, was considered too broad and unspecific.

Any non-compete clause must be specific, not only with regard to time and territorial scope, but also in terms of its business scope. The fact that an exception to the non-compete clause may be granted by way of a shareholders´ resolution was also not deemed sufficient for the court to hold the clause valid. The articles did not specify in detail when such an exception was to be granted. Further, a shareholder/director pursuing potentially competitive activities cannot be expected to wait for a final court decision on the matter. Finally, the clause may also not be saved by way of the court reducing its scope to an acceptable degree. A reduction to an acceptable degree has in some cases been considered by the courts in connection with temporal scope but not where other situations are concerned. This was confirmed by a decision of the Nuremberg Court of Appeal.[52]

49 *Bürgerliches Gesetzbuch* (BGB) (Civil Code) 1900, s138 (FRG).

50 *Gesetz gegen Wettbewerbsbeschränkungen* (GWG) (Act against Restrictions of Competition), 1 (FRG).

51 Regarding non-compete obligations for managing directors in a GmbH, see also Section 107.

52 File no. 12 U 681/09, decision of 25 November 2009.

The court ruled that a non-compete clause excluding a managing director of a GmbH from doing business with any customer of the group of the GmbH (which comprised 120 companies) was too excessive and therefore invalid in its entirety. The court refused to accept a reduction of the clause to, for example, customers of the GmbH or to those customers with whom the director had personal contact. Similarly, in the same decision, the court refused to reduce a contractual penalty it considered too high to an acceptable amount in the specific case (€100,000 for each violation).

In the event of a violation of the obligation not to compete, the company may file for injunctive relief or claim damages against the violator.

62. Confidentiality obligation

The shareholders in a GmbH have the right to inform themselves comprehensively regarding the affairs of the company.[53] The corresponding obligation in return for being granted full inspection rights regarding the business affairs of the company is the shareholder's duty to keep confidential all information received from the company or obtained while inspecting its books and records. Moreover, a shareholder must refrain from disclosing any confidential information about the company, irrespective of its source. The obligation to keep the information confidential derives from the duty of loyalty of each shareholder.

62a. Obligations during insolvency

Regarding the obligations of the shareholders of a GmbH during the insolvency of the company, see Section 109.

63. Auxiliary and additional obligations

Within the articles of association, the shareholders may assume any and all kinds of additional and auxiliary obligations towards the company or towards other shareholders. Such additional obligations are not unusual and may typically be found in personalised companies. Additional obligations may only be established for several or all shareholders. These may be of a financial nature, but may also comprise the provision of services to supply goods or intellectual property rights or to acquire goods from the company.

---

53 *Gesetz betreffend die Gesellschaft mit beschränkter Haftung* (GmbHG) (Act on Limited Liability Companies) 1892, s51a (FRG). For details see Section 41.

64. Duty of loyalty

Aside from any particular obligations based on statutory law and the articles, the shareholders of a GmbH (and any other corporation or partnership) are subject to a general duty of loyalty. This duty of loyalty requires the shareholders to act loyally towards the company, meaning that they must actively support its purpose and prevent it from being exposed to harm. The duty serves to resolve conflicts within the company which cannot be resolved by statutory or case law, or by the articles of association. It applies in the first place to the relationship between the shareholders and the company, and secondly to the relationship between the shareholders themselves. The duty of loyalty requires a shareholder to duly take into account the interests of the other shareholders and of the company when exercising a membership right. The duty does not prevent shareholders from exercising their rights in a manner most favourable to them. Its aim is merely to avoid unacceptable outcomes when the justified interests of other shareholders or of the GmbH are not sufficiently taken into account and shareholders pursue their own interests in an inappropriate way. The duty of loyalty provides the courts with an instrument to balance the contradicting interests of the shareholders and the company in order to find appropriate solutions on a case-by-case basis.

However, a duty of loyalty does not exist in a single shareholder company. In such a company, there are no conflicts of interest between the company and the shareholder.[54]

C. Liability of shareholders towards third parties (piercing the corporate veil)

65. General

According to statutory law, a GmbH's liability *vis-à-vis* its creditors is solely limited to its assets, that is, the shareholders of the GmbH are not personally liable towards third parties.[55] Nevertheless, aside from the establishment of a personal liability of a shareholder in a GmbH by way of an individual agreement with a creditor of the company (eg, guarantee, suretyship, lien, pledge, etc), German case

---

54 28 September 1992, *Bundesgerichtshof* (German Federal Supreme Court) (II ZR209/91) – BGHZ 119, 257.

55 *Gesetz betreffend die Gesellschaft mit beschränkter Haftung* (GmbHG) (Act on Limited Liability Companies) 1892, s13, para. 2 (FRG).

law recognises that, under certain circumstances, the shareholders in a GmbH may be held personally liable for the liabilities of the GmbH. These cases are, however, highly exceptional and shall be outlined in the following.

66. Confusion of goods (*Vermögensvermischung*)

A confusion of goods typically arises in single shareholder companies, but can also occur within a multi-shareholder GmbH. In the event of a confusion of goods, the assets of the GmbH and the private assets of the shareholders are not, or not sufficiently, separated from each other. The confusion of goods must be so extreme that it is no longer possible to separate the two types of assets, making it in turn impossible for the creditors to distinguish which assets are available to satisfy their claims. Separation usually becomes impossible as a result of a non-transparent, or incomprehensive accounting system or a substantial lack of such a system, resulting in the situation that it cannot be determined whether or not the stipulations regarding the maintenance of the share capital have been observed (a so-called *Waschkorblage* – 'laundry basket situation').[56] Such a situation gives rise to the personal liability of the shareholders, who are responsible for this kind of negligence in connection with the accounting and bookkeeping of the company, *vis-à-vis* the creditors of the GmbH. Typically, this would be the majority shareholder in the company, but it may also be any other shareholder who has sufficient influence on the company to be able to control or manipulate the way in which the books and records are kept.

67. Confusion of spheres (*Sphärenvermischung*)

The situation of a confusion of spheres is very closely related to the situation of the confusion of goods. A confusion of spheres occurs when, in dealings with third parties, shareholders fail to sufficiently distinguish whether they are representing themselves or the company. It thus becomes difficult for the third party to distinguish who is the actual contract partner. In cases such as these, many legal scholars argue that if the corporation assumes responsibility for all liabilities the shareholder gives rise to, this would constitute an unacceptable misuse of the said corporation. The shareholder

56 13 April 1994, *Bundesgerichtshof* (German Federal Supreme Court) (IIZR 16/93) – BGHZ 125, 366 *et seq.*

must therefore be personally liable for the liabilities he or she gives rise to on behalf of the company.

68. Undercapitalisation

One highly disputed situation in connection with which a piercing of the corporate veil is discussed is the undercapitalisation of the GmbH. A distinction is often drawn between two different kinds of undercapitalisation. A 'material' undercapitalisation is present if the share capital of the company does not reach an adequate level in comparison with the scope of its business, that is, the (anticipated) business activities of the company far exceed the stated capital (often when only the minimum required share capital of €25,000 was raised). The other kind of undercapitalisation, so-called 'formal' or nominal undercapitalisation, is present if the company actually dispose of the necessary share capital in a manner commensurate to the range of its activities. However, this kind of share capital is only (or to a large extent) provided by means of shareholder loans rather than equity. This creates problem in particular if the company should become insolvent later on. Whether and on which legal ground a direct liability on the part of the shareholders may be established in these situations is a matter of dispute amongst legal scholars. The lower courts, too, are undecided on this matter. In one case, the Federal Supreme Court applied section 826 of the German Civil Code (*Bürgerliches Gesetzbuch* – BGB), which grants damages in the event of deliberate immoral damage being caused to a third party. In its decision of 28 April 2008,[57] the Federal Supreme Court ruled that at least occurrences of 'material' undercapitalisation do not constitute a case of destructive intervention (see immediately below under Section 69) and thus do not give rise to an internal liability on the part of the shareholders *vis-à-vis* the GmbH itself. The court ruled that the failure to furnish a GmbH with the necessary share capital may not be equated with a shareholder actively intervening and taking away equity from the company to the detriment of its creditors. The legal provisions regarding the maintenance of the share capital[58] are considered sufficient and the Federal Supreme Court saw no reason to establish further rules in this regard. The specific function of a GmbH, namely to limit the

---

57 28 April 2008, *Bundesgerichtshof* (German Federal Supreme Court) (II ZR 264/06) – BGH NJW 2008, 2437 *et seq.*

58 See Section 163 *et seq.* for further details.

liability of the shareholders to the stated share capital, would otherwise be endangered. In its decision, however, the Federal Supreme Court also clearly stated that the potential direct liability of a shareholder towards third parties on the basis of tort law (in particular based on section 826 of the German Civil Code) remains unaffected.

69. Destructive intervention (*Existenzvernichtender Eingriff*)

A destructive intervention occurs if a shareholder intervenes in the financial situation of the company (in particular the stated share capital) such that it is no longer able to satisfy its obligations towards its creditors. Prior to July 2007, intervention of this nature resulted in personal liability on the part of the intervening shareholder towards the creditors of the GmbH. In its decision of 16 July 2007,[59] however, the Federal Supreme Court ruled that in the event of a destructive intervention, the shareholders would no longer be personally and directly liable towards the creditors. Only the company itself has a claim towards the respective shareholder based on section 826 of the German Civil Code (*Bürgerliches Gesetzbuch*) (deliberate immoral damage). These rules also apply during the liquidation process if the GmbH goes into liquidation.[60] In other words, a direct liability on the part of the shareholders towards the creditors of the company has been abolished in this regard. Instead, the ruling has established an internal, unlimited liability on the part of the shareholders towards the company to repay to the company the funds required to satisfy its creditors and to maintain its operations. The creditors of the company are nevertheless entitled to appropriate the internal claim of the company towards the shareholder and afterwards claim payment from the shareholder directly. In order to do so, however, the creditor would need to establish a claim against the company first and may not directly claim compensation from the shareholder.[61]

70. Misuse of the corporate structure

It continues to be an issue of dispute amongst legal scholars and courts whether – apart from the cases cited above – (other categories

---

59 16 July 2007, *Bundesgerichtshof* (German Federal Supreme Court) (II ZR 3/04) – BGH NJW 2007, 2689 *et seq.*

60 9 February 2009, *Bundesgerichtshof* (German Federal Supreme Court) (II ZR 292/07) – BGH NJW 2009, 2127 *et seq.* For further details on the liquidation process see Section 263 *et seq.*

61 For further details, see Section 262.

of) the misuse of the corporate structure by the shareholders gives rise to a personal and direct liability towards the creditors of the GmbH. The Federal Supreme Court has not yet issued a definite ruling on this question, nor have the lower courts reached agreement on this issue. It is therefore possible that a misuse of the corporate structure could give rise to personal liability on the part of the shareholders. However, this would have to be decided on a case-by-case basis, and exceptional circumstances would certainly be a prerequisite in this regard. Furthermore, a situation involving an intervention as regards the financial situation of a GmbH which does not already fall under the situations outlined above is hardly conceivable.

V. Shareholders' meeting

71. General

The meeting of the shareholders is the principal corporate body of a GmbH. As opposed to the case where a stock corporation is concerned, where the exact distribution of powers between the shareholders, the management and the supervisory board is prescribed by mandatory law, to a large extent, the Act on Limited Liability Companies entitles the shareholders themselves to determine and change the distribution of powers between the managing directors and the shareholders as prescribed by law, in the articles of association and accompanying by-laws.

For the purposes of legal certainty, however, the GmbH is mandatorily represented by the managing directors in dealings with third parties. Internally, the articles of association and the by-laws may either provide for strong managing directors practically subject to just a few of the mandatory provisions of the Act on Limited Liability Companies, or for a strong position in the shareholders' favour, requiring prior consent from the shareholders for each (significant) action the managing directors take on behalf of the company. The flexibility of the Act on Limited Liability Companies has contributed to the GmbH being the most successful legal entity within Germany and, in its comparable legal forms, also in other European countries.

A. Statutory rights and obligations; transferral of rights and powers

72. Statutory rights and obligations of the shareholders' meeting

The Act on Limited Liability Companies sets out an optional list of powers on the part of the shareholders in the event that the articles of association do not provide otherwise by either limiting this list, adding powers thereto, or transferring certain powers listed herein (to the extent legally permitted) to another corporate body. The powers in question are:

- approval of the annual financial statement and the allocation of the surplus;[1]

---

1 *Gesetz betreffend die Gesellschaft mit beschränkter Haftung* (GmbHG) (Act on Limited Liability Companies) 1892, s46, no. 1 (FRG).

- resolution on the publication of an individual annual financial statement according to international accounting standards and on the approval of the annual statement prepared by the managing directors;[2]
- approval of the group annual financial statement prepared by the managing directors;[3]
- calling in unpaid capital contributions;[4]
- repayment of supplementary contributions;[5]
- splitting, grouping and redemption of shares;[6]
- the appointment and removal of managing directors and the discharging thereof (*Entlastung*);[7]
- determining the guidelines for assessing and supervising the managing directors;[8]
- appointment of proxies and authorised signatories (*Handlungsbevollmächtigte*) for the whole business;[9] and
- the enforcement of damage claims to which the company is entitled against the managing directors or the shareholders and relating to the establishment or the management of the company, and the representation of the company in court proceedings which the company conducts against the managing directors.[10]

In addition, the shareholders' meeting has the competence to decide upon amendments to the articles of association, including

2 *Gesetz betreffend die Gesellschaft mit beschränkter Haftung* (GmbHG) (Act on Limited Liability Companies) 1892, s46, no. 1a (FRG).

3 *Gesetz betreffend die Gesellschaft mit beschränkter Haftung* (GmbHG) (Act on Limited Liability Companies) 1892, s46, no. 1b (FRG).

4 *Gesetz betreffend die Gesellschaft mit beschränkter Haftung* (GmbHG) (Act on Limited Liability Companies) 1892, s46, no. 2 (FRG).

5 *Gesetz betreffend die Gesellschaft mit beschränkter Haftung* (GmbHG) (Act on Limited Liability Companies) 1892, s46, no. 3 (FRG).

6 *Gesetz betreffend die Gesellschaft mit beschränkter Haftung* (GmbHG) (Act on Limited Liability Companies) 1892, s46, no. 4 (FRG).

7 *Gesetz betreffend die Gesellschaft mit beschränkter Haftung* (GmbHG) (Act on Limited Liability Companies) 1892, s46, no. 5 (FRG).

8 *Gesetz betreffend die Gesellschaft mit beschränkter Haftung* (GmbHG) (Act on Limited Liability Companies) 1892, s46, no. 6 (FRG).

9 *Gesetz betreffend die Gesellschaft mit beschränkter Haftung* (GmbHG) (Act on Limited Liability Companies) 1892, s46, no. 7 (FRG).

10 *Gesetz betreffend die Gesellschaft mit beschränkter Haftung* (GmbHG) (Act on Limited Liability Companies) 1892, s46, no. 8 (FRG).

amendments pertaining to the stated share capital,[11] and upon the liquidation of the GmbH.[12]

73. Transferring powers to other corporate bodies

As outlined above, the GmbH is very flexible where the distribution of powers amongst the respective corporate bodies is concerned. This means for instance that it is possible to transfer powers from the shareholders to an optional supervisory board, or that certain shareholders may be granted additional rights compared to other shareholders (subject to the consent of the affected shareholders). If, however, the articles of association transfer certain powers from the shareholders' meeting to another corporate body (eg, the supervisory board), but this other corporate body is unable to act for whichever reason, the shareholders' meeting is again responsible for taking the respective measures. In other words, the shareholders' meeting, as the supreme corporate body, has unwritten subsidiary competence.

The shifting of responsibilities from one corporate body to another is, nevertheless, subject to certain limits. Transferring responsibilities from the shareholders' meeting to another corporate body cannot result in a complete reversal of the position of the shareholders as the supreme corporate body. The law requires that the shareholders must retain certain core powers. These core powers generally relate to all measures which constitute a substantial intervention with regard to the economic or legal basis of the GmbH, such as for instance the sale of an essential portion of the assets of the company or a substantial change in the business activities of the company. These measures require the consent of the shareholders.[13] Aside from this general principle, the Act on Limited Liability Companies mandatorily stipulates that a shareholders' resolution is required in specific circumstances, these being, *inter alia*, amendments to the articles of association, including measures to increase or decrease the stated share capital;[14] the calling in of

11 *Gesetz betreffend die Gesellschaft mit beschränkter Haftung* (GmbHG) (Act on Limited Liability Companies) 1892, s53 *et seq.* (FRG).

12 *Gesetz betreffend die Gesellschaft mit beschränkter Haftung* (GmbHG) (Act on Limited Liability Companies) 1892, s60, para. 1, no. 2 (FRG).

13 25 February 1982, *Bundesgerichtshof* (Federal Supreme Court) (II ZR 184/80) (*Holzmüller*) – BGHZ 83, 122 *et seq.*

14 *Gesetz betreffend die Gesellschaft mit beschränkter Haftung* (GmbHG) (Act on Limited Liability Companies) 1892, s53 *et seq.* (FRG).

additional contributions;[15] the liquidation of the company and the appointment and removal of the liquidators;[16] and changes in the corporate form (*Umwandlung*) based on the German Law Regulating the Transformation of Companies (*Umwandlungsgesetz* – UmwG). In all of these cases, a transferral of competence to another corporate body is not possible, or only under very limited circumstances.

B. Calling of shareholders' meetings

73a. Passing of resolutions at a shareholders' meeting

Shareholder resolutions may be passed during formally called shareholders' meetings or outside of shareholders' meetings (see Section 88a for details). The following sections outline the formalities which must be observed for a shareholders' resolution to be passed during a (physical) meeting of the shareholders and when a shareholders' meeting has to be called.

74. Responsibility for convening the shareholders' meeting

The managing directors are responsible for convening the shareholders' meeting.[17] If the company has several managing directors, each managing director is individually entitled to call a shareholders' meeting. In companies which are subject to one of the Co-Determination Acts,[18] or which have an optional supervisory board according to the statutory regulations contained in the Act on Limited Liability Companies,[19] a shareholders' meeting may also be called by the supervisory board if the shareholders' meeting is deemed necessary for the benefit of the company.[20] Shareholders holding at least 10% of the stated share capital may request the managing directors to call a shareholders' meeting.[21] If the managing directors refuse to call a shareholders' meeting upon such

---

15 *Gesetz betreffend die Gesellschaft mit beschränkter Haftung* (GmbHG) (Act on Limited Liability Companies) 1892, s26 *et seq.* (FRG).

16 *Gesetz betreffend die Gesellschaft mit beschränkter Haftung* (GmbHG) (Act on Limited Liability Companies) 1892, s60, para. 1, no. 2, 66 (FRG).

17 *Gesetz betreffend die Gesellschaft mit beschränkter Haftung* (GmbHG) (Act on Limited Liability Companies) 1892, s49, para. 1 (FRG).

18 For further details, refer to Sections 141–156.

19 *Gesetz betreffend die Gesellschaft mit beschränkter Haftung* (GmbHG) (Act on Limited Liability Companies) 1892, s52, para. 1 (FRG).

20 *Aktiengesetz* (AktG) (Stock Corporation Act) 1965, s111, para. 3 (FRG) accordingly.

21 *Gesetz betreffend die Gesellschaft mit beschränkter Haftung* (GmbHG) (Act on Limited Liability Companies) 1892, s50, para. 1 (FRG).

a request, the (minority) shareholders may call the shareholders' meeting themselves by stating the purpose and the agenda of the meeting.[22]

The right to call a meeting of the shareholders may also be transferred to another corporate body by the articles of association. Typically, the right to call a shareholders' meeting is assigned to the supervisory board or another advisory board. It may, however, also be transferred to a single shareholder or even a third person. However, according to the prevailing opinion, the right of shareholders holding at least 10% of the share capital to call a shareholders' meeting in the event that the managing directors refuse to do so may not be excluded by the articles of association.

75. Reasons for convening a shareholders' meeting

A shareholders' meeting may be convened by the persons named in Section 74 for any reasonable cause which necessitates consultation between the shareholders or a subsequent resolution. It is not a prerequisite that the calling of the shareholders' meeting is absolutely necessary or in the best interests of the GmbH. There must, however, be grounds of some kind for a meeting. As regards how often the meetings are convened, the number of shareholders and the distance from the place where the meeting is to take place must be taken into consideration. The meetings usually take place at the place of business of the GmbH. However, the articles or the shareholders may provide for convening at any other place they deem appropriate.

76. Reasons for convening the shareholders' meeting: explicitly defined cases

The Act on Limited Liability Companies stipulates that a shareholders' meeting must be convened in the cases explicitly defined therein.[23] Explicitly defined cases are those stipulated in the articles of association or those which apply when it is necessary to pass a resolution in connection with any of the powers accorded as per the optional list of responsibilities of the shareholders outlined

---

22 *Gesetz betreffend die Gesellschaft mit beschränkter Haftung* (GmbHG) (Act on Limited Liability Companies) 1892, s50, para. 3 (FRG).

23 *Gesetz betreffend die Gesellschaft mit beschränkter Haftung* (GmbHG) (Act on Limited Liability Companies) 1892, s49, para. 2, or, alternatively, 1 (FRG).

above (for details see Section 72). In larger GmbHs with more than one shareholder, at least one shareholders' meeting per year is good practice, as is the case in a stock corporation.

77. Reasons for convening a shareholders' meeting: interests of the company

A shareholders' meeting must be convened by the competent corporate body if such a meeting appears necessary in terms of the interests of the company.[24] Such a necessity is deemed present if the GmbH is in danger of suffering significant damage without the shareholders' meeting or if the managing directors must reasonably assume that the shareholders of the company wish to pass a resolution prior to the managing directors entering into a risky or costly transaction. Generally, a shareholders' meeting appears to be in the interest of a company if the managing directors or the competent corporate body must have reasonable grounds to believe that the shareholders would not allow the implementation of the respective matter without their prior consent. Whether this is the case depends on various factors such as the size of the company compared with the risk associated with the business in question, and the personal relationship between the managing directors and the shareholders.

78. Reasons for convening a shareholders' meeting: loss of half of the stated share capital

A shareholders' meeting must be convened mandatorily if the annual balance sheet or a balance sheet drawn up during the course of the business year shows that half of the stated share capital of the GmbH has been lost.[25] An obligation to call a shareholders' meeting also arises if, based on their reasonable judgement, the managing directors have grounds to believe that half of the share capital has been lost. If the managing directors assume that this is the case, they may be obliged to draw up a balance sheet to evaluate whether or not their assumption is correct, unless it is obvious that this is the case.

---

24 *Gesetz betreffend die Gesellschaft mit beschränkter Haftung* (GmbHG) (Act on Limited Liability Companies) 1892, s49, para. 2, or, alternatively, 2 (FRG).

25 *Gesetz betreffend die Gesellschaft mit beschränkter Haftung* (GmbHG) (Act on Limited Liability Companies) 1892, s49, para. 3 (FRG).

79. Reasons for convening a shareholders' meeting: request submitted by minority shareholders

Minority shareholders holding at least 10% of the stated share capital may also call a shareholders' meeting if the managing directors refuse to do so upon their prior request.[26] When convening the shareholders' meeting, the minority shareholders must state the facts which entitle them to call the shareholders' meeting and communicate the topics of such a meeting.

80. Formal requirements for calling a shareholders' meeting

According to the applicable law in this regard, shareholders' meetings must be convened by way of registered letter to all shareholders. The invitation must be issued at least one week prior to the date on which the meeting is due to take place.[27] The invitation must be sent to all shareholders at their last known address.

The invitation must set forth the place and date, including the exact hour, where and when the shareholders' meeting is to take place. The meeting date and time and the venue must be commensurate to and customary for the type and size of the company, wherein the interests of the shareholders must be taken into account, in particular the distance of the shareholders from the venue of the shareholders' meeting and conflicting appointments. Usually, the articles stipulate the place where meetings are held (eg, the place of business of the GmbH). Additionally, the invitation must set forth the purpose of the shareholders' meeting, in particular the issues to be discussed among the shareholders.[28] The shareholders must be given sufficient time to prepare themselves for the discussion and to make up their mind as to how they wish to vote on the respective topics. The topics may be amended and additional topics may be set forth on the agenda of the shareholders' meeting at the latest three days prior to it taking place.[29]

These formal requirements may be freely amended in the articles of association. The articles may stipulate more or less stringent

26 *Gesetz betreffend die Gesellschaft mit beschränkter Haftung* (GmbHG) (Act on Limited Liability Companies), 1892, s50, para. 1, 3 (FRG). See also Section 74.

27 *Gesetz betreffend die Gesellschaft mit beschränkter Haftung* (GmbHG) (Act on Limited Liability Companies), 1892, s51, para. 1 (FRG).

28 *Gesetz betreffend die Gesellschaft mit beschränkter Haftung* (GmbHG) (Act on Limited Liability Companies), 1892, s51, para. 2 (FRG).

29 *Gesetz betreffend die Gesellschaft mit beschränkter Haftung* (GmbHG) (Act on Limited Liability Companies), 1892, s51, para. 4 (FRG).

requirements as regards the convening of the shareholders' meeting. In practice, notice may not only be given by registered letter but also via facsimile or other means of communication (eg, email). The notice period is usually more than one week (typically two weeks) for ordinary meetings and a shorter notice period applies in the case of extraordinary meetings.

In the event of a violation of the provisions prescribed by statutory law or set forth in the articles of association regarding the convening of a shareholders' meeting, the resulting shareholders' resolution may either be contestable or void. However, if all the shareholders of the company are present at the shareholders' meeting, either personally or by means of sending an agent (*Universalversammlung*), if none of the shareholders issues an objection regarding the mistakes relating to the invitation, and if the shareholders pass resolutions on the topics of the agenda, the corresponding shareholders' resolutions are considered valid.[30] In other words, if claims are not asserted regarding the formal mistakes associated with the invitation and if all shareholders participate in the voting, the errors in connection with the invitation are considered remedied.

81. Formal requirements for a shareholders' meeting

The Act on Limited Liability Companies does not establish many formal requirements with regard to the process of obtaining a shareholders' resolution, which means that most issues must be addressed in the articles.

Each shareholder has an inalienable right to actively and passively participate in the shareholders' meeting. This also applies in the event that a shareholder is excluded from voting on a particular topic.[31] Additionally, a shareholder may be represented by a proxy based on a written power of attorney.[32] Third parties are only entitled to participate in the shareholders' meeting if the shareholders explicitly consent to this. Managing directors themselves have no intrinsic right to participate in a shareholders' meeting. They are, however, obliged to appear at the shareholders'

30 *Gesetz betreffend die Gesellschaft mit beschränkter Haftung* (GmbHG) (Act on Limited Liability Companies) 1892, s51, para. 3 (FRG).

31 *Gesetz betreffend die Gesellschaft mit beschränkter Haftung* (GmbHG) (Act on Limited Liability Companies) 1892, s47, para. 4 (FRG). For further details see Section 86.

32 *Gesetz betreffend die Gesellschaft mit beschränkter Haftung* (GmbHG) (Act on Limited Liability Companies) 1892, s47, para. 3 (FRG).

meeting upon the request of the shareholders, which is usually the case. If a mandatory supervisory board exists, the members of the supervisory board are entitled to participate in the shareholders' meeting.[33] In the case of an optional supervisory board, the participation right of the respective members must be established by the articles of association.

Even though not required by law, it is recommended that the articles of association of a multi-shareholder GmbH determine that each shareholders' meeting has a chairperson and define how the chairperson is to be nominated (either by way of resolution, by way of function (eg, chair of supervisory board) or by way of other criteria (eg, age, participation in the GmbH or another way)). The chairperson is responsible for directing the shareholders' meeting. In particular, he or she needs to ensure that all of the issues on the agenda are properly discussed and that resolutions are passed in accordance with the applicable laws.

Unlike the Stock Corporation Act, the Act on Limited Liability Companies does not generally require that minutes are taken at shareholders' meetings unless this is mandatorily prescribed by law. In particular, this is the case when the articles of association are amended or when resolutions are passed regarding the transformation of the company's corporate structure.[34] Apart from these cases, where a notarial deed must be issued, the taking of minutes at a shareholders' meeting is nevertheless usual and standard practice. The appropriate content of these minutes is often specified in the articles of association, and usually comprises the place, time and date of the meeting, when it begins and ends, confirmation that the meeting has been properly convened, the persons present, the petitions put forward by the shareholders, the topics to be resolved, the manner and results of the voting on the respective topics and the signature of the chairperson. The articles may, however, also stipulate other formal details which must be recorded.

---

33 *Gesetz über die Mitbestimmung der Arbeitnehmer* (MitbestG) (Co-Determination Act) 1976, s25, para. 1, no. 2 (FRG); see also *Aktiengesetz* (AktG) (Stock Corporation Act) 1965, s118, para. 3 (FRG); where the participation of the management board and of the supervisory board in the shareholders' meetings is considered normal.

34 *Gesetz betreffend die Gesellschaft mit beschränkter Haftung* (GmbHG) (Act on Limited Liability Companies) 1892, s53, para. 2 (FRG); *Umwandlungsgesetz* (UmwG) (Law Regulating the Transformation of Companies) 1994, s193, para. 3, sentence 1 (FRG).

If one shareholder holds all the shares in the company, mandatory law requires that he or she must approve and sign the minutes immediately after passing a resolution.[35]

C. Passing of resolutions

82. Classes of voting rights

According to statutory law, each euro of the nominal amount of a share grants one vote at the shareholders' meeting.[36] The articles of association may provide for a different distribution of voting rights amongst the shareholders. It is possible to exclude or reduce the voting rights of a shareholder, or give the shareholder additional voting rights within the articles of association. In the event of such a deviation from statutory law, the consent of all shareholders whose rights will be negatively affected by such a provision is required. This consent may be given when the articles of association are drawn up or at any later point in time in connection with a change of the voting rights.

83. Proxy voting

As outlined above,[37] a shareholder is not required to appear personally at a shareholders' meeting, but may send a proxy in his or her place. Unless otherwise stipulated by the articles, this form of representation requires a written power of attorney.[38] The articles may also set forth more stringent criteria for the participation rights and stipulate that only a personal appearance of the shareholders at the shareholders' meeting is allowed, that is, that proxy voting is excluded. A common regulation is that a shareholder may only be represented by other shareholders or by persons practising certain professions where they are subject to a professional duty of confidentiality, such as legal or tax advisers. A written power of attorney granted to a proxy for participation in the shareholders' meeting can, in principle, be revoked at any time. It will not prevent the shareholder issuing the power of attorney from being able

---

35 *Gesetz betreffend die Gesellschaft mit beschränkter Haftung* (GmbHG) (Act on Limited Liability Companies) 1892, s48, para. 3 (FRG).

36 *Gesetz betreffend die Gesellschaft mit beschränkter Haftung* (GmbHG) (Act on Limited Liability Companies) 1892, s47, para. 2 (FRG).

37 See Section 81.

38 *Gesetz betreffend die Gesellschaft mit beschränkter Haftung* (GmbHG) (Act on Limited Liability Companies) 1892, s47, para. 3 (FRG).

to appear in person at the shareholders' meeting and exercise his or her participation rights. If an irrevocable power of attorney were to be granted, this would be very similar to a situation in which the voting right is separated from the shareholding, which is not acceptable under German law. It would have to be considered in each individual case in question whether or not a failure to observe the restrictions in this regard is present.

84. Voting agreements and pools

Within the limits prescribed by mandatory statutory law[39] and standards of morality,[40] shareholders are entitled to commit themselves to exercising their voting rights in a shareholders' meeting in a certain way. The typical situation would be when a shareholder enters into a voting agreement with another person (this person being a shareholder or a third party), thereby committing him- or herself to exercising his or her voting rights according to the instructions of such a person. Such an arrangement is often found in the form of a supplementary provision attached to a pledge or lien agreement in which the pledgee is granted the right to instruct the shareholder as to how to execute his or her voting right relating to the pledged share. The pledging of the shares does not in itself grant or transfer the voting rights in these shares.[41]

Also not untypical are voting arrangements between the shareholders themselves whereby the shareholders promise to exercise their voting rights in a certain uniform way. The way in which the voting right is exercised is either determined by a majority vote of the 'pooling shareholders', by instructions given by one shareholder, or by any other way stipulated in the pooling agreement between the shareholders. By entering into such a pooling agreement, the shareholders establish a civil law partnership (*Gesellschaft bürgerlichen Rechts*). A valid voting arrangement may be enforced before the courts. It is, however, highly disputed among legal scholars and the courts whether an arrangement stipulated in such a voting agreement may also be enforced by way of injunctive relief.

Apart from the limits prescribed by statutory law and standards of morality, voting arrangements or voting pools may not be used

39 *Bürgerliches Gesetzbuch* (BGB) (Civil Code) 1900, s134 (FRG).
40 *Bürgerliches Gesetzbuch* (BGB) (Civil Code) 1900, s138 (FRG).
41 For details see Section 192.

to circumvent the exclusion of the voting right of one shareholder with regard to a certain resolution.[42]

85. Fiduciary duties to vote in a certain way

All shareholders are in principle entitled to exercise their voting rights at the shareholders' meeting at their sole and unlimited discretion. In certain individual cases, shareholders may, however, be restricted in terms of the way they exercise their voting right, in particular on the basis of their fiduciary duties (also called duty of loyalty) towards their fellow shareholders and the GmbH.[43] The fiduciary duties may even result in the consequence that a shareholder is obliged to exercise his or her voting rights in a certain way in order to prevent damages occurring to the company or other shareholders. If a shareholder votes contrary to his fiduciary duty, the respective vote is considered void. It will not be taken into account when establishing the outcome of the specific shareholders' resolution. If the vote is taken into account and plays a decisive role as regards the outcome, the resolution is contestable.

86. Exclusion of voting rights

Under certain circumstances, a shareholder might not be entitled to make use of his or her voting right in a shareholders' meeting with regard to a specific resolution to be passed. If a case such as this applies, the shareholder, or his or her agent or proxy, may not participate in the respective voting process. The same applies if solely the agent but not the shareholder is subject to exclusion rights of this nature. The reason for the exclusion of the voting right is to avoid an obvious collision of interests between the interests of the shareholder in question on the one hand and those of the company and the other shareholders on the other. No person is entitled to decide whether the company should enter into business with him or her or be a judge in his or her own case. The exclusion of the voting right, however, does not exclude the right of the shareholder to participate in the shareholders' meeting and to speak on the issue. The shareholder is only excluded from casting his or her vote.

The first scenario in which a shareholder is excluded from taking part in the voting process is when a resolution is to be passed on

---

42 For details see Section 86.
43 For details on the duty of loyalty, see Section 64.

whether he or she should be discharged (*Entlastung*).[44] This scenario comprises situations in which a shareholder additionally holds an office as managing director or as a member of the supervisory board, liquidator, etc. The shareholder will not only be excluded from voting if the shareholders' meeting is to reach a resolution on the discharging of an individual member of the corresponding corporate body (which it is entitled to do), but also if the respective corporate body to which the shareholder belongs is to be discharged in its entirety. Whether or not the exclusion also applies if the shareholders' meeting reaches a resolution on discharging a fellow member of the respective corporate body is a matter of controversy.

Secondly, shareholders are not entitled to exercise their voting rights if this results in them being exempted from liability.[45] The term 'exemption' must be interpreted broadly and includes any and all measures by means of which the shareholder is even partly relieved of such liability (also deferral of payment). The word 'liability' must equally be interpreted broadly and means any and all liabilities which may arise in the relationship between the company and a shareholder, irrespective of its legal basis. The exclusion of the voting right also applies to security grantors who are also shareholders and who provide security for a shareholder liability from which the respective shareholder in question would be exempted.

Thirdly, the voting right may not be exercised if the resolution relates to a legal transaction (*Rechtsgeschäft*) to be entered into between the GmbH and a shareholder.[46] A legal transaction comprises agreements of all kinds as well as unilateral declarations (such as, eg, revocation, rescission, declaration of termination, etc) and the retroactive approval of legal transactions into which the company and the shareholder have entered.

In the last scenario in this regard, a shareholder is prohibited from casting his or her vote if the shareholders decide to initiate or settle a legal dispute with this shareholder.[47] A legal dispute

44 *Gesetz betreffend die Gesellschaft mit beschränkter Haftung* (GmbHG) (Act on Limited Liability Companies) 1892, s47, para. 4, sentence 1, or, alternatively, 1 (FRG).

45 *Gesetz betreffend die Gesellschaft mit beschränkter Haftung* (GmbHG) (Act on Limited Liability Companies) 1892, s47, para. 4, sentence 1, or, alternatively, 2 (FRG).

46 *Gesetz betreffend die Gesellschaft mit beschränkter Haftung* (GmbHG) (Act on Limited Liability Companies) 1892, s47, para. 4, sentence 2, or, alternatively, 1 (FRG).

47 *Gesetz betreffend die Gesellschaft mit beschränkter Haftung* (GmbHG) (Act on Limited Liability Companies) 1892, s47, para. 4, sentence 2, or, alternatively, 2 (FRG).

comprises proceedings of any kind, not only court proceedings but also arbitration proceedings and any other extrajudicial proceedings or proceedings preparatory to trial in court (eg, foreclosure or injunctive relief). In the same way, the initiation of a legal dispute not only comprises measures leading to a court trial but also other measures prior to such proceedings, such as the request of payment, threatening court proceedings etc. Finally, the settlement of a legal dispute comprises any and all measures leading to the conclusive termination thereof (eg, settlement or waiver).

In addition to the cases cited above, a shareholder who at the same time acts as a managing director is also excluded from taking part in the voting process if a resolution is to be reached regarding his or her removal as managing director 'for cause'. The typical example for such a resolution is the aforementioned removal of a managing director for cause or the termination of his or her service agreement for cause. In these cases, the shareholder in question is not entitled to vote, as this would mean that he or she would be a judge in his or her own case.

Nevertheless, shareholders may always exercise their voting rights when the shareholders' meeting votes on a 'social act' (*Sozialakt*). Social acts are measures which relate to internal company relations between the shareholders and the legal transactions relating thereto. Social acts are, in particular, the appointment and removal of managing directors (unless removed for cause, see previous paragraph) and members of the supervisory board, the forfeiture of a share, resolutions on the liquidation of the company, amendments to the articles of association, entering into control or profit and loss pooling agreements, transformation agreements, approval of the transfer of shares etc. This means, in particular, that a shareholder may vote in his or her own favour to become a managing director of the GmbH.

The statutory regulations on the exclusion of the voting right may be freely amended in the articles of association if the reasons for an exclusion are specified in detail. On the other hand, a limitation or even exclusion is only possible to a very limited extent. The details in this regard remain an issue of great contention in jurisprudence and amongst scholars. It is, however, recognised that in the case of discharge, of exemption from a liability and with regard to all measures taken for cause against a shareholder, the exclusion of the voting right is mandatory law which may not be amended by the articles of association.

87. Majority requirements

Unless otherwise stipulated by law or the articles of association, the resolutions in a shareholders' meeting are passed with a simple majority of the votes cast.[48] Votes are given with either a 'yes' or a 'no'. Abstentions from voting are not taken into account. Each one euro of the nominal amount of a share grants one vote.[49]

A qualified majority of three quarters of the votes cast is required for the passing of important resolutions such as, for example, amendments to the articles of association (including capital increase or decrease),[50] the liquidation of the company,[51] measures under the Law Regulating the Transformation of Companies (*Umwandlungsgesetz*), the conclusion of domination or profit and loss transfer agreements, the exclusion of a shareholder, etc.

The articles of association may stipulate other majority requirements. In cases where mandatory law requires (at least) three quarters of the votes cast, the articles may increase, but not decrease, the percentage of the votes required for a resolution to be passed. In all other cases, where a simple majority is sufficient, the articles of association may provide for an increase of the votes cast for the passing of resolutions. It is, however, recognised that it is not possible to reduce the threshold for the passing of resolutions to a level below the minimum requirement for a simple majority.

88. Formal declaration and announcement of resolutions

Under German stock corporation law, a resolution passed by the shareholders' meeting only becomes valid if it has been formerly declared (*Feststellung*) and announced (*Verkündung*).[52] The Act on Limited Liability Companies does not require this kind of formal declaration and announcement in order for shareholders' resolutions to become valid. The articles of association may, however, provide otherwise. If a formal declaration of a resolution is announced at a shareholders' meeting and accordingly recorded in

---

48 *Gesetz betreffend die Gesellschaft mit beschränkter Haftung* (GmbHG) (Act on Limited Liability Companies) 1892, s47, para. 1 (FRG).

49 *Gesetz betreffend die Gesellschaft mit beschränkter Haftung* (GmbHG) (Act on Limited Liability Companies) 1892, s47, para. 2 (FRG).

50 *Gesetz betreffend die Gesellschaft mit beschränkter Haftung* (GmbHG) (Act on Limited Liability Companies) 1892, s53, para. 2 (FRG).

51 *Gesetz betreffend die Gesellschaft mit beschränkter Haftung* (GmbHG) (Act on Limited Liability Companies) 1892, s60, para. 1, no. 2 (FRG).

52 *Aktiengesetz* (AktG) (Stock Corporation Act) 1965, s130, para. 2 (FRG).

the minutes, the resolution passed with the content as described in the minutes is binding on the shareholders even if the content of such a declaration deviates from what has actually been resolved. If the declaration deviates from the resolution passed, the resolution must be challenged or reversed by a corresponding reverse resolution in order to render null and void the shareholders' resolution underlying the declaration.

88a. Passing of resolutions outside of shareholders' meetings

Shareholders' resolutions may also be passed outside of a shareholders' meeting. In this regard, the Act on Limited Liability Companies requires that all shareholders either agree in writing upon the content of the resolution to be passed or agree in writing to a resolution being passed outside the shareholders' meeting.[53] The written form requirement is also deemed satisfied if a vote is cast by way of facsimile or if a circular has been signed by all shareholders.

Typically, the articles of association further define whether and how a shareholders' resolution may be passed outside of a shareholders' meeting which takes place in person. In this context, other means of communication for the passing of resolutions are permitted and stipulated, for example, telephone, email or videoconference. A resolution may also be passed by way of circular resolution (*Umlaufbeschluss*). In some cases, however, the passing of a resolution outside of a shareholders' meeting is not allowed and a physical meeting of all shareholders or their proxies is required. In particular, this is the case with resolutions to be passed under the Law Regulating the Transformation of Companies or otherwise requiring the participation of a notary public (ie, amendments to the articles of association). Resolutions passed outside of a shareholders' meeting should subsequently be recorded in the minutes of the meeting.

D. Defective shareholders' resolutions

89. General

The Act on Limited Liability Companies does not contain any particular provisions regarding defective shareholders' resolutions and their consequences. It also does not contain regulations on how to

53 *Gesetz betreffend die Gesellschaft mit beschränkter Haftung* (GmbHG) (Act on Limited Liability Companies) 1892, s48, para. 2 (FRG).

challenge such resolutions. In the jurisprudence and amongst scholars this gap has been filled by applying the regulations contained in the Stock Corporation Act[54] accordingly and adapting them to suit the particular characteristics of the GmbH where necessary.

Both in a GmbH and in a stock corporation, a distinction can usually be drawn between four different types of resolution: non resolutions or mock resolutions (*Nichtbeschlüsse* and *Scheinbeschlüsse*), invalid resolutions, void resolutions and contestable resolutions.

90. Defective shareholder resolutions: non or mock resolutions

These kinds of 'resolutions' only appear to be shareholders' resolutions. In fact they are so obviously defective that they are not even considered resolutions and no one must be bound by them. In other words, 'resolutions' of this nature are immediately recognisably invalid. By way of example, the courts have qualified the following situations as constituting resolutions which only have the appearance of being shareholders' resolutions: the calling of a shareholders' meeting by a person who has no power to do so (eg, a third party which does not hold any share in the GmbH) and the passing of resolutions by non-shareholders or by shareholders involving the participation of several non-shareholders. If such a non-resolution is passed, it does not have any legal effect and anyone affected by the resolution (ie, also third parties) is entitled to claim that it is invalid without having to file a motion in court.

91. Defective shareholder resolutions: invalid resolutions

Invalid resolutions are resolutions which fail to satisfy one or several conditions which must be fulfilled in order for the resolution to become valid. A condition of this nature could for instance be the necessary consent of certain shareholders or of third parties. Another example in this regard would be when an agent without proper authorisation participates in the resolution and the consent of the represented shareholder has not yet been given. Until this consent is granted, the resolution remains provisionally invalid (*schwebend unwirksam*). As soon as the requisite condition for the resolution has been satisfied, the resolution becomes valid. If, on the other hand, the unsatisfied condition is not going to be satisfied any more, the resolution becomes ultimately invalid and void.

---

54 *Aktiengesetz* (AktG) (Stock Corporation Act) 1965, s241 *et seq.* (FRG).

92. Defective shareholder resolutions: void resolutions

The German stock corporation law sets out certain serious errors which may occur in connection with a shareholders' resolution, making the resolution null and void.[55] It is recognised that a shareholders' resolution of a GmbH may be null and void under the same circumstances. The grounds set out in the Stock Corporation Act leading to a shareholders' resolution becoming null and void are mandatory law and may neither be extended nor limited by the articles of association.

First, a shareholders' resolution is considered void if it has been passed in a meeting which has not been properly convened.[56] Examples for defective notices of meetings would be the convening of a shareholders' meeting by a person who is not competent or when there is a failure to properly invite all shareholders. This consequence, namely the resolution being rendered null and void, will, however, not apply in the event that all of the shareholders appear at the shareholders' meeting and none of the shareholders contradict the passing of resolutions during the meeting.

Secondly, a shareholders' resolution is deemed void if a notarisation of the resolution is required by law and the notarisation has not been undertaken.[57] As opposed to the case where a stock corporation is concerned, where all shareholders' resolutions must be notarised, the resolutions of a GmbH only need to be notarised if this is explicitly prescribed by mandatory law. Included among the important cases in which notarisation to this effect is required are amendments of the articles of association,[58] resolutions under the Law Regulating the Transformation of Companies (*Umwandlungsgesetz*) and resolutions regarding the issue of entering into domination, or profit and loss transfer agreements.

Thirdly, resolutions are considered void if they are not compatible with the character of a GmbH or if the content of a resolution violates regulations which are either exclusively or predominantly designed to protect the interests of the creditors of the company or if these have been adopted in the public interest.[59] Given the broad wording, it is difficult to establish general rules as to when a

---

55 *Aktiengesetz* (AktG) (Stock Corporation Act) 1965, s241 (FRG) accordingly.
56 *Aktiengesetz* (AktG) (Stock Corporation Act) 1965, s241, no. 2 (FRG) accordingly.
57 *Aktiengesetz* (AktG) (Stock Corporation Act) 1965, s241, no. 2 (FRG) accordingly.
58 *Gesetz betreffend die Gesellschaft mit beschränkter Haftung* (GmbHG) (Act on Limited Liability Companies) 1892, s53, para. 2 (FRG).
59 *Aktiengesetz* (AktG) (Stock Corporation Act) 1965, s241, no. 3 (FRG) accordingly.

resolution will be void under this provision. It must be determined on a case-by-case basis whether a resolution violates regulations which are in force to protect the interests of creditors or of the general public. One example of a violation of regulations adopted in the interest of the creditors of the company would be shareholders' resolutions which violate mandatory statutory rules on the raising and maintenance of the share capital.

A shareholders' resolution may also be void if, by way of its content, it violates standards of morality (*gute Sitten*).[60] Again, given the extensive scope of this provision, it is necessary to examine on a case-by-case basis whether or not a resolution violates this standard. However, a violation of this nature will not occur often, since the requirements associated with this standard are rather high. Additionally, a shareholders' resolution is considered void if it has been declared so by a court as a result of an action of opposition (*Anfechtungsklage*).[61] A shareholders' resolution is further void if the respective resolution has been deleted from the commercial register based on a final court decision.[62]

In addition to these cases, the Stock Corporation Act sets out further grounds leading to the invalidity of a shareholders' resolution which also apply accordingly in the case of a GmbH. These further grounds for the invalidity of a resolution include, for example, the election of members of the supervisory board subject to certain serious violations of statutory law,[63] resolutions on the use of the net profits for the financial year if the resolution on the approval of the annual financial statement is null and void,[64] and resolutions on the approval of the annual financial statement if this resolution is subject to major defects.[65]

However, as is the case in a stock corporation, the invalidity of a shareholders' resolution of a GmbH is subject to the statute of limitations. If a shareholders' resolution which has not been properly notarised is registered in the commercial register, it is no longer possible to claim its invalidity. Generally, other grounds which give rise to invalidity can no longer be claimed if three years have passed since the invalid resolution was registered in the commercial

60 *Aktiengesetz* (AktG) (Stock Corporation Act) 1965, s241, no. 4 (FRG) accordingly.
61 *Aktiengesetz* (AktG) (Stock Corporation Act) 1965, s241, no. 5 (FRG) accordingly.
62 *Aktiengesetz* (AktG) (Stock Corporation Act) 1965, s241, no. 6 (FRG) accordingly.
63 *Aktiengesetz* (AktG) (Stock Corporation Act) 1965, s250 (FRG) accordingly.
64 *Aktiengesetz* (AktG) (Stock Corporation Act) 1965, s253 (FRG) accordingly.
65 *Aktiengesetz* (AktG) (Stock Corporation Act) 1965, s256 (FRG) accordingly.

register.[66] Besides, as a general principle of law, the right to challenge a void resolution is subject to forfeiture (*Verwirkung*).

93. Defective shareholder resolutions: contestable resolutions
Aside from being invalid, a resolution may also contain errors which are not considered so severe as to make the resolution void, but which merely entitle the party in question to challenge (*anfechten*) the resolution in court. A shareholders' resolution is contestable in the event of a violation of statutory law or the articles of association if the violation in question does not in itself lead to the resolution being null and void.[67] Such resolutions remain valid despite their legal flaws unless they are challenged by way of an action of opposition (*Anfechtungsklage*). Should the action be successful, the court will declare the resolution void. If such an action of opposition is not filed, the resolution becomes incontestable once the period for opposition (*Anfechtungsfrist*) has elapsed (for details, see Section 94).

As opposed to the case where errors which make a shareholders' resolution void are concerned, a successful annulment of a resolution not only requires that the resolution violates the law or the articles of association. In addition, since any violation of the law or the articles of association gives rise to the right to challenge the respective shareholders' resolution, a violation will only lead to a successful challenge of the resolution if the violation of the law or the articles bore relevance for the resolution passed. Whether or not a violation was 'relevant' mainly depends on whether it was the intention of the violated rule to protect the interest of all shareholders in adequately participating in the decision-making process of the company. Each case must be considered individually, taking into account the specific rule in question. A relatively substantial body of case law has been developed by the courts and legal scholars in this regard. The burden of proof as regards this lack of relevance lies with the company, wherein the shareholder filing the claim must specify the violation of the provision in question to the extent reasonably possible. This depends largely upon whether he or she had insight into the reasons for the violation of the provision.

However, a resolution can (also) no longer be challenged if it has been confirmed by a (proper) new resolution and this new resolution has not been challenged within the period for opposition.[68]

---

66 *Aktiengesetz* (AktG) (Stock Corporation Act) 1965, s242 (FRG) accordingly.
67 *Aktiengesetz* (AktG) (Stock Corporation Act) 1965, s243, para. 1 (FRG) accordingly.
68 *Aktiengesetz* (AktG) (Stock Corporation Act) 1965, s244 (FRG) accordingly.

94. Defective shareholder resolutions: legal remedies before state courts

Defective resolutions may be challenged in court in a number of different ways. Resolutions which are void are challenged by way of an action for nullity (*Nichtigkeitsklage*).[69] The aim of such an action is to obtain the confirmation (*Feststellung*) of the nullity of the resolution by a court. Resolutions which are not void in themselves but are contestable are typically challenged by way of an action of opposition leading to the court declaring that the respective resolution is void.[70] In practice, actions for nullity and actions of opposition are filed in parallel, as it is often not exactly clear whether a resolution is void or only contestable.

Sometimes, a so-called action for a positive declaratory judgment (*positive Beschlussfeststellungsklage*) may be filed. This kind of action is usually combined with an action for nullity or an action of opposition as the former action only declares the respective resolution void, but does not replace the void resolution with another valid resolution. Actions for a positive declaratory judgment may typically be filed when votes are not properly counted or when a shareholder has exercised his or her voting right even though he or she was excluded from doing so. In these cases, the court may itself rule on what the proper resolution was that should have been passed. Furthermore, shareholders may also file a simple action for a declaratory judgment (*Feststellungsklage*) if they want the court to confirm that a resolution has been passed with a certain content. However, if at the same time the nullity of the resolution should be confirmed or the resolution should be declared void, the shareholder must file an action for nullity or an action of opposition. Finally, in the event that a shareholder's vote constitutes a violation of his or her fiduciary duties, the person's fellow shareholders may file an action (*Leistungsklage*) with the aim of replacing the vote cast in contravention of the fiduciary duties with a vote which complies with such duties.

All shareholders are entitled to file such claims with a court, irrespective of whether or not they have participated in the relevant shareholders' resolution. As opposed to the case where a stock corporation is concerned, the managing directors are generally not entitled to challenge a resolution. By way of exception, they are

---

69 *Aktiengesetz* (AktG) (Stock Corporation Act) 1965, s249 (FRG) accordingly.

70 *Aktiengesetz* (AktG) (Stock Corporation Act) 1965, s243 *et seq*. (FRG) accordingly.

granted such a right if the resolution needs to be executed by the managing directors and such an execution would constitute a violation of statutory law or a failure to observe due diligence as prudent businessmen. If the GmbH has a supervisory board, the members of the board are entitled to challenge a shareholders' resolution if its execution would constitute a criminal offence or could result in damage claims against the members of the supervisory board. The action must be filed against the company only.[71] The GmbH is represented by its managing directors.[72]

An action of opposition must be filed within a reasonable period of time. The courts have defined that a reasonable period of time should usually not exceed four weeks following the passing of the resolution in so far as there are no particular circumstances which would justify an extension of this time period.[73] Shareholders filing claims after the aforementioned time period must provide grounds as to why they were not able to file the claim earlier. The action for nullity, however, is not subject to such a time restriction. The time limit for the filing of an action for nullity is prescribed by the three-year period, upon expiration of which a void resolution registered with the commercial register becomes valid.[74]

The regional court (*Landgericht*) which is the competent court for the place of business of the GmbH shall have exclusive jurisdiction with regard to any actions filed against shareholders' resolutions.[75] A court decision rendered in an action for nullity or an action of opposition and affirming the motion of the plaintiff(s) applies for and against all persons (company, shareholders, managing directors, supervisory board and third parties). In the event that the motion is dismissed, however, the dismissal only applies with effect for the relationship between the company and the plaintiff.

---

71 *Aktiengesetz* (AktG) (Stock Corporation Act) 1965, s246, para. 2, sentence 1 (FRG) accordingly.

72 *Aktiengesetz* (AktG) (Stock Corporation Act) 1965, s246, para. 2, sentence 2 (FRG) accordingly.

73 For example, 1 June 1987, *Bundesgerichtshof* (German Federal Supreme Court) (II ZR 128/86) – BGHZ 101, 113 *et seq.*

74 See Section 91.

75 *Aktiengesetz* (AktG) (Stock Corporation Act) 1965, s246, para. 3, sentence 1 (FRG) accordingly.

95. Defective shareholder resolutions: legal remedies before arbitration courts

Until recently, the question of whether shareholder resolutions may be subjected to arbitration was an issue of great contention between legal scholars and the courts. In its decision of 6 April 2009,[76] the Federal Supreme Court made it clear that – under certain circumstances which shall be outlined below – shareholder resolutions may also be brought before an arbitration court if this is provided by either the articles of association or an individual agreement extraneous to the articles which is to be entered into by all shareholders (not only the shareholders involved in the dispute) and the company. The arbitration court may then decide on the relevant issues in the same way as a state court with binding effect in particular on the GmbH, its shareholders, the managing directors and, if applicable, any members of a supervisory or advisory body ('*inter omnes*').

The court clarified that the decision of an arbitration court would only be of the same legal nature as a decision issued by a state court if the legal proceedings before the arbitration court were to grant at least the same degree of protection for the (potential) parties involved in a dispute as a state court would. In order to meet this requirement, the arbitration clause in the articles of association or an individual agreement must satisfy the following requirements:

- The arbitration clause must either be part of the articles of association or of an individual agreement to be entered into between all shareholders and the company.
- Each shareholder and each corporate body must be informed about the initiation of an arbitration proceeding and must thus be enabled to participate in the proceeding as an intervening party (*Nebenintervenient*).
- All shareholders must participate in the selection of the arbitrators if these are not selected by a third, neutral party. A simple majority of the votes may be considered sufficient if so provided in the articles or the agreement.
- Finally, it must be ensured that all proceedings relating to the same shareholders' resolution and to the same subject matter are jointly heard by one arbitration court.

76 6 April 2009, *Bundesgerichtshof* (German Federal Supreme Court) (II ZR 255/08) – BGH NJW 2009, 1962.

Only once all of these criteria have been met, may the decision of an arbitration court called upon by the shareholders and the company replace a decision of a state court. If none or some of these criteria have not been met, the state courts shall have proper jurisdiction.

VI. Managing directors

A. Appointment and removal of managing directors

96. Appointment of the managing directors

A GmbH may have one or more managing directors which are appointed by the shareholders' meeting by a simple majority of the votes cast.[1] The right to nominate the managing directors may, however, be transferred to another corporate body such as the supervisory board or a committee of the shareholders' meeting. The articles of association may also provide that a single shareholder shall be entitled to appoint the managing directors. If the company is subject to the Co-Determination Act (*Mitbestimmungsgesetz*), the managing directors are appointed by the mandatory supervisory board. In cases where the managing directors are appointed by the shareholders' meeting, a resolution with a simple majority of the votes cast is sufficient. The articles of association may stipulate a higher majority requirement. If the managing directors are appointed by a mandatory supervisory board, a two-third majority of the votes cast is required.[2]

Unlike the Stock Corporation Act, the Act on Limited Liability Companies does not provide for a specific or limited term in office where the managing directors are concerned. They will thus be appointed for life in so far as the articles of association or the service agreements do not stipulate otherwise. On the other hand, the managing directors of a GmbH may be removed much more easily than those of an AG (see Section 97). An exception to the unlimited term exists where the company is subject to the Co-Determination Act. In this case, the managing directors – like in a stock corporation – may only be appointed for a term of five years with the possibility of re-nomination.[3]

1 *Gesetz betreffend die Gesellschaft mit beschränkter Haftung* (GmbHG) (Act on Limited Liability Companies) 1892, s46, no. 5, 47, para.1 (FRG).

2 *Gesetz über die Mitbestimmung der Arbeitnehmer* (MitbestG) (Co-Determination Act) 1976, s31, para. 2 (FRG).

3 *Gesetz über die Mitbestimmung der Arbeitnehmer* (MitbestG) (Co-Determination Act) 1976, s31 p. 2 (FRG); *Aktiengesetz* (AktG) (Stock Corporation Act) 1965, s84, para. 1, sentence 1 (FRG).

The appointment of a managing director must be registered with the commercial register,[4] wherein the managing director must confirm that he or she is not aware of any circumstances preventing his or her nomination as managing director (prohibition from practising certain professions, criminal offences),[5] that he or she has been instructed either by a domestic or foreign notary or by a consular officer, either orally or in written form, and that he or she is subject to an unrestricted duty of disclosure towards the court.[6] This registration must be published in the commercial register. The registration of the managing director's appointment in the commercial register is not a prerequisite which has to be satisfied for it to become effective. It is merely declaratory. The nomination becomes valid the moment the competent corporate body (see above) has resolved that a certain person shall become managing director of the company and the nominated person has accepted being appointed managing director on the basis of this resolution. No person may be forced to become a managing director without his or her consent.

97. Removal of managing directors

A managing director of a GmbH may be removed at any time without notice and without any particular reason being required.[7] According to statutory law, the shareholders' meeting is responsible for removing a managing director by simple majority of the votes cast.[8] The articles of association may confer upon another corporate body or an individual shareholder the right to remove the managing directors. In contrast to the case where a stock corporation is concerned, where a director may only be removed for cause, the managing directors of a GmbH are largely unprotected against their removal and are effectively at the mercy of the goodwill of the shareholders. The reason for this difference lies in the dissimilar structure of the two types of companies. Since a GmbH is designed to be far more personalised, and usually has a small

---

4 *Gesetz betreffend die Gesellschaft mit beschränkter Haftung* (GmbHG) (Act on Limited Liability Companies) 1892, s39, 8, para. 1, no. 2, para. 3 (FRG).

5 For further details see Section 98.

6 *Gesetz betreffend die Gesellschaft mit beschränkter Haftung* (GmbHG) (Act on Limited Liability Companies) 1892, s8, para. 3, sentence 2 (FRG).

7 *Gesetz betreffend die Gesellschaft mit beschränkter Haftung* (GmbHG) (Act on Limited Liability Companies) 1892, s38, para. 1 (FRG).

8 *Gesetz betreffend die Gesellschaft mit beschränkter Haftung* (GmbHG) (Act on Limited Liability Companies) 1892, s46, no. 5, 47, para. 1 (FRG).

circle of shareholders which generally have a closer day-to-day relationship with the managing directors compared to the situation in an AG. According to the law, the interests of the shareholders in replacing a managing director they no longer have faith in are deemed to have priority over the interest the managing director might have in remaining in office.

The right to remove a managing director freely and at any time may be limited in the articles of association so that removal is only possible for cause[9] or for any other reasons the shareholders deem appropriate (if not completely arbitrary). If the GmbH is subject to the Co-Determination Act, the managing directors may only be removed for cause, as the provisions of the Stock Corporation Act will apply accordingly.[10]

Such a cause for the removal of the managing director from office is given if it would be unacceptable to the company and/or the shareholders if he or she were to remain in office. This applies typically in the case of a gross violation of assigned duties on the part of the managing director or the inability to properly manage the company. Another cause for removal could be a (substantial) disagreement between the managing director and the majority of the shareholders. In a case decided upon by the Cologne Court of Appeal,[11] through gross negligence a managing director ignored the competence of the shareholders' meeting when deciding on an issue which was of essential importance for the company (in the case in question, the termination of a loan agreement). The court ruled that the conditions for removing the managing director for cause were satisfied, since the necessary trust between director and shareholders no longer existed and the director thereby became unacceptable to the company and its shareholders.

The reasons for the removal do not necessarily have to relate to the person of the managing director him- or herself, but may also be found in the specific situation of the company or other surrounding circumstances. It is also not required that the managing director is responsible for the grounds leading to his or her removal.

It has to be noted that the removal from office as managing director does not automatically lead to a termination of the service

---

9 *Gesetz betreffend die Gesellschaft mit beschränkter Haftung* (GmbHG) (Act on Limited Liability Companies) 1892, s38, para. 2, sentence 1 (FRG).

10 *Mitbestimmungsgesetz* (MitbestG) (Co-Determination Act) 1976, s1, para. 1, 6, para. 1, 31, para. 1 (FRG); *Aktiengesetz* (AktG) (Stock Corporation Act) 1965, s84, para. 3 (FRG).

11 1 June 2010, *Oberlandesgericht Köln* (Cologne Court of Appeal) (18 U 72/09).

agreement between the managing director and the GmbH.[12] The position as managing director and the underlying service agreement are two separate legal relationships to be considered separately from and independently of each other. However, in most cases, a removal from office for cause also entails a right to terminate the service agreement for cause, even though this is not necessarily always the case.

Managing directors may also resign from office themselves at any time and without observing any notice period. A cause for resignation is not required. The resignation needs to be declared *vis-à-vis* the corporate body which appoints the managing directors (ie, shareholders' meeting, supervisory board, etc). However, a resignation may be considered legally abusive and therefore invalid if it occurs at an improper time or if it puts the company in a difficult position.

98. Personal requirements for appointment to the position of managing director

Statutory law does not stipulate many personal requirements which must be satisfied by a potential managing director. In particular, the law does not require that the managing director should have any particular qualifications. A managing director may either be a shareholder of the company or a third person not holding any shares in the company (*Fremdgeschäftsführer*).[13] He or she must be an individual with full legal capacity (ie, over 18 years of age) who is not under legal guardianship (*Betreuung*).[14] A legal entity does not qualify as a managing director of a GmbH. It is not required that the managing directors are German citizens, nor must they reside in Germany. Based on recent court decisions,[15] it is not even a requirement that the managing director of a GmbH has permission to enter Germany at any time. Since the Act to Modernise the Law Governing GmbHs and Combat Abuses came into force, a German GmbH may also have its place of business and pursue its business

---

12 For further details see Section 99.

13 *Gesetz betreffend die Gesellschaft mit beschränkter Haftung* (GmbHG) (Act on Limited Liability Companies) 1892, s6, para. 3, sentence 1 (FRG).

14 *Gesetz betreffend die Gesellschaft mit beschränkter Haftung* (GmbHG) (Act on Limited Liability Companies) 1892, s6, para. 2, sentence 2, no. 1 (FRG).

15 17 December 2009, *Oberlandesgericht München* (Munich Court of Appeal) (31 Wx 142/09); 16 April 2009, *Oberlandesgericht Düsseldorf* (Düsseldorf Court of Appeal) (3 Wx 85/09).

activities (exclusively) outside Germany.[16] It is only required that the place of business as set out in the articles of association must be located in Germany.[17] Against this background, the courts have ruled that it is no legal prerequisite for the managing director of a GmbH to be able to enter Germany at any time, even if its actual business activities and place of business are located within Germany. It is also not a prerequisite that the managing directors are in command of the German language. However, since a managing director will have to communicate in multiple ways with the German authorities and potentially with banks where German is the official language of communication, a managing director who is not in command of the German language is advised to have external or internal advisers or employees who are in sufficient command of the German language.

Furthermore, the Act on Limited Liability Companies requires that a managing director may not be prohibited by a court decision or an administrative order from practising certain professions or be active in a certain branch if the profession or branch he is prohibited from being active in (at least partly) coincides with the business purpose of the company.[18] Moreover, a managing director may not have been sentenced, either in Germany or abroad, for certain criminal offences relating to property, insolvency, fraud, accounting and bookkeeping.[19] In the event that the managing director has been sentenced for any such criminal offences, he or she is prohibited from being a managing director of the company for a period of five years onwards from the issuing of the final court decision. Periods during which the managing director was held in

---

16 *Gesetz betreffend die Gesellschaft mit beschränkter Haftung* (GmbHG) (Act on Limited Liability Companies) 1892, s4a (FRG).

17 For details see Section 15.

18 *Gesetz betreffend die Gesellschaft mit beschränkter Haftung* (GmbHG) (Act on Limited Liability Companies) 1892, s6, para. 2, sentence 2, no. 2 (FRG).

19 *Gesetz betreffend die Gesellschaft mit beschränkter Haftung* (GmbHG) (Act on Limited Liability Companies) 1892, s6, para. 2, sentence 2, no. 3, sentence 3 (FRG); *Insolvenzordnung* (InsO) (Insolvency Ordinance) 1994, s15a, para. 4 (delay of insolvency) (FRG); *Strafgesetzbuch* (StGB) (German Criminal Code) 1871, ss283–283d, 263–264a, 265b–266a (bankruptcy, fraudulent preference of creditors or debitors, fraud and breach of trust) (FRG); *Gesetz betreffend die Gesellschaft mit beschränkter Haftung* (GmbHG) (Act on Limited Liability Companies) 1892, s82 (FRG); *Aktiengesetz* (AktG) (Stock Corporation Act) 1965, ss399, 400 (FRG); *Handelsgesetzbuch* (HGB) (Commercial Code) 1897, s331 (FRG); *Umwandlungsgesetz* (UmwG) (Law Regulating the Transformation of Companies) 1994, s313 (FRG); *Publizitätsgesetz* (PublG) (Act on the Accounting of Certain Companies and Groups) 1969, s17 (false information and false depiction) (FRG).

custody will not be taken into account where the calculation of the five-year period is concerned.[20]

99. Service agreement

The appointment as managing director is almost always accompanied by the conclusion of a service agreement with the said managing director. An exception may apply in cases where the managing director is already under contract with the GmbH or another group company. The service agreement is not subject to any particular requirements in terms of form and may also be concluded verbally. Nevertheless, in practice almost all service agreements are entered into in written form. The service agreement usually contains regulations on the tasks and responsibilities of the managing director, on his or her compensation and on the termination of the agreement.

If the articles of association do not provide otherwise, the shareholders' meeting is responsible for entering into and amending the service agreement with the managing director on behalf of the GmbH. This is considered a responsibility which is supplementary to the right to appoint and remove the managing director. Nevertheless, the articles of association may also provide that another corporate body will be responsible for entering into and amending the service agreement on behalf of the company, for example, the supervisory board or a shareholders' committee. In a company which is subject to the Co-Determination Act, the company is mandatorily represented by the supervisory board when entering into or amending the service agreement with the managing director.[21] The service agreement does not have to specify a certain term, but it usually does.

The service agreement is typically entered into with the GmbH itself. Nevertheless, it is also possible to conclude this with a third party which does not have to be a shareholder of the GmbH, even though this would normally be the case. A typical example in practice is that the managing director of a GmbH enters into a service agreement with a parent or another company of the group of the GmbH. Such a construction, despite being legally accepted, creates

---

20 *Gesetz betreffend die Gesellschaft mit beschränkter Haftung* (GmbHG) (Act on Limited Liability Companies) 1892, s6, para. 2, sentence 2 (FRG).

21 *Mitbestimmungsgesetz* (MitbestG) (Co-Determination Act) 1976, s1, para. 1, 6, para. 1, 31, para. 1 (FRG); *Aktiengesetz* (AktG) (Stock Corporation Act) 1965, s84, para. 1, sentence 1 (FRG).

certain difficulties in the relationship between the managing director and its GmbH on the one hand, and the parent company employing the managing director on the other hand. The latter may receive instructions from both sides and then end up in a situation where the instructions are conflicting. This issue should already be addressed at the point of entering into the service agreement with the parent or other group company or when the position as managing director is assumed, whichever occurs earlier.

The Act on Limited Liability Companies does not contain a regulation, as the German Stock Corporation Act does, which stipulates that the compensation must be adequate in view of the tasks of the director and the overall situation of the company.[22] However, it is recognised that the basic concept underlying this provision also applies in a GmbH, even though the shareholders in a GmbH have more freedom to determine what they consider to be appropriate compensation. In determining adequate compensation, the company may take into account all kinds of circumstances, such as the respective business segment of the company, the overall business situation of the company, the capital structure, whether or not there are other directors, the responsibility of the director, his or her age and experience, the business goals to be achieved and the commensurate salary in comparable companies etc. Again, the generally personalised structure of the GmbH with only a few shareholders offers more freedom and flexibility in regulating these issues compared with a stock corporation in which there are typically a larger number of (often anonymous) shareholders. As is the case in any other corporation, the remuneration for a managing director in a GmbH typically consists of a fixed element and a bonus element (bonus for achievement of certain financial aims etc) plus a pension scheme. With the newly introduced possibility of creating authorised capital in a GmbH,[23] a shares option plan may also be established. In addition, a customary element of a service agreement with a managing director is that the company bears half of the costs for the usual insurances such as health insurance, invalidity insurance or accident insurance. Apart from these typical compensation components, the specific details may be freely negotiated between the company and the managing director.

22 *Aktiengesetz* (AktG) (Stock Corporation Act) 1965, s87, para. 1 (FRG).

23 *Gesetz betreffend die Gesellschaft mit beschränkter Haftung* (GmbHG) (Act on Limited Liability Companies) 1892, s55a (FRG).

The service agreement is subject to the general rules prescribed by the German Civil Code.[24] Since a managing director in a corporation is seen to hold the position of an employer rather than of an employee, the prevailing opinion amongst the courts and scholars is that the provisions contained in various employment laws designed for the protection of employees do not apply when it comes to managing directors. However, this does not preclude the applicability of certain employment law regulations to a managing director if this is called for in the specific situation. The courts apply the regulations on a case-by-case basis, taking into account the particular situation of the managing director. Many employment regulations already in themselves exclude their applicability to managing directors such as the Protection against Unfair Dismissal Act (*Kündigungsschutzgesetz*) and the law on working hours (*Arbeitszeitgesetz*).

In a remarkable decision issued by the Federal Labour Court (*Bundesarbeitsgericht*),[25] the court ruled that managing directors of a GmbH are to be considered 'consumers' (*Verbraucher*) within the meaning of the German Civil Code[26] if they are not at the same time shareholders in the company who hold at least a blocking minority (*Sperrminorität*). If directors do not hold such a blocking minority, they are to be treated like consumers, as they are bound by the instructions given by the shareholders' meeting. As a consequence, in the court's view, the service agreements of managing directors would be subject to the German regulations on general terms and conditions.[27] These regulations in particular stipulate that the clauses used by the company in the service agreement are "clear, easily understandable and not surprising in terms of their content". In view of the great volume of case law on labour agreements with (ordinary) employees, this means that the jurisprudence has in many cases established extremely high standards when it comes to a clause being accepted under the regulations on general terms and conditions, and that it has become very difficult to meet these standards. It is currently uncertain whether the ruling of the Federal Labour Court merely constitutes a one-off reference to general terms and conditions in order to resolve a particular case

24 *Gesetz betreffend die Gesellschaft mit beschränkter Haftung* (GmbHG) (Act on Limited Liability Companies) 1892, s55a (FRG).

25 19 May 2010, *Bundesarbeitsgericht* (German Federal Labour Court) (5 AZR 253/09), NRW 2010, 2827.

26 *Bürgerliches Gesetzbuch* (BGB) (Civil Code) 1900, s13 (FRG).

27 *Bürgerliches Gesetzbuch* (BGB) (Civil Code) 1900, s 305 *et seq.* (FRG).

or – as is to be feared – that the court and following it also the Federal Supreme Court will resort to the rules on general terms and conditions if they deem a specific provision in a service agreement with a managing director to be inappropriate. In the future, this will create more uncertainty when drafting and negotiating service agreements with managing directors and means that the rules on general terms and conditions must be given special consideration. Legal scholars have criticised the application of the rules on general terms and conditions to managing directors as going beyond the intention behind these rules, namely to protect (ordinary) consumers in undertaking their daily business. It is doubtful whether managing directors really need (or even desire) this kind of protection. One solution in this regard, however, could be to insert at least certain regulations which do not necessarily have to be included in the service agreement in the by-laws or the articles of association of the GmbH. These regulations are agreements according to corporate law and as such are not subject to the regulations on general terms and conditions prescribed by the German Civil Code.[28]

The service agreement is a legal relationship the managing director enters into which is independent from the office of managing director itself. Since the service agreement and the office of managing director exist independently of each other, the removal of a person from the office of managing director will not automatically result in a termination of the service agreement. The termination of the service agreement is subject to the provisions contained therein and the additional regulations of the German Civil Code.[29] Grounds which entitle the company to remove a managing director from his or her office may not necessarily at the same time be grounds to terminate the service agreement, even if in practice this is often the case. The parties to the service agreement may, however, agree that when the managing director is removed from office, the underlying service agreement will also be terminated automatically, or that the removal of the managing director from office gives rise to the right to terminate the service agreement, either with or without notice.

The right to the extraordinary termination (*außerordentliche Kündigung*) of the service agreement is mandatory law and may not be excluded. An extraordinary termination is only possible for

28 *Bürgerliches Gesetzbuch* (BGB) (Civil Code) 1900, s310, para. 4 (FRG).
29 *Bürgerliches Gesetzbuch* (BGB) (Civil Code) 1900, s620 *et seq.* (FRG).

cause.[30] Usually, the grounds which permit an extraordinary termination of the service agreement must be more substantial than the grounds permitting the removal of a managing director from his or her office for cause. Grounds which typically allow the company to extraordinarily terminate the service agreement are criminal offences, the misuse of corporate powers, severe incompetence or severe violations of fiduciary duties. An extraordinary termination must be issued within two weeks from the date upon which the person entitled to terminate the agreement becomes aware of such grounds. Such grounds usually also give rise to the right to remove the managing director from office, even when the articles only allow removal from office for cause.

Finally, service agreements usually include a post-contractual non-compete obligation. For further details see Section 107.

B. Rights and obligations

100. Duty of loyalty

The rights and obligations listed below represent the most important rights and obligations a managing director has during his or her term in office.

First, to the same extent as a shareholder or member of the supervisory board, a managing director has a permanent duty of loyalty towards the GmbH while exercising these rights and obligations. In some cases, the duty of loyalty will even extend beyond the end of the term in office or the end of the service agreement with the managing director.

In simple terms, the duty of loyalty obliges a managing director to refrain from doing anything which may harm the company and to actively do everything reasonably possible which would be to its benefit. This very general rule is to a certain extent further defined by the relevant stipulations below. It remains, however, a measurement when assessing a specific activity taken by a managing director, in particular when determining whether or not managing directors have violated their obligations towards the GmbH as a prudent business person.[31]

---

30 *Bürgerliches Gesetzbuch* (BGB) (Civil Code) 1900, s626, para. 1 (FRG).

31 For details refer to Section 112 *et seq*.

101. Management (*Geschäftsführung*) of the GmbH

German law distinguishes between the management (*Geschäftsführung*) of a company and its representation (*Vertretung*) towards third parties.

The management of the company comprises all internal measures of the company not directed towards third parties which are aimed at accomplishing the purpose of the company. In other words, the management of the company comprises the internal affairs of the company relating to its daily business.

The duty of loyalty obliges a managing director to actively manage the company. However, the management powers of the managing director are limited in various ways. According to mandatory statutory law, the managing director is obliged to comply with the individual instructions given by the shareholders regarding the management of the company.[32] Furthermore, certain fundamental measures having a significant impact on the company as a whole or its shareholders are excluded from the management powers of the managing directors. Usually, the articles of association or the bylaws of the company stipulate that the directors may only take such measures with the (prior) consent of the shareholders' meeting. If the articles fail to stipulate such a list of situations in which consent is required, there is an unwritten limitation of the management powers of directors if they must assume that they cannot take a measure without the consent of the shareholders' meeting. If and when this is the case must be decided on a case-by-case basis and depends on the particular circumstances of the company. Typical fundamental measures in this respect would be, for example, the transfer of the place of business, a change in the company's trade name, a change regarding the business purpose of the company, a transfer of production or production stop, an amendment of the articles of association, the admission of new shareholders to the company, the sale of the company or its assets as a whole or of significant parts thereof, the creation of liabilities or granting of security above certain amounts etc. Decisions of such calibre which have a significant influence on the internal relations of the shareholders or of the overall situation of the GmbH require the consent of the shareholders or of any other competent corporate body.

---

32 *Gesetz betreffend die Gesellschaft mit beschränkter Haftung* (GmbHG) (Act on Limited Liability Companies) 1892, s37, para. 1 (FRG).

102. Representation (*Vertretung*) of the GmbH

The GmbH is mandatorily represented by its managing directors, both *vis-à-vis* third parties and before the courts. A managing director is obliged to use his or her power of representation in line with his or her duty of loyalty. If the company has one managing director, the company is represented by this managing director alone. If the company has several managing directors, the Act on Limited Liability Companies stipulates that the company is represented by all managing directors jointly.[33] The articles of association may – and in practice often do – amend this regulation in various ways. They may stipulate that each managing director is entitled to represent the company individually or that several managing directors are entitled to represent the company individually, whereas others may only represent the company collectively. A regulation which is often found in the articles of association is that the company is represented either by two managing directors or a managing director together with a proxy holder (*Prokurist*). In the event that a GmbH has no managing director (either in factual terms or for legal reasons – so-called '*Führungslosigkeit*'), by way of exception the company will be represented by the shareholders for the purpose of serving declarations of will or documents[34] and during insolvency.[35] Any declarations of will or documents may be served upon the GmbH under its business address published in the commercial register or upon a third person who is registered as being entitled to receive declarations on behalf of the GmbH.[36]

Aside from the question of how many managing directors or proxies are required to represent the GmbH, the power of the managing directors to represent the company *vis-à-vis* third parties may not be limited by internal measures of the company.[37] The articles or the by-laws of the company may not for instance prescribe (with effect *vis-à-vis* third parties) that a managing director may only legitimately represent the GmbH in transactions of a certain

---

33 *Gesetz betreffend die Gesellschaft mit beschränkter Haftung* (GmbHG) (Act on Limited Liability Companies) 1892, s35, para. 2, sentence 1 (FRG).

34 *Gesetz betreffend die Gesellschaft mit beschränkter Haftung* (GmbHG) (Act on Limited Liability Companies) 1892, s35, para. 1, sentence 2 (FRG).

35 *Insolvenzordnung* (InsO) (Insolvency Ordinance) 1994, s15a, para. 3. For further details see Section 109.

36 *Gesetz betreffend die Gesellschaft mit beschränkter Haftung* (GmbHG) (Act on Limited Liability Companies) 1892, s35, para. 2, sentence 3, 10, para. 2 (FRG).

37 *Gesetz betreffend die Gesellschaft mit beschränkter Haftung* (GmbHG) (Act on Limited Liability Companies) 1892, s37, para. 2 (FRG).

value, only in certain business areas, or only during a certain period of time. When entering into a legal transaction with a managing director of a GmbH, a third party must be certain that the person acting on behalf of the company is also entitled to represent the company in this particular transaction. Otherwise, legal relations with GmbHs would be significantly hampered. Whereas the factual statement as to whether a managing director may represent the company individually or only jointly in combination with other managing directors or proxies represents information which must be registered in the commercial register and is thus publicly available,[38] any further restrictions on the power of representation may not be registered. Therefore, such additional internal limitations (eg, business requiring prior consent of the shareholders) are only valid *vis-à-vis* third parties if the third party knows, or through gross negligence is not aware, that the managing director is acting beyond the internal limits of his or her power of representation. The same applies if the third party and the managing director act together in a collusive manner transcending the internal limits which apply to the managing director in order to damage the company. There is disagreement amongst scholars and the courts with regard to the exact consequences which result when the third party knows of the internal limitation or acts in collusion together with the managing director. Some scholars and appellate courts assume in this regard that the legal act is provisionally invalid, which entails the possibility that the company can agree to the transaction, thus making it valid and binding; other scholars and the Federal Supreme Court[39] are of the opinion that the respective transaction is void (section 138 German Civil Code). Shareholders, managing directors and members of the supervisory board are not considered third parties in this context, and are always considered to be aware of the internal restrictions on the power of representation.

The above may not, however, be understood to mean that a managing director may ignore the internal limitations set out in the articles, the by-laws or an instruction of the shareholders.[40] Managing directors are bound by their duty of loyalty and their service agreement to respect such internal restrictions of their power

38 *Gesetz betreffend die Gesellschaft mit beschränkter Haftung* (GmbHG) (Act on Limited Liability Companies) 1892, s10, para. 1, sentence 2 (FRG).

39 5 November 2003, *Bundesgerichtshof* (German Federal Supreme Court) (VIII ZR 218/01) – BGH NJW-RR 2004, 247 *et seq.*

40 For details see Section 54.

of representation when acting *vis-à-vis* third parties. If they ignore such limitations, the legal transaction *vis-à-vis* the third party will be valid and binding on the GmbH, but they may be held liable for any damages the company may suffer as a consequence of their acting in a manner which goes beyond the scope of their authority. Ignoring internal limitations of the company, on whatever legal grounds, may also constitute a reason to remove the managing director from office and/or to terminate the service agreement.

According to the German Civil Code,[41] a managing director of a GmbH may not enter into a legal transaction where he or she represents the company on the one hand and himself or a third party on the other hand (prohibition of self-contracting). This also applies in the case of a single-person company.[42] The articles of association may, and in practice often do, exempt all or several managing directors from the prohibition of self-contracting. It is disputed whether such an exemption may also be granted based on a simple shareholders' resolution or if only the articles of association entitle the shareholders to resolve in this way. In any case, an exemption of this nature must (also) be registered in the commercial register.

103. Bookkeeping and accounting

The managing directors are responsible for ensuring that the company undertakes proper bookkeeping and accounting.[43] This obligation in particular comprises the duty to provide a balance sheet and a profit and loss statement, and, where required, an annual report (*Lagebericht*) for the GmbH at the end of the business year in accordance with the German generally accepted accounting principles (GAAP) as set forth in the German Commercial Code (*Handelsgesetzbuch* – HGB). The managing directors may either do the bookkeeping and accounting themselves or they may commission third parties to do it for them (eg, accountants); the managing directors must duly select, instruct, and supervise these commissioned third parties.[44]

---

41 Bürgerliches Gesetzbuch (BGB) (Civil Code) 1900, s181 (FRG).

42 *Gesetz betreffend die Gesellschaft mit beschränkter Haftung* (GmbHG) (Act on Limited Liability Companies) 1892, s35, para. 3 (FRG).

43 *Gesetz betreffend die Gesellschaft mit beschränkter Haftung* (GmbHG) (Act on Limited Liability Companies) 1892, s41 (FRG).

44 For further details see Sections 194–197.

104. Tax obligations

The managing directors represent the GmbH in any tax-related matters. They are required to inform the tax authorities about any matters which are relevant in terms of taxation and are obliged to maintain proper records and provide proper bookkeeping – not only due to obligations arising under corporate law, but also under tax law. The annual tax balance sheet is to be developed on the basis of the (commercial) balance sheet under the German GAAP. It constitutes the basis for the taxation of the company and must be disclosed to the tax authorities. Additionally, the managing directors are responsible for filing any required tax returns on behalf of the GmbH. Furthermore, the managing directors are responsible for the quarterly prepayments of corporate income tax (*Körperschaftsteuer*) and trade tax (*Gewerbesteuer*).[45] In the case of a tax audit, the managing directors must disclose the books and records to the tax auditors. Finally, the directors have to ensure the proper withholding of taxes from the salary of the employees to be transferred directly to the tax authorities.

105. Social security obligations

The managing directors of a GmbH must ensure that the company complies with the obligations of an employer towards its employees with regard to social security issues. Like with taxes, they must withhold certain social security contributions (eg, pension insurance, health insurance, unemployment insurance and disability insurance) and transfer the amounts to the relevant social security authorities. Usually, half of this contribution to the social security system is paid by the employer (the GmbH) and the other half by the employee via deduction from his or her salary in advance. If this duty to deduct and transfer the social security contributions from the salaries of the employees is not properly fulfilled, this may result in criminal and civil liability on the part of the managing directors themselves.

106. Information to be filed/submitted and registration

The Act on Limited Liability Companies and other laws require that important information of various kinds is filed with or submitted to (depending on the specific legal requirements) the commercial register. All notifications must be given/all information must be

45 For further details on the tax obligations of a GmbH, see Sections 238–241.

filed by the managing directors.[46] The most important information to be filed with the commercial register for registration is as follows: registration of the company upon its formation;[47] registration of the managing directors or a change in managing director/s, including their power of representation;[48] registration of any amendments to the articles of association;[49] and the registration of the liquidation of the company.[50] The right to file information with the commercial register is generally linked to the right to represent the company and information can be filed by any director who is entitled to represent the company. Some very important information, however, can only be filed by all directors jointly in combination. This includes, *inter alia*, the registration of the company upon its formation and increases in the share capital.[51]

Moreover, the managing directors must submit a new list of shareholders to be registered in the commercial register after each change in the shareholder structure, particularly subsequent to each transfer of shares from one shareholder to a third party.[52] If the managing directors fail to do so, this may result in personal liability on the part of the managing directors *vis-à-vis* the parties whose shareholding in the GmbH has changed and towards the creditors of the company for any and all damages arising from the breach of their duties to submit the new list of shareholders.[53] However, since the Act to Modernise the Law Governing GmbHs and Combat Abuses came into force, the main responsibility for submitting this list of new shareholders has been shifted from the managing directors to the notary where a notary has participated in the act leading to a change in the shareholder structure, for example, a transfer of shares

46 *Gesetz betreffend die Gesellschaft mit beschränkter Haftung* (GmbHG) (Act on Limited Liability Companies) 1892, s78 (FRG).

47 *Gesetz betreffend die Gesellschaft mit beschränkter Haftung* (GmbHG) (Act on Limited Liability Companies) 1892, s7 (FRG).

48 *Gesetz betreffend die Gesellschaft mit beschränkter Haftung* (GmbHG) (Act on Limited Liability Companies) 1892, s39 (FRG).

49 *Gesetz betreffend die Gesellschaft mit beschränkter Haftung* (GmbHG) (Act on Limited Liability Companies) 1892, s54 *et seq*. (FRG).

50 *Gesetz betreffend die Gesellschaft mit beschränkter Haftung* (GmbHG) (Act on Limited Liability Companies) 1892, s65 (FRG).

51 *Gesetz betreffend die Gesellschaft mit beschränkter Haftung* (GmbHG) (Act on Limited Liability Companies) 1892, s78 (FRG).

52 *Gesetz betreffend die Gesellschaft mit beschränkter Haftung* (GmbHG) (Act on Limited Liability Companies) 1892, ss16, 40 (FRG).

53 *Gesetz betreffend die Gesellschaft mit beschränkter Haftung* (GmbHG) (Act on Limited Liability Companies) 1892, s40, para. 3 (FRG).

by way of a share purchase agreement.[54] If, however, a change in the ownership of a share occurs without the participation of a notary (eg, in of the event of the death of a shareholder where the share goes to his or her heirs), it remains the responsibility of the managing directors to file this change with the commercial register.

Aside from the registration and publication of certain facts, the Act on Limited Liability Companies in some cases merely requires that the commercial register is notified with regard to certain circumstances occurring in the GmbH. The most important notification duties in this context are the duty to submit the annual financial statement, the annual report of the company[55] and a complete list of the members of the supervisory board each time the composition of the supervisory board changes.[56]

107. Non-compete obligation

The Act on Limited Liability Companies does not contain a comparable regulation to that included in the Stock Corporation Act[57] explicitly stipulating that the managing directors are not entitled to compete against the company. Nevertheless, it is commonly recognised that a managing director of a GmbH is not entitled to pursue activities within the scope of the business purpose of the company or to be a managing director in a competing company. Furthermore, the obligation to refrain from competition prohibits the managing director and the shareholders from seizing, for their own benefit, business opportunities they might become aware of in their capacity as managing directors or shareholders (duty of loyalty).

The managing directors may be exempted from this obligation to refrain from competition in the articles of association. It is disputed whether an exemption is also possible by means of a (mere) shareholders' resolution. It is therefore recommendable (if required) to stipulate such an exemption in the articles themselves or to explicitly allow in the articles that a corresponding resolution is passed. In the event of a violation of the obligation to refrain from competition, this may give rise to damage claims against the managing director. The GmbH may also seek injunctive relief. The

---

54 For further details see Sections 179–184.

55 *Handelsgesetzbuch* (HGB) (Commercial Code) 1897, s325 (FRG).

56 *Gesetz betreffend die Gesellschaft mit beschränkter Haftung* (GmbHG) (Act on Limited Liability Companies) 1892, s52, para. 2, sentence 2 (FRG).

57 *Aktiengesetz* (AktG) (Stock Corporation Act) 1965, s88 (FRG).

rules outlined above do not apply to a sole shareholder in a GmbH (being at the same time its director) who is not subject to any non-compete obligations.

The non-compete obligation ceases automatically with the end of the term of the managing director. In practice, the service agreement or the articles of association often provide for a post-contractual obligation not to compete. The regulations for such post-contractual obligations are subject to the assessment and weighing of the courts based on standards of morality.[58] The non-compete obligation must be in the justified business interest of the company. To a certain extent, the courts also apply the regulations as set out in the German Commercial Code (*Handelsgesetzbuch – HGB*) regarding the post-contractual obligations of commercial clerks accordingly, even though they are not applicable directly to managing directors.[59] The courts require a temporal, territorial and objective (*gegenständlich*) limitation of a post-contractual non-compete obligation. A non-compete obligation for a period of up to two years following the end of the term is usually possible without giving rise to legal problems. Non-compete periods of between two and four years following the termination of the service agreement have been accepted in certain individual cases, but usually require additional justification. It is unlikely that a post-contractual non-compete obligation for a period of more than four years would be accepted by the courts unless extraordinary circumstances are present. If a non-compete clause exceeds the acceptable temporal scope (and only then), it is possible for the courts to reduce the duration thereof to an acceptable length. As regards territorial restrictions, the obligation not to compete must be limited to the territories in which the company (and its subsidiaries, if any) is active, or at least into which it has specific and serious plans to expand in the near future, when the non-compete obligation begins to apply. Furthermore, the non-compete obligation is to be restricted to the business purpose pursued by the company and/or its subsidiaries. A restriction to refrain from any and all post-contractual business activities irrespective of whether they are similar to the business activities of the company and its subsidiaries would not be acceptable, particularly in view of the protection of occupational freedom.[60]

---

58 *Bürgerliches Gesetzbuch* (BGB) (Civil Code) 1900, s138 (FRG).

59 *Handelsgesetzbuch* (HGB) (Commercial Code) 1897, s74 *et seq.* (FRG).

60 See also *Grundgesetz* (GG) (Constitutional Law) 1949, Art. 12 (FRG).

The managing director is generally entitled to receive adequate compensation during the post-contractual non-compete period. However, there is disagreement on the details in this regard. A managing director who is not at the same time a shareholder is usually entitled to receive at least half of his or her last annual salary for each calendar year of the post-contractual obligation. Managing directors who are also shareholders and thereby participate directly in the profits of the company may not be entitled to such additional compensation if the profits they receive as shareholders provide sufficient compensation. Income generated from other sources by the managing director will generally not be deducted from his or her compensation claim, but the service agreement may provide otherwise. Furthermore, the courts also tend to take into account other compensations the director may be entitled to even though he or she is leaving the company (eg, pension claims, compensation for shares in the company).

Note that other concepts pertaining to managerial or shareholder duties can play a role in this context. For instance, the duty of loyalty has a post-contractual effect. Even in the absence of a post-contractual non-compete obligation, managing directors may nevertheless be prevented from seizing – for their own purposes, or the purposes of a company newly established by them – business opportunities and making use of business contacts of which they have become aware during their term in office.

108. Secrecy obligation

Managing directors are obliged to hold strictly confidential any and all secrets relating to the company, in particular business and trade secrets they become aware of in their capacity as managing directors and they may not disclose these to third parties. In the event of a breach of this obligation, the managing director may be fined or sentenced to imprisonment for a period of up to one year. If the managing director discloses the confidential information for money, with the intention of enriching him- or herself or a third party, of damaging a third party (including the company), or misuses a company secret, he or she may be fined or sentenced to imprisonment for a period of up to two years. However, an offence of this kind would only be pursued at the request of the company, that is, the supervisory board or a representative nominated by the shareholders.[61] The managing director is only entitled to disclose

61 *Gesetz betreffend die Gesellschaft mit beschränkter Haftung* (GmbHG) (Act on Limited Liability Companies) 1892, s85 (FRG).

secrets of the company if he or she is entitled (eg, based on an agreement or a shareholders' resolution) or obliged (eg, based on the law, or the order of a court or an authority) to do so. The shareholders and the members of a supervisory board are not third parties in the above sense, since they have explicit information rights *vis-à-vis* the company or the managing directors.[62] The employees of the company, however, are usually third parties if they are not specifically responsible for dealing with the relevant information.

The secrecy obligation does not cease after the term in office has come to an end unless otherwise agreed between the managing director and the company.

During a due diligence process, a managing director must carefully weigh the interest of the company in keeping the relevant information confidential against the interest of the potential buyer in receiving the information. Since the shareholders are the ultimate 'holders' of the confidential information, a managing director should obtain their consent if he or she wishes to ensure that the disclosure of certain information does not constitute a breach of his or her secrecy obligations.

109. Obligations during insolvency

If a GmbH becomes insolvent (*zahlungsunfähig*) or overindebted (*überschuldet*), the managing directors of a GmbH must file for insolvency without undue delay, at the latest three weeks after the insolvency or over-indebtedness has occurred, irrespective of their knowledge of the situation.[63]

Before the Act to Modernise the Law Governing GmbHs and Combat Abuses came into force, it was a regular occurrence that companies or managing directors attempted to avoid filing for insolvency proceedings by physically disappearing or being removed from their position as managing directors. In such a situation, the company was virtually without management. Since no other corporate body was entitled to file for the opening of insolvency proceedings and in order to avoid such a misuse of the corporate structure, the Act to Modernise the Law Governing GmbHs and Combat Abuses introduced the new legal concept of a 'lack of management' (*Führungslosigkeit*).[64] Now, in a situation

---

62 *Gesetz betreffend die Gesellschaft mit beschränkter Haftung* (GmbHG) (Act on Limited Liability Companies) 1892, s51a (FRG) (Shareholders); s52 (FRG) (Supervisory board).

63 *Insolvenzordnung* (InsO) (Insolvency Ordinance) 1994, s15a, para. 1 (FRG).

64 *Insolvenzordnung* (InsO) (Insolvency Ordinance) 1994, s10, para. 2, sentence 2 (FRG).

where there is a lack of management, the Act on Limited Liability Companies stipulates that, in the place of the managing directors, the shareholders of the company are obliged to file for insolvency unless the respective shareholder has no positive knowledge of the insolvency or over-indebtedness or the lack of management of the company.[65] The burden of proof lies with the shareholders. If the shareholders fail to file for insolvency and are not able to prove that they were not obliged to do so, they may face a term of imprisonment for a period of up to three years.[66] The shareholders thus now have a much greater responsibility to keep themselves informed regarding a potential lack of managerial direction and with respect to the financial situation of the company.[67]

110. Provision of particulars on business letters

The managing director must also ensure that the GmbH's letterhead is correctly drafted in compliance with mandatory law. The letterhead of the company must at least contain the legal form and place of business of the company, the commercial register wherein the company is registered along with the registration number in the commercial register, the full name of all managing directors and, if the company has a supervisory board, the full name of the chairman of the supervisory board.[68] It is not required that the letterhead indicates the stated share capital of the company.

111. Compliance with laws

Aside from the specific obligations of the managing directors as outlined above, the directors of a GmbH are generally required to ensure that the company complies with any and all regulations applicable to it. This applies not only to general rules to which a GmbH is subject in themselves, but also to the specific rules which apply to the business sector in which the GmbH is currently active. If the activities of the GmbH necessitate obtaining permission from the authorities to undertake these activities, the managing directors are obliged to obtain this permission before commencing business.

---

65 *Insolvenzordnung* (InsO) (Insolvency Ordinance) 1994, s15a, para. 3 (FRG).

66 *Insolvenzordnung* (InsO) (Insolvency Ordinance) 1994, s15a, para. 4 (FRG).

67 For further details on insolvency proceedings refer to Section 268 *et seq.*

68 *Gesetz betreffend die Gesellschaft mit beschränkter Haftung* (GmbHG) (Act on Limited Liability Companies) 1892, s35a (FRG).

C. Liability

112. Liability towards the GmbH

Managing directors have certain liabilities and duties towards the GmbH as outlined in the previous paragraph. This raises the question as to the circumstances under which these duties are deemed to be breached and the consequences resulting from such breaches. The following sections will endeavour to illuminate these issues further.

113. Liability towards the GmbH: diligence of a prudent businessman

The most important provision regarding the liability of a managing director towards the GmbH is set out in section 43 paragraph 1 of the Act on Limited Liability Companies, which requires that a managing director must apply the diligence of a prudent businessman when handling the business affairs of the company. The provision is mandatory law and may not be amended by the articles of association. A violation of this obligation will give rise to a damage claim on the part of the GmbH against the managing director. The degree of diligence the managing director must apply is to a large extent defined by the size of the company and the business sector in which the company is active. Nevertheless, the standard of diligence is an objective standard subject to assessment by the courts, which have developed a large volume of case law in this regard. The Act on Limited Liability Companies itself defines two specific cases wherein the diligence of a prudent businessman is deemed to be lacking: (i) if managing directors make payments from the assets of the company which are required to maintain the stated share capital;[69] and (ii) if the company acquires its own shares in contravention of the Act on Limited Liability Companies.[70]

In the event that damage has been brought about by several managing directors, these are jointly and severally liable for the damage.[71] If the responsibilities of the shareholders are divided

---

69 *Gesetz betreffend die Gesellschaft mit beschränkter Haftung* (GmbHG) (Act on Limited Liability Companies) 1892, s43, para. 3, sentence 1, or, alternatively 1, 30 (FRG).

70 *Gesetz betreffend die Gesellschaft mit beschränkter Haftung* (GmbHG) (Act on Limited Liability Companies) 1892, s43, para. 3, sentence 1, or, alternatively 2, 33 (FRG).

71 *Gesetz betreffend die Gesellschaft mit beschränkter Haftung* (GmbHG) (Act on Limited Liability Companies) 1892, s43, para. 2 (FRG).

between specific business segments (finance, HR, production, sales, etc), managing directors may nevertheless be held liable for a breach of the duties of their fellow managing directors if they are in breach of their own obligation to inform themselves regarding the activities in the other business segments. Managing directors may not argue that their liability is limited to their specific segment because the management is divided into specific segments. A director is always responsible for the management of the business in its entirety. Therefore, as soon as the managing director becomes aware of irregularities in the respective other business segment, he or she is obliged to immediately gain a clear understanding of the facts and – if necessary – intervene.

Furthermore, a managing director may not be held directly liable for the actions of the employees of the company. The managing director is only liable for the proper selection, instruction and supervision of the respective employee. If the company is too large for the directors to do this entirely by themselves, they must put appropriate control mechanisms in place by installing subordinate employees (who are nonetheless managerial staff).

As outlined above, the managing directors in a GmbH are subject to the instructions issued by the shareholders. Therefore, if a managing director acts on the basis of a shareholders' resolution or another instruction, in principle he or she is exempted from liability for not acting with the necessary diligence of a prudent businessman. On the other hand, he or she is not exempted if the shareholders' resolution proves to be void, constitutes an obvious violation of applicable law or if the instructions are issued by a corporate body which is not entitled to do so.

The courts and legal scholars are in disagreement on the issue of whether the standard of liability set out under section 43 paragraph 1 of the Act on Limited Liability Companies may be eased so that a managing director is only liable in the case of wilful misconduct or gross negligence or if the liability may perhaps even be excluded. The question of whether such a reduction of the standard of liability is acceptable must be decided upon on a case-by-case basis given the specific situation of the company. However, it is hard to imagine a blanket exemption in advance for all kinds of violations of the obligation to be diligent as a managing director.

Any claims against a managing director based on a breach of his or her diligence obligation are subject to the statute of limitations after a period of five years.[72] The five-year period commences as soon as the grounds for the claim are present, that is, the moment the company is at least able to file an action for declaratory judgment (*Feststellungsklage*). It is neither necessary that the total amount of the damage is certain nor that the GmbH (ie, other directors, shareholders or a supervisory board) are aware of the damage. When acting in breach of their obligations, managing directors may also be held liable on the basis of tort law. Claims under tort law and under the Act on Limited Liability Companies exist independently alongside each other and are subject to their own applicable regulations under the statute of limitations respectively. Usually, claims based on tort will become subject to the statute of limitations within three years.

Furthermore, breach of the duty to act as a prudent businessman typically also constitutes a breach of the obligations of the managing director under the terms of his or her service agreement, and gives rise to contractual damage claims on the part of the GmbH. The obligations violated under the service agreement may either be primary or secondary obligations. Any contractual claims stand independently and alongside any claims based on the Act on Limited Liability Companies or tort law. Damage claims against a director under contract law are also subject to the statute of limitations five years after the breach of the contractual obligation by the managing director and in accordance with the same principles outlined in the previous section.

114. Liability towards the GmbH: payments during insolvency

The managing directors are liable to the company for any payments they make after the occurrence of insolvency (*Zahlungsunfähigkeit*) or the discovery of the over-indebtedness of the company. However, payments that are made with the diligence of a prudent businessman during this period will not give rise to such liability. The managing directors are equally liable for payments they make towards the shareholders only in so far as these contribute to the insolvency of the company unless the insolvency could not have been predicted even if the diligence of a prudent businessman had been applied.[73]

---

72 *Gesetz betreffend die Gesellschaft mit beschränkter Haftung* (GmbHG) (Act on Limited Liability Companies) 1892, s43, para. 4 (FRG).

73 *Gesetz betreffend die Gesellschaft mit beschränkter Haftung* (GmbHG) (Act on Limited Liability Companies) 1892, s64 (FRG).

The question as to what kinds of payments are deemed to be in compliance with the requisite diligence of a prudent businessman cannot always be clearly answered. The issue of whether or not a payment made by the directors is allowed must always be decided upon on a case-by-case basis, taking into account the particular situation of the company. The relevant criterion here is whether, from an ex-ante perspective, the payment is likely to create more benefits than disadvantages for the creditors of the company.[74] Payments that are typically in compliance with the requisite diligence of a prudent businessman are usually those which: (i) are required to avoid the immediate breakdown of the company (eg, leases, water, electricity and heating supply, salaries (this point is disputed)), and (ii) payments which are compensated by an adequate consideration, (eg, payment against simultaneous receipt of goods).

Regarding social security contributions and taxes, the Federal Supreme Court has ruled in two important decisions[75] that the payment of social security contributions on behalf of the employees (not for the employers!) and the payment of sales tax (VAT) and income tax (*Lohnsteuer*) are always in compliance with the requisite diligence of a prudent businessman and therefore do not constitute a breach of the obligations of the directors. The court has emphasised that this applies to the future payment (ie, payments made after the company has become insolvent) of such taxes and social security contributions and to payments in arrears. For details see also Sections 123 and 124.

115. Liability towards the GmbH: liability under other provisions of the Act on Limited Liability Companies

In addition, the Act on Limited Liability Companies stipulates further liabilities of the managing directors in the event of a breach of their duties, in particular if the managing director gives false information during the formation of the company[76] or during a capital increase.[77] This liability applies in particular when a managing

---

74 5 November 2007, *Bundesgerichtshof* (German Federal Supreme Court) (II ZR 262/06), NGZ 2008, 75.

75 14 May 2007, *Bundesgerichtshof* (German Federal Supreme Court) (II ZR 48/06); 25 January 2011, *Bundesgerichtshof* (German Federal Supreme Court) (II ZR 196/09), NRW 2011, 196.

76 *Gesetz betreffend die Gesellschaft mit beschränkter Haftung* (GmbHG) (Act on Limited Liability Companies) 1892, s9a (FRG).

77 *Gesetz betreffend die Gesellschaft mit beschränkter Haftung* (GmbHG) (Act on Limited Liability Companies) 1892, s57, para. 4 (FRG).

director incorrectly states at the point in time of the formation of the company that the stated share capital has been properly paid in and is at his or her free disposal.

116. Liability towards the GmbH: responsibility based on tort law

Aside from the liability based on the Act on Limited Liability Companies, the managing directors may be held liable under tort law. Tort claims may result in particular from of a breach of trust (*Untreue*)[78] or from immoral behaviour.[79] Additionally, the managing directors may be held liable for the violation of any protective laws (*Schutzgesetze*) which then give rise to a civil law liability under tort law.[80]

117. Liability towards the GmbH: discharge from claims (*Entlastung*)

In principle, the GmbH is entitled to amicably settle or waive a claim for compensation under section 43 paragraph 1 of the Act on Limited Liability Companies. The corporate body responsible for deciding whether a claim should be enforced or settled, or whether a managing director should be discharged for acting on behalf of the company is the shareholders' meeting,[81] in so far as the authority in this regard has not been transferred to another corporate body (eg, a supervisory body).

The legal effect of a discharge from claims is that the company waives any claims it may have against the managing director based on his or her business conduct and which were recognisable to the responsible corporate body deciding on the said discharge from claims after applying due diligence when examining the respective reports and any other documents available to it. The most important report available to the responsible corporate body is usually the annual financial statement and the attachments thereto. However, the resolution may also be based on other available information. The corporate body generally reaches a resolution on the discharge from claims at its free discretion. According to case law, however, granting managing directors a discharge from claims is considered

78 *Bürgerliches Gesetzbuch* (BGB) (Civil Code) 1900, s823 p. 2 (FRG); *Strafgesetzbuch* (StGB) (German Criminal Code) 1871, s266 (FRG).

79 *Bürgerliches Gesetzbuch* (BGB) (Civil Code) 1900, s826 (FRG).

80 *Bürgerliches Gesetzbuch* (BGB) (Civil Code) 1900, s823, para. 2 (FRG).

81 *Gesetz betreffend die Gesellschaft mit beschränkter Haftung* (GmbHG) (Act on Limited Liability Companies) 1892, s46, no. 5, or, alternatively, 3, no. 8 (FRG).

invalid if they have severely breached their obligations, if their misconduct leads to the company suffering significant damage or if they have seriously violated applicable law or the articles of association. Moreover, in the cases specified by the law itself (eg, repayment of assets required to maintain the stated share capital or acquisition of their own shares contrary to statutory provisions), a settlement or waiver of claims based on the breaches of duty is only possible if the respective compensation payments are not required for the satisfaction of creditor claims.[82] In addition, the law provides that if the compensation claim against the managing director is required to satisfy creditor claims, the liability of the managing director will also not be excluded even if he or she was acting on the basis of a (valid) shareholders' resolution.[83] Here the law makes it clear that a valid shareholders' resolution usually exempts the managing directors from their liability.

On the other hand, if the management of the company does not give rise to any significant complaints, the managing director has a right to be discharged from claims.

118. Liability towards the GmbH: requirement of a shareholders' resolution for the enforcement of claims

The enforcement of any claims the company has against a managing director on whatever legal grounds requires a corresponding shareholders' resolution.[84] The articles of association may provide otherwise or shift the responsibility for deciding on the enforcement of such claims to another corporate body. According to the prevailing opinion, a resolution in this regard must be reached prior to the enforcement of a claim. Otherwise, the enforcement would be considered illegal and would be rejected by the courts on the merits. The company must prove it has suffered the respective damage and that this was (or at least with reasonable certainty could have been) caused by the breach of duty on the part of the managing director. The managing director bears the burden of proof regarding any circumstances which would relieve him or her of his or her

82 *Gesetz betreffend die Gesellschaft mit beschränkter Haftung* (GmbHG) (Act on Limited Liability Companies) 1892, s43, para. 3, sentence 2, 9b (FRG).

83 *Gesetz betreffend die Gesellschaft mit beschränkter Haftung* (GmbHG) (Act on Limited Liability Companies) 1892, s43, para. 3, sentence 3 (FRG).

84 *Gesetz betreffend die Gesellschaft mit beschränkter Haftung* (GmbHG) (Act on Limited Liability Companies) 1892, s46, no. 8 (FRG).

obligation (eg, waiver, settlement, time barring, discharge etc). In addition, the principles outlined in Section 56 apply accordingly.

119. Liability towards the shareholders

As a general rule, a managing director is not directly liable towards the shareholders of the GmbH. The above-mentioned regulations are designed to protect the company as such and not the individual shareholders. A liability towards the shareholders may, however, be based on a particular legal agreement between the shareholder and the managing director. One exception wherein the managing directors are directly liable towards the shareholders is stipulated in the Act on Limited Liability Companies itself.[85] According to this provision, managing directors may be held directly liable by the shareholders if they are repaying assets which are required to maintain the stated share capital and the shareholder receiving such payments is not able to repay them. In this case, the principles outlined under Section 113 apply accordingly.

In addition, there is always the possibility of a liability of a managing director towards the shareholders based on tort law.

120. Liability towards third parties

Managing directors can also become liable towards third parties, in particular in the context of insolvency, contractual liability, tax and social security obligations, as will be discussed in detail in the following sections.

121. Liability towards third parties: delayed filing of insolvency

The managing directors of a GmbH are obliged to file for insolvency of the company at the latest three weeks after the insolvency or over-indebtedness of the company has occurred.[86] If the managing directors fail to file for insolvency within this time period, they may be held personally liable by the creditors of the company.[87]

Regarding the creditors who are entitled to claim damages, a distinction must be drawn between the so-called 'old creditors'

---

85 *Gesetz betreffend die Gesellschaft mit beschränkter Haftung* (GmbHG) (Act on Limited Liability Companies) 1892, s31, para. 6 (FRG).

86 *Insolvenzordnung* (InsO) (Insolvency Ordinance) 1994, s15a, para. 1 (FRG); formerly *Gesetz betreffend die Gesellschaft mit beschränkter Haftung* (GmbHG) (Act on Limited Liability Companies) 1892, s64, para. 1 (old version) (FRG).

87 *Bürgerliches Gesetzbuch* (BGB) (Civil Code) 1900, s823, para. 2 (FRG); *Insolvenzordnung* (InsO) (Insolvency Ordinance) 1994, s15a, para. 1 (FRG).

(*Altgläubiger*) and 'new creditors' (*Neugläubiger*). Old creditors are creditors who already had a claim towards the GmbH prior to the insolvency or over-indebtedness occurring. These creditors are only entitled to proportional compensation resulting from the fact that the filing for insolvency has been delayed and the assets of the company available for their satisfaction have been diminished due to the delay. The new creditors, on the other hand, are those who have entered into legal relationships with the GmbH only after grounds for filing for insolvency have occurred. These creditors are entitled to be compensated in full for any damages they suffer from entering into legal relationships with the company rather than just proportional compensation for the damages.

In addition to the liability described above, a delayed or false filing for insolvency or the failure to do so may result in imprisonment for a period of up to three years.[88]

121a. Liability towards third parties: filing of changes to the shareholders' list

The managing directors must submit a new list of shareholders to the commercial register following each change in the shareholder structure, in particular after each transfer of shares from one shareholder to a third party.[89] If the managing directors fail to do so, this may result in personal liability on the part of the managing directors towards the parties whose shareholding in the GmbH has changed as well as towards the creditors of the company for any and all damages resulting from the breach of the duty to submit the new list of shareholders.[90] Since the enacting of the Act to Modernise the Law Governing GmbHs and Combat Abuses, the duty to submit a new shareholders' list has been shifted to the notaries if a notary was involved in the change of the shareholders' structure.[91] In such a case, the responsibility of the directors is replaced by that of the notary. In the unlikely case that the notary should not comply with the duty to file the new shareholders' list, the directors remain responsible to file the new list.

---

88 *Insolvenzordnung* (InsO) (Insolvency Ordinance) 1994, s15a, para. 4 (FRG).

89 *Gesetz betreffend die Gesellschaft mit beschränkter Haftung* (GmbHG) (Act on Limited Liability Companies) 1892, s16, 40 (FRG).

90 *Gesetz betreffend die Gesellschaft mit beschränkter Haftung* (GmbHG) (Act on Limited Liability Companies) 1892, s40, para. 3 (FRG).

91 See Section 183 for details.

122. Liability towards third parties: contractual liability

A liability on the part of a managing director towards a third party is obviously present in cases in which a contractual basis for such a liability exists. Such a relationship may be established, for example, by entering into a guarantee agreement, through the granting of a surety, the signing of a joint liability agreement, or any other kind of agreement by which the managing director assumes a personal liability apart from the company. Usually this occurs in connection with the granting of a loan.

Another circumstance which may give rise to personal liability for a managing director is one involving negotiations in bad faith (*culpa in contrahendo*). In such cases, the managing director acts on behalf of the GmbH but negotiates in bad faith by violating pre-contractual disclosure and diligence obligations. The liability arising from such misconduct usually affects the GmbH itself as the represented entity but not the managing director. The Federal Supreme Court, however, has recognised a personal liability on the part of the managing director in two specific cases. The first case is in situations in which the managing director encourages confidence in his or her person in an extraordinary way, for instance by indicating his or her own willingness to satisfy the obligations of the company or his or her personal creditworthiness.[92] Additionally, a managing director may be held personally liable if he or she has a strong individual economic interest in the particular business and draws his or her own profit (apart from the regular management compensation) from the business.[93] The interest of the managing director must be of a nature which makes the transaction appear as if it is his or her own. In recent years, stringent standards have been established in the case law for the affirmation of a personal liability on the part of a managing director in such cases.

Finally, managing directors may be held personally liable by third parties if they have entered into legal relationships with third parties on behalf of the GmbH prior to the GmbH being registered in the commercial register.[94] Such a liability, however, expires the moment the GmbH is registered with the commercial register,

---

92 6 June 1994, *Bundesgerichtshof* (German Federal Supreme Court) (II ZR 292 / 91) – BGHZ 126, 181 *et seq*. BGHZ 126, 181 *et seq*.

93 2 March 1988, *Bundesgerichtshof* (German Federal Supreme Court) (VIII ZR 380 / 86) – BGH NJW 1988, 2234.

94 *Gesetz betreffend die Gesellschaft mit beschränkter Haftung* (GmbHG) (Act on Limited Liability Companies) 1892, s11, para. 2 (FRG).

unless the managing director was acting in a way that exceeded his or her power of representation.

123. Liability towards third parties: breach of tax obligations
The managing directors of the company are responsible for satisfying the tax obligations of the company and may be held personally liable if such obligations are breached on the basis of wilful misconduct or gross negligence.[95] However, the managing directors can only be held personally liable (for the breach of this specific obligation) if the company was able to satisfy its tax obligations in the first place. If the company was unable to do so due to its economic situation, the managing directors may not be held liable for not making outstanding tax payments. In this respect, the managing directors are not obliged to preferentially pay the tax authorities over other creditors if the tax obligations are due. At the same time, however, they also may not discriminate against the tax authorities in favour of other creditors.

As outlined above (see Section 114), a managing director is not entitled to make any payments on behalf of the company if the company is either insolvent, over-indebted or if such payments would result in an over-indebtedness of the company, assuming that such payments are not in accordance with the obligations of a prudent business person. In the context of such a company crisis, it is disputed amongst the courts and legal scholars whether tax payments are deemed to be in accordance with the requisite due care and diligence of a prudent business person. Whereas some scholars believe that the crisis does indeed exempt the GmbH from having to make tax payments, the German Federal Supreme Courts for Civil, Criminal and Tax Law in the meantime tend towards the opinion that in a crisis the company is nevertheless obliged (and entitled) to satisfy its tax obligations, since such payments would be in accordance with the due care and diligence of a prudent business person. Only by these means can the managing directors prevent personal liability on the grounds of withholding tax. This point of view was confirmed by the Federal Supreme Court in two important decisions.[96] The court ruled that the payment of sales tax (VAT) and of income tax (*Lohnsteuer*) are always in accordance

95 *Abgabenordnung* (AO) (Fiscal Code) 1976, s34, 69 (FRG).
96 14 May 2007, *Bundesgerichtshof* (German Federal Supreme Court) (II ZR 48/06); 29 January 2011, *Bundesgerichtshof* (German Federal Supreme Court) (II ZR 196 / 09), NZI 2011, 196.

with the due care and diligence of a prudent business person and therefore do not constitute a breach of the obligations of the directors. The court underlined that this applies to the future payment (ie, payments made after the company has become insolvent) of such taxes and to payments in arrears. In outlining their argument, the court explained that the directors are subject to a conflict of interest between their obligations to pay taxes on behalf of the company and not to undertake payments if the company is insolvent or over-indebted. Failure to pay such taxes would not only give rise to personal liability, but also to criminal liability on the part of the managing directors.[97] On the other hand, paying these taxes could put the directors in a position of conflict with their obligations to refrain in principle from making payments if the company is in an economic crisis.[98] In order to provide clarity in connection with such conflicts, the Federal Supreme Court ruled that it is not acceptable for directors to be threatened by the danger of committing a criminal offence if they do not make tax payments, and therefore considered the payment of VAT and income tax to be in accordance with the obligations of a prudent business person.

124. Liability towards third parties: social security obligations

Contributions to the social security systems in Germany are usually paid by the employer and the employee in equal parts. The employer is therefore obliged to deduct the social security contributions of the employees from their salaries and to transfer these to the respective social security authority.[99] The managing directors must carry out this task on behalf of the GmbH as the employer. This obligation takes precedence over any other payment obligations of the GmbH. In other words, the social security contributions take precedence over the payment of salaries. Regarding the payment of social security contributions in a crisis (ie, when insolvency must be filed), the Federal Supreme Court has ruled in the same two decisions as mentioned in the paragraph before[100] that the payment of the social security contributions pertaining to the employee's part (but not that of the employer) is always deemed to be in accordance with

---

97 *Abgabenordnung* (AO) (Fiscal Code) 1976, s369 *et seq.* (FRG).

98 *Gesetz betreffend die Gesellschaft mit beschränkter Haftung* (GmbHG) (Act on Limited Liability Companies) 1892, s64 (FRG).

99 *Sozialgesetzbuch IV* (SGB IV) (Social Security Code IV) 1976, s28e, para. 1 (FRG).

100 14 May 2007, *Bundesgerichtshof* (German Federal Supreme Court) (II ZR 48/06); 29 January 2011, *Bundesgerichtshof* (German Federal Supreme Court) (II ZR 196/09).

the requisite due care and diligence of a prudent business person and therefore not a violation of the obligations of the directors. The court emphasised that this applies both to the future payment (ie, payments made after the company has become insolvent) of such social security contributions and to payments in arrears. The arguments of the court were similar to those outlined for the payment of taxes in the event that the company becomes insolvent (see Section 123 above). If the social security contributions are not duly paid, the managing directors may be held personally liable for the non-payment thereof.[101] Additionally, the non-payment of social security contributions may lead to a criminal offence on the part of the managing director.[102] In this regard, the managing directors are only liable for the non-payment of the employees' contributions to the social security system, but not for the employer's share. Failure to pay the social security contributions could therefore lead to criminal and civil liability, whereas a failure to pay the contributions could result in a breach of the duties as managing director. The court provided clarification with regard to this conflict by declaring the payment of the employees' share of the social security contributions to be in accordance with the requisite due care and diligence of a prudent business person. Since only the non-payment of the employees' share of the social security contributions is subject to criminal and civil liability but not the non-payment of the employer's share, the court also clarified the fact that paying the employer's part of the social security contributions after the company has become insolvent is not deemed to be in accordance with the obligations of a prudent business person. Paying this share of the contributions would give rise to personal liability on the part of the directors under the Act on Limited Liabilities Companies.

Notwithstanding the above, the managing directors may not be held liable if the company is completely insolvent and lacks sufficient funds to satisfy any of its obligations.

125. Liability towards third parties: failure to file the list of shareholders

As outlined under Section 106 and as will be discussed in more detail below under Section 183, the managing directors are obliged to file

101 *Bürgerliches Gesetzbuch* (BGB) (Civil Code) 1900, s823, para. 2 (FRG); *Strafgesetzbuch* (StGB) (German Criminal Code) 1871, s266a (FRG).

102 *Strafgesetzbuch* (StGB) (German Criminal Code) 1871, s266, 266a (FRG).

a new list of shareholders with the commercial register each time a change in terms of the persons who are shareholders occurs and there is no notary involved in this change in the shareholder structure.[103] If they are in breach of this obligation, managing directors may be held personally liable by the persons whose shareholding has changed and the creditors of the company for any and all damages resulting from the failure to file the new list of shareholders. If there are several managing directors, these are jointly and severally liable.

126. D&O insurance

Nowadays, it has become good practice to provide directors and officers insurance (D&O insurance) for the managing directors and other officers of the company to cover potential liability arising from breaches of their duties. This means that, at least to a considerable degree, the managing directors and officers will not have to pay out of their own pocket for damages caused by their potential failure to apply the requisite due care and diligence of a prudent business person. This generally tends to attract managing directors of a higher calibre or will encourage directors to act more vigorously when pursuing the business of the GmbH. The premiums for this kind of insurance are usually paid by the company and are addressed in the service agreement. D&O insurances typically only cover monetary damages but not acts of bodily harm or acts of wilful misconduct or gross negligence. They will neither cover intentional nor grossly negligent breaches of the obligations of a managing director. The insurances often stipulate a maximum amount covered, subject to the conditions of the respective insurance.

103 *Gesetz betreffend die Gesellschaft mit beschränkter Haftung* (GmbHG) (Act on Limited Liability Companies) 1892, s40, para. 1 (FRG).

VII. Supervisory board

127. **General**

The Act on Limited Liability Companies does not in itself prescribe the installation of a supervisory board in a GmbH. A supervisory board may either be voluntarily established in the articles of association or may be mandatorily required if the GmbH is subject to one of the Co-Determination Acts (*Mitbestimmung*). In Germany, there are four principal Co-Determination Acts: the One-Third Participation Act for companies which generally have more than 500 employees, the Co-Determination Act 1976 for companies which generally have more than 2,000 employees, the Co-Determination Act for the Coal and Steel Industry (*Montanmitbestimmungsgesetz*) for companies active in the coal and steel industry and the Capital Investment Act (*Kapitalanlagegesetzbuch*) for financial institutions whose business purpose is the administration of investment assets. All of these Acts prescribe the mandatory installation of a supervisory board also in a GmbH. The specific details with regard to optional and mandatory supervisory boards will be outlined in the following sections.

If a GmbH is not subject to one of the aforementioned Co-Determination Acts, it may nevertheless voluntarily install such a board. It may have various names (supervisory board, advisory board (*Beirat*), family board (*Familienrat*), administrative board (*Verwaltungsrat*), board of experts (*Sachverständigenrat*) etc) and various kinds of authority. The decisive question of whether such a board is to be qualified as a supervisory board in the proper sense of the term is dependent upon whether the board has the right (and obligation) to supervise the management of the GmbH. A body which is not entitled to supervise the management is typically not considered a supervisory board in the original meaning of the term. On the other hand, a body which is entitled to carry out at least certain specific supervising tasks is a supervisory board in the proper sense of the term irrespective of its denomination.

If a GmbH is subject to a Co-Determination Act, but it is unclear which Act is actually applicable, the Stock Corporation Act provides for a particular proceeding in which the applicable Co-Determination

Act is determined by the court.[1] The rules apply accordingly in a GmbH.[2] This status proceeding (*Statusverfahren*) mainly applies in the case of a transformation of another entity into the legal form of a GmbH according to the Law Regulating the Transformation of Companies and, as a consequence, a supervisory board must be established for the first time, or if the existing supervisory board is no longer in compliance with applicable statutory law.

When it is required that a mandatory supervisory board must be established, the question often arises as to whether, aside from this supervisory board, other corporate bodies, in particular an advisory board, are permitted. There is disagreement as to how this question should be answered. The prevailing opinion assumes that such competing boards are permitted as long as the mandatory rights of the mandatory supervisory board are not restricted or factually transferred to the respective other corporate body. Whether this is the case must be determined on a case-by-case basis.

A. Optional supervisory board

128. Basic freedom of installation and operation

If a GmbH is not subject to any Co-Determination Act which prescribes a supervisory board, the shareholders are free to provide for the establishment of a supervisory board in the articles of association. The articles may also provide that the shareholders may establish a supervisory board based on a shareholders' resolution to this effect. The Act on Limited Liability Companies itself provides some basic regulations in the event that the articles stipulate the establishment of a supervisory board, but remain silent on the applicable rules for such a supervisory board.[3] In the relevant paragraph, the Act on Limited Liability Companies lists certain provisions of the Stock Corporation Act (where a supervisory board is mandatory) which may apply to a GmbH accordingly. Despite this regulation in the Act on Limited Liability Companies, the shareholders in a GmbH are free to amend the list of applicable provisions of the

1 *Aktiengesetz* (AktG) (Stock Corporation Act) 1965, ss97–99 (FRG); *Einführungsgesetz zum Aktiengesetz* (EGAktG) (Introduction Act to the Stock Corporation Act) 1965, s27 (FRG).

2 *Mitbestimmungsgesetz* (MitbestG) (Co-Determination Act) 1976, s6, para. 2 (FRG); *Drittelbeteiligungsgesetz* (DrittelbG) (One Third Employee Participation Act) 2004, s1, para. 1, no. 3 (FRG).

3 *Gesetz betreffend die Gesellschaft mit beschränkter Haftung* (GmbHG) (Act on Limited Liability Companies) 1892, s52 (FRG).

Stock Corporation Act in the GmbH by either excluding all or some of them, by amending them or by providing a completely independent set of rights and obligations of the supervisory board. In other words, the regulations set out in the articles always prevail over the subsidiary regulations pertaining to the supervisory board in the Act on Limited Liability Companies. Whether the corporate body installed is then indeed a supervisory board in the proper sense of the term depends on the type of authority it has (see Section 127).

129. Number of members

If the articles of association do not provide otherwise, the optional supervisory board has three members.[4] The articles may, however, provide for a different number of members. The number of members does not have to be divisible by three and the prevailing opinion even admits a one-person supervisory board. If, on the other hand, a supervisory board is established which is too large in view of the size and business of the company, a corresponding shareholders' resolution could be considered invalid due to a violation of the duty of loyalty. However, rather stringent standards apply in terms of the burden of proof for the alleged fact that this duty is violated.

130. Eligibility

The shareholders may freely decide who shall be eligible to become a member of the supervisory board. It is highly disputed whether legal entities themselves may become members of the supervisory board or only individuals. The articles may provide that the eligibility is dependent on the fulfilment of certain personal criteria such as age, membership of a certain family, certain knowledge of the market, professional qualifications etc. It is also disputed whether a managing director may also become a member of such supervisory board. In a stock corporation and where the GmbH is subject to a Co-Determination Act this would be prohibited.

If the articles of association give no indication of the eligibility criteria for the members of the supervisory board, the subsidiarily applicable Stock Corporation Act provides that only persons who have full legal capacity (*unbeschränkt geschäftsfähig*),[5] but who are

---

4 *Gesetz betreffend die Gesellschaft mit beschränkter Haftung* (GmbHG) (Act on Limited Liability Companies) 1892, s52, para. 1 (FRG); *Aktiengesetz* (AktG) (Stock Corporation Act) 1965, s95, sentence 1 (FRG).

5 *Aktiengesetz* (AktG) (Stock Corporation Act) 1965, s100, para. 1 (FRG).

not legal representatives of subsidiaries[6] and managing directors or their permanent substitutes, proxies or authorised signatories[7] of the company, may be members of the supervisory board.

131. Nomination, term and revocation

If the articles of association do not provide otherwise, the members of the supervisory board are elected by the shareholders' meeting with a simple majority of the votes cast.[8] Often, the articles of association grant a delegation right (*Entsendungsrecht*) in favour of certain shareholders or members of a certain family. The delegation right may alternatively be linked to a certain share, meaning that the actual holder of the respective share is entitled to exercise the right. A delegation right once granted may only be revoked with the consent of the entitled person or for cause. Furthermore, the establishment of such a particular right for a specific shareholder requires the consent of other shareholders who are not being granted such a right. It is disputed whether and under which conditions a third party which is not a shareholder in the company (eg, banks, customers, creditors) may be granted a delegation right for membership of the supervisory board.

The term of office of a member is not prescribed by the GmbHG, as the latter does not refer to the corresponding section of the Stock Corporation Act.[9] If the articles of association or the shareholders' resolution by means of which the member of the supervisory board has been nominated do not provide otherwise, the member is nominated for an indefinite period of time. Therefore, the articles should reasonably provide for a mechanism for the removal of the members of the supervisory board or stipulate a certain maximum term or age limit.

Members of the supervisory board who have been elected by the shareholders may be removed prior to the end of their term in office by way of a shareholders' resolution requiring three quarters of the votes cast.[10] The articles may stipulate other regulations regarding

6 *Aktiengesetz* (AktG) (Stock Corporation Act) 1965, s100, para. 2, no. 2 (FRG).

7 *Aktiengesetz* (AktG) (Stock Corporation Act) 1965, s105, para. 1 (FRG).

8 *Gesetz betreffend die Gesellschaft mit beschränkter Haftung* (GmbHG) (Act on Limited Liability Companies) 1892, s52, para. 1 (FRG); *Aktiengesetz* (AktG) (Stock Corporation Act) 1965, s101, para. 1, sentence 1 (FRG).

9 *Aktiengesetz* (AktG) (Stock Corporation Act) 1965, s102 (FRG).

10 *Gesetz betreffend die Gesellschaft mit beschränkter Haftung* (GmbHG) (Act on Limited Liability Companies) 1892, s52, para. 1 (FRG); *Aktiengesetz* (AktG) (Stock Corporation Act) 1965, s103, para. 1, sentences 1 and 2 (FRG).

the removal of members of the supervisory board. Typically, if a person is granted the right to delegate a member to the supervisory board, he or she is also entitled to remove this member.[11] A right to this effect is recognised by the prevailing opinion. In the articles, the right to remove a board member usually goes along with the obligation to nominate a new member in case of removal of a board member. A person entitled to delegate the member will typically also be required to remove a member of the supervisory board on the basis of his or her fiduciary duties towards the company if a cause to do so exists (eg, gross violation of duties). The term of office of a member of the supervisory board may also cease by way of the death of the member, if the member no longer satisfies the personal requirements for membership of the supervisory board prescribed by law or the articles of association, or if the company undergoes a transformation under the Law Regulating the Transformation of Companies. Additionally, an optional supervisory board may be abolished at any time by the shareholders by way of an amendment to the articles of association to this effect. Finally, a member of the supervisory board is also entitled to resign from office in so far as this does not put the company in a difficult situation (*zur Unzeit*).

According to mandatory law, any changes with regard to the members of the supervisory board must be filed with the commercial register by the managing director by way of setting forth a complete list of the current members of the supervisory board. The list must contain the family name, first name, profession and residence of the respective members.[12] The fact that this list has been filed with it must be published in the commercial register.

132. Convening of board meetings and resolutions

With regard to an optional supervisory board, the Act on Limited Liability Companies merely sets out very rudimentary regulations regarding the formal requirements for meetings of the board and the way in which resolutions should be passed. The Act on Limited Liability Companies only provides for regulations on the convening of meetings of the supervisory board and the number of meetings to be held in an indirect manner by referring to the Stock Corporation

11 *Aktiengesetz* (AktG) (Stock Corporation Act) 1965, s103, para. 2 (FRG) accordingly.

12 *Gesetz betreffend die Gesellschaft mit beschränkter Haftung* (GmbHG) (Act on Limited Liability Companies) 1892, s52, para. 2 (FRG).

Act.[13] According to these provisions, a board meeting is to be called by the chairman of the board by giving two weeks' notice at the request of a managing director or a member of the board. A meeting may also be called by the director or a board member him- or herself if the chairman refuses to call a meeting upon request. In addition, it is highly recommendable to establish rules regarding the formal criteria for board meetings, including rules on the nomination of a chairman and deputy chairman of the supervisory board. The regulations may be set out in the articles of association themselves or within the by-laws of the supervisory board.

132a. Passing of supervisory board resolutions and quorum

The supervisory board reaches decisions by way of resolution.[14] In order for a resolution to be passed, a simple majority of the votes cast is sufficient. Abstentions from voting are not taken into account.

In principle, resolutions of the supervisory board are reached in meetings. It is, however, recommendable (and this is often done in practice) to also allow other means of passing resolutions. This can include resolutions in writing, by phone, by facsimile, by email, by video conference, etc. Resolutions may also be passed in this way even if the articles of association do not provide so explicitly in so far as no member of the supervisory board objects thereto.[15]

Each member of the supervisory board is entitled to participate in the meetings of the board and has a right to all issues being discussed. There is disagreement as to how many members of the supervisory board must participate in a meeting or participate in the voting in order to have a quorum. This question should generally be addressed in the articles of association. If the articles do not refer to this issue, according to the opinion of some, a quorum is deemed to be given if one member of the supervisory board is present, whereas others require that there is only a quorum if the majority of the members of the supervisory board are present. The articles should also set forth details on the taking of minutes of supervisory board meetings.

---

13 *Gesetz betreffend die Gesellschaft mit beschränkter Haftung* (GmbHG) (Act on Limited Liability Companies) 1892, s52, para. 1 (FRG); *Aktiengesetz* (AktG) (Stock Corporation Act) 1965, s110 (FRG).

14 *Gesetz betreffend die Gesellschaft mit beschränkter Haftung* (GmbHG) (Act on Limited Liability Companies) 1892, s52, para. 1 (FRG); *Aktiengesetz* (AktG) (Stock Corporation Act) 1965, s108, para.1 (FRG).

15 *Aktiengesetz* (AktG) (Stock Corporation Act) 1965, s108, para. 4 (FRG) accordingly.

Furthermore, it is recognised as a general corporate principle that a member of the supervisory board is not entitled to exercise his or her voting right if the supervisory board resolves to enter into a legal transaction with this member or if the supervisory board resolves to settle a legal dispute between the member and the GmbH. The same applies if the member would be relieved of a liability. In this respect, the same principles apply as those pertaining to the exclusion of a shareholder from voting in a shareholders' meeting as set out in Section 86.

132b. Challenging of supervisory board resolutions

In the event that a resolution of the supervisory board violates the law or the articles of association, the legal consequences of such a violation are disputed. It is recognised that serious errors may render such a resolution void. If the violation in question is minor in nature, in particular if it only relates to formalities as opposed to the content of the resolution, it is disputed whether such a resolution is also void or whether it is merely contestable under the regulations set out in the Stock Corporation Act with respect to the challenging of shareholders' resolutions.[16] In some decisions, the Federal Supreme Court has ruled that the regulations set out in the Stock Corporation Act do not apply accordingly and that resolutions of the supervisory board which violate the law or the articles of association are in principle void.[17] However, there is dispute on the details in this regard, and discussion on the topic continues. The validity of resolutions of the supervisory board may be claimed by an action for a declaratory judgment (*Feststellungsklage*) to confirm that the respective resolution is either void or not. A prerequisite for the filing of such an action is the presence of a particular legal interest (*Rechtsschutzinteresse*). Usually, members of the supervisory board, shareholders and managing directors of a GmbH will have such a particular interest. The courts endeavour to limit the number of actions brought against resolutions of supervisory boards by denying a particular legal interest in cases where the violation is of interest in formal terms or in the event that the error had no effect on the outcome of the resolution passed. The action must be filed against the GmbH itself, not against the supervisory

16 *Aktiengesetz* (AktG) (Stock Corporation Act) 1965, s243 *et seq.* (FRG) accordingly.

17 For example, 21 April 1997, *Bundesgerichtshof* (German Federal Supreme Court) (II ZR 175/95) – BGHZ 135, 244 *et seq.*

board. The action does not have to be brought within a specific time period after the resolution was passed but the claim is subject to forfeiture (*Verwirkung*).

133. Rights and obligations: supervision of management

If the articles of association do not provide otherwise, the predominant task of the supervisory board is the supervision of the managing directors.[18] This right is exclusively limited to the measures taken by the managing directors but not those taken by the shareholders' meeting or other corporate bodies. It is not the task of the supervisory board to run the daily management of the company.

In the first place, the supervisory board is responsible for monitoring whether the measures taken by the managing directors are lawful (in particular in compliance with statutory law and the articles of association). Additionally, the supervisory board must evaluate whether the measures are appropriate and economically reasonable. If the GmbH holds subsidiaries or affiliates, the supervisory board is also entitled to supervise the administration and management of such subsidiaries by the managing directors of the GmbH. In order to perform its duties, the supervisory board is entitled to review the books and records of the company along with all of its assets. It may do this itself or may engage external experts to undertake this monitoring on behalf of the supervisory board.[19] The board members may also question the directors in order to perform their duties. The articles of association may provide for other control rights to which the supervisory board is entitled or specify these statutory rules.

In principle, the supervisory board is at liberty to determine the measures by which it exercises its control, provided that the supervision is pursued effectively. If the supervisory board considers it necessary in the interests of the company, it may also call a shareholders' meeting.[20]

---

18 *Gesetz betreffend die Gesellschaft mit beschränkter Haftung* (GmbHG) (Act on Limited Liability Companies) 1892, s52, para. 1 (FRG); *Aktiengesetz* (AktG) (Stock Corporation Act) 1965, s111, para. 1 (FRG).

19 *Gesetz betreffend die Gesellschaft mit beschränkter Haftung* (GmbHG) (Act on Limited Liability Companies) 1892, s52, para. 1 (FRG); *Aktiengesetz* (AktG) (Stock Corporation Act) 1965, s111, para. 2, sentences 1 and 2 (FRG).

20 *Gesetz betreffend die Gesellschaft mit beschränkter Haftung* (GmbHG) (Act on Limited Liability Companies) 1892, s52, para. 1 (FRG); *Aktiengesetz* (AktG) (Stock Corporation Act) 1965, s111, para. 3, sentence 1 (FRG).

134. Rights and obligations: information rights

In order to properly perform its duties as the controlling corporate body, the supervisory board must be invested with certain information rights *vis-à-vis* the managing directors. Along with the right to review the books and records of the GmbH, the supervisory board may request from the managing directors at any time a report on the status of the company, including its legal relationships with subsidiaries and affiliated companies and regarding the business situation in these companies which could bear a significant influence on the GmbH itself.[21] The reports must be submitted in a proper and diligent manner. The law also requires that these reports must be submitted in due course, so as to enable the supervisory board to consider them prior to making its own decisions.[22] It is usually required that they are submitted in written form, although this is not a mandatory requirement. Each member of the supervisory board is entitled to gain knowledge of such reports. If the reports are submitted in written form, any member is entitled to receive a copy.[23] Notwithstanding these legal provisions, it is also customary that the articles of association provide for a regulation specifically designed to meet the information needs of the supervisory board in the specific GmbH at hand. As regards the receiving of such information, a member of the supervisory board is subject to the same confidentiality obligations as a managing director.[24] If a member of the supervisory board is also a shareholder of the company, his or her information rights as a shareholder[25] remain unaffected. This person may use the information gained as a shareholder when performing his or her duties as a member of the supervisory board.

---

21 *Gesetz betreffend die Gesellschaft mit beschränkter Haftung* (GmbHG) (Act on Limited Liability Companies) 1892, s52, para. 1 (FRG); *Aktiengesetz* (AktG) (Stock Corporation Act) 1965, s90, para. 3 (FRG).

22 *Gesetz betreffend die Gesellschaft mit beschränkter Haftung* (GmbHG) (Act on Limited Liability Companies) 1892, s52 p. 1 (FRG); *Aktiengesetz* (AktG) (Stock Corporation Act) 1965, s90, para. 4 (FRG).

23 *Gesetz betreffend die Gesellschaft mit beschränkter Haftung* (GmbHG) (Act on Limited Liability Companies) 1892, s52, para. 1 (FRG); *Aktiengesetz* (AktG) (Stock Corporation Act) 1965, s90, para. 5, sentences 1 and 2 (FRG).

24 For details see Section 108.

25 *Gesetz betreffend die Gesellschaft mit beschränkter Haftung* (GmbHG) (Act on Limited Liability Companies) 1892, s51a (FRG).

135. Rights and obligations: assessment of the annual financial statements

Subject to the articles of association providing otherwise, the managing directors must submit the annual financial statement (*Jahresabschluß*) and the annual report (*Lagebericht*) to the supervisory board and in addition, if the GmbH is the parent company of a group, the group annual financial statement (*Konzernabschluß*) and the group annual report (*Konzernlagebericht*).[26] If the annual financial statement and the annual report need to be audited by an auditor or an audit company,[27] the auditor is usually chosen by the shareholders' meeting.[28] It is, however, the supervisory board which engages the auditor on behalf of the company and instructs him or her to carry out the respective audit.[29] The articles of association may combine these two obligations to select and engage the auditor or assign the right to engage the auditor to the managing directors or another corporate body. In so far as the supervisory board engages the auditor, the auditor must submit his or her auditing report to the supervisory board directly.[30] The managing directors have the right to comment on this auditing report prior to it being handed over to the supervisory board. If the auditor is engaged by the managing directors or the shareholders' meeting itself, it is nevertheless advisable to submit the respective report to the supervisory board immediately after it has been received by the GmbH.

In addition to submitting the annual financial statements and the annual report to the supervisory board, the managing directors must submit to the supervisory board a proposal on the use of the balance sheet profits.[31] Once the (audited) annual financial statement and annual report and the proposal for the use of the balance sheet profit have been submitted to the supervisory board, the supervisory

---

26 *Gesetz betreffend die Gesellschaft mit beschränkter Haftung* (GmbHG) (Act on Limited Liability Companies) 1892, s52, para. 1 (FRG); *Aktiengesetz* (AktG) (Stock Corporation Act) 1965, s170, para. 1 (FRG).

27 *Handelsgesetzbuch* (HGB) (Commercial Code) 1897, ss316, 267 (FRG). Any company not classified as a small corporation must be audited. For the definition of small corporations see Section 194.

28 *Handelsgesetzbuch* (HGB) (Commercial Code) 1897, s318, para. 1 (FRG).

29 *Gesetz betreffend die Gesellschaft mit beschränkter Haftung* (GmbHG) (Act on Limited Liability Companies) 1892, s52, para. 1 (FRG); *Aktiengesetz* (AktG) (Stock Corporation Act) 1965, s111, para. 2, sentence 3 (FRG).

30 *Handelsgesetzbuch* (HGB) (Commercial Code) 1897, s321, para. 5, sentence 2 (FRG).

31 *Gesetz betreffend die Gesellschaft mit beschränkter Haftung* (GmbHG) (Act on Limited Liability Companies) 1892, s52, para. 1 (FRG); *Aktiengesetz* (AktG) (Stock Corporation Act) 1965, s170, para. 2 (FRG).

board must review and assess these documents. Within one month after receiving all of these documents, the supervisory board must issue to the shareholders' meeting a written report on the results of the assessment. In this report, the supervisory board must also indicate the manner in and extent to which it has exercised its control obligations throughout the business year. If the annual financial statement requires auditing, the auditor must participate in the discussions of the supervisory board in which it assesses the (group) annual financial statement. Additionally, the supervisory board must submit its report to the managing directors one month after it has received the annual financial statement, the annual report and, if required, the audit report of the respective auditor. If such a report is not submitted to the managing directors within the specified period, the managing directors must request that the report be delivered within a period not exceeding one month. If this additional deadline is also not met, the annual financial statement or a group annual financial statement must be considered as not being approved.[32]

136. Rights and obligations: representation of the company *vis-à-vis* managing directors

Unless otherwise provided by the articles of association, the members of the supervisory board represent the company *vis-à-vis* the managing directors.[33] However, unless this is stipulated explicitly, the supervisory board is not entitled to appoint and remove the managing directors or to enter into a service agreement with them on behalf of the company. The supervisory board represents the company *vis-à-vis* both current and former managing directors in the event that the shareholders' meeting resolves to enforce damage claims against the managing directors for business conduct[34] in so far as the articles do not provide otherwise or if the shareholders' meeting does not resolve on the installation of a special representative (*besonderer Vertreter*).

---

32 *Gesetz betreffend die Gesellschaft mit beschränkter Haftung* (GmbHG) (Act on Limited Liability Companies) 1892, s52, para.1 (FRG); *Aktiengesetz* (AktG) (Stock Corporation Act) 1965, s171 (FRG).

33 *Gesetz betreffend die Gesellschaft mit beschränkter Haftung* (GmbHG) (Act on Limited Liability Companies) 1892, s52, para. 1 (FRG); *Aktiengesetz* (AktG) (Stock Corporation Act) 1965, s112 (FRG).

34 *Gesetz betreffend die Gesellschaft mit beschränkter Haftung* (GmbHG) (Act on Limited Liability Companies) 1892, s46, no. 8 (FRG).

137. Rights and obligations: influence on the management

Within an optional supervisory board, the articles of association may provide that the responsibility for certain measures in connection with the management of the company is transferred to the managing directors and/or that the directors may only take certain kinds of measures or undertake certain business activities with the consent of the supervisory board. In addition, if the articles do not provide otherwise or are silent on the topic, an optional supervisory board may also by itself stipulate that certain kinds of business activity require its prior consent.[35] However, this may not result in a situation where the directors require the consent of the supervisory board for any action they take, that is, the supervisory board taking over the management of the company. Otherwise, the company would hardly be able to run its daily business. The business measures or decisions subject to the consent of the supervisory board are to be decided upon by the board according to their best judgment. Decisions of this nature are typically those associated with a considerable risk or which may otherwise have a substantial influence on the business of the company.

If the supervisory board refuses to give its consent, the managing directors may request that a shareholders' meeting replace the consent of the supervisory board. According to the Stock Corporation Act,[36] a shareholders' resolution replacing the consent of the supervisory board requires a majority of three quarters of the votes cast. The prevailing opinion, however, interprets this section of the Stock Corporation Act in a narrower sense for the purposes of a GmbH and assumes that a simple majority of the votes cast within such a shareholders' meeting is sufficient to replace the missing consent of the supervisory board. The reasons for the lower majority requirement are, first, that the corporate constitution of the GmbH respects the shareholders' meeting as the supreme corporate body despite the possibility of being able to establish further corporate bodies. Furthermore, a managing director is always bound by the instructions issued by the shareholders' meeting, wherein these instructions merely require a simple majority of the votes cast. In other words, a reservation pertaining to the need to obtain

---

35 *Gesetz betreffend die Gesellschaft mit beschränkter Haftung* (GmbHG) (Act on Limited Liability Companies) 1892, s52, para. 1 (FRG); *Aktiengesetz* (AktG) (Stock Corporation Act) 1965, s111, para. 4 (FRG).

36 *Aktiengesetz* (AktG) (Stock Corporation Act) 1965, s111, para. 4, sentence 4 (FRG).

consent from the supervisory board may not exclude the right of the shareholders' meeting to issue instructions to the managing directors based on a simple majority of the votes cast.

138. Rights and obligations: assignment of competences of the shareholders' meeting

In the articles of association, many areas of competences of the shareholders' meeting may be transferred to the supervisory board (except for some fundamental competences which will be discussed directly below). These transferable areas of authority are in particular those stipulated in the list of areas of authority of the shareholders' meeting[37] as already introduced above under Section 72.

There are, however, certain areas of authority of the shareholders' meeting which cannot be transferred to another corporate body, as they are of a fundamental nature and must remain with the shareholders themselves. Such fundamental competences include, amongst others, the undertaking of any amendments to the articles of association,[38] including in turn changes in the stated share capital by way of capital increase or capital decrease,[39] any measures to be taken under the Law Regulating the Transformation of Companies (eg, merger, splitting or conversion), entering into control and profit and loss transfer agreements and other corporate agreements (*Unternehmensverträge*) and the dissolution of the company.[40]

Apart from these areas of authority which must remain with the shareholders' meeting, the articles of association may freely assign rights and obligations to the supervisory board.

139. Compensation and side agreements

According to statutory law, the members of the supervisory board may receive compensation for their services if this compensation is provided for in the articles of association or is approved by the shareholders' meeting.[41] If neither the articles of association nor a

---

37 *Gesetz betreffend die Gesellschaft mit beschränkter Haftung* (GmbHG) (Act on Limited Liability Companies) 1892, s46 (FRG).

38 *Gesetz betreffend die Gesellschaft mit beschränkter Haftung* (GmbHG) (Act on Limited Liability Companies) 1892, s53 (FRG).

39 *Gesetz betreffend die Gesellschaft mit beschränkter Haftung* (GmbHG) (Act on Limited Liability Companies) 1892, s55 *et seq.* (FRG).

40 *Gesetz betreffend die Gesellschaft mit beschränkter Haftung* (GmbHG) (Act on Limited Liability Companies) 1892, s60, para. 1, no. 2 (FRG).

41 *Gesetz betreffend die Gesellschaft mit beschränkter Haftung* (GmbHG) (Act on Limited Liability Companies) 1892, s52, para. 1 (FRG); *Aktiengesetz* (AktG) (Stock Corporation Act) 1965, s113, para. 1, sentences 1 and 2 (FRG).

shareholders' resolution provide for compensation of the members of the supervisory board, the prevailing opinion presumes that an appropriate compensation is agreed implicitly.

The amount of the compensation shall be appropriate to the duties of the members and the situation of the company.[42] The compensation may also consist of a bonus element, either in the form of cash or non-cash benefits (such as insurance premiums, company car, office, etc). These extra benefits call for the establishment of a special legal basis and may not be agreed upon implicitly. Additionally, the members of the supervisory board are entitled to be compensated for their appropriate out-of-pocket expenses.[43]

It is not prohibited for a member of the supervisory board to enter into a separate (service) agreement with the company. Such agreements are, however, subject to certain restrictions. If the articles of association do not provide otherwise, the obligations of the member of the supervisory board as stipulated in the agreement must be obligations outside of his or her regular duties as a member of the supervisory board. Such an agreement requires the consent of the supervisory board as a whole.[44] If, however, the scope of the agreement identically matches the regular duties as a member of the supervisory board, the agreement is considered void; it would circumvent the regulation that the compensation received by a member of the supervisory board must be set out in the articles of association or a shareholders' resolution.[45] Side agreements between members of the supervisory board and the company itself typically relate to areas which are not already inherent to the regular duties of the supervisory board (eg, legal, tax or technical advice).

140. Liability

When fulfilling their obligations, the members of the supervisory board must act with the due care and diligence of a proper and prudent business person.[46] Any members of the supervisory board

---

42 *Gesetz betreffend die Gesellschaft mit beschränkter Haftung* (GmbHG) (Act on Limited Liability Companies) 1892, s52, para. 1 (FRG); *Aktiengesetz* (AktG) (Stock Corporation Act) 1965, s113, para. 1, sentence 3 (FRG).

43 *Bürgerliches Gesetzbuch* (BGB) (Civil Code) 1900, ss670, 675 (FRG).

44 *Gesetz betreffend die Gesellschaft mit beschränkter Haftung* (GmbHG) (Act on Limited Liability Companies) 1892, s52, para. 1 (FRG); *Aktiengesetz* (AktG) (Stock Corporation Act) 1965, s114, para. 1 (FRG).

45 *Aktiengesetz* (AktG) (Stock Corporation Act) 1965, s113, para. 1 (FRG) accordingly.

46 *Gesetz betreffend die Gesellschaft mit beschränkter Haftung* (GmbHG) (Act on Limited Liability Companies) 1892, s52, para. 1 (FRG); *Aktiengesetz* (AktG) (Stock Corporation Act) 1965, s93, 116, para. 1 (FRG).

violating this standard of care are jointly and severally liable towards the company. In other words, a member of the supervisory board may not claim that another member of the supervisory board is more experienced with regard to the question at hand or that the respective matter falls within the other member's internal sphere of responsibility (just as a director also cannot do this).

The most important obligations of the members of the supervisory boards include the obligation to keep the business and trade secrets of the company confidential and to ensure that the rules and regulations relating to a GmbH are observed, in particular that the managing directors are properly supervised. The latter obligation has been specifically confirmed by a decision of the Federal Supreme Court.[47] In this decision, the court ruled that the members of a voluntary supervisory board may not generally be held personally liable if the managing directors of a GmbH effect payments in breach of their obligation not to do so during the insolvency of the GmbH (see Section 124 for details). The decisive argument for the court was that payments of the directors in the event of insolvency would only reduce the funds available for creditors, but would not directly damage the company. The court also found it unreasonable to hold the members of a voluntary supervisory board, who often act without remuneration or for very little remuneration, liable for the sometimes considerable amounts involved (in the case where this decision was concerned, roughly €1.1 million). The above exclusion from liability, however, does not apply if the member of the supervisory board was actually aware that illegal payments were being made by the managing directors.

Like the shareholders and the managing directors, the members of the supervisory board are furthermore subject to a duty of loyalty towards the GmbH.

The members of the supervisory board bear the burden of proof if it is disputed whether or not they have complied with their obligations as prudent business people.[48] Any damage claim resulting from a breach of their obligations is a claim held by the GmbH itself, not its shareholders. The shareholders may, however, have their own claim against the members of the supervisory

47 20 September 2010, *Bundesgerichtshof* (German Federal Supreme Court) (II ZR 78/09), NRW 2011, 221.

48 *Gesetz betreffend die Gesellschaft mit beschränkter Haftung* (GmbHG) (Act on Limited Liability Companies) 1892, s52, para. 1 (FRG); *Aktiengesetz* (AktG) (Stock Corporation Act) 1965, s116, 93, para. 2, sentence 2 (FRG).

board if they can prove that they have incurred damage which goes beyond damage to the company itself or if they have a particular legal relationship with the members of the supervisory board.

Any claims against the members of the supervisory board are time-barred five years after the damaging event occurred.[49] The time-barring regulation is mandatory law. A shortening of the time-barring period is therefore possible, but it is not possible to extend it.

The supervisory board may be granted discharge (*Entlastung*) by the shareholders' meeting. As a result of being discharged, any claims on the part of the company against the members of the supervisory board based on their misconduct as prudent business persons are waived, unless the shareholders' meeting is not aware of the facts giving rise to such claims. If these requirements are satisfied, the members of the board have a claim to be discharged.

B. Mandatory supervisory board under the One Third Employee Participation Act

141. Requirements and ramifications

A GmbH which generally has between 500 and no more than 2,000 employees is subject to the provisions of the One Third Employee Participation Act (*Drittelbeteiligungsgesetz – DrittelbG*).[50] For the purpose of calculating the number of employees, the employees of a company that has entered into a domination agreement with or which is integrated (*eingegliedert*) into the (parent) GmbH must be taken into account when determining the total number of employees. Companies which directly and predominantly pursue a religious, political, educational, scientific, artistic or charitable purpose or which are engaged in reporting or activities relating to freedom of speech are exempted from the Act.[51] The law also does not apply to religious groups.

A GmbH subject to the One Third Employee Participation Act is mandatorily required to establish a supervisory board, wherein at least one third of its members must be employee representatives.[52]

---

49 *Gesetz betreffend die Gesellschaft mit beschränkter Haftung* (GmbHG) (Act on Limited Liability Companies) 1892, s52, para. 3 (FRG).

50 *Drittelbeteiligungsgesetz* (DrittelbG) (One Third Employee Participation Act) 2004, s1, para. 1, no. 3 (FRG).

51 *Drittelbeteiligungsgesetz* (DrittelbG) (One Third Employee Participation Act) 2004, s1, para. 2 (FRG).

52 *Drittelbeteiligungsgesetz* (DrittelbG) (One Third Employee Participation Act) 2004, s4, para. 1 (FRG).

142. Number of members and eligibility

The supervisory board has at least three members, with the option of increasing this number in the articles of association as long as the total number of members is divisible by three.[53] The maximum number of members of the supervisory board is limited to nine if the GmbH has a stated share capital of up to €1.5 million, to 15 if the stated share capital is higher than €1.5 million and to 21 if the GmbH has a stated share capital of more than €10 million.

Regarding the eligibility of the supervisory board members, effectively, the same rules apply as those applicable to the members of an optional supervisory board.[54] The articles of association may only provide for other or additional personal requirements for those members of the supervisory board who are representatives of the shareholders but not of the employees. In addition to the personal requirements for eligibility in an optional supervisory board, a person who is already a member of the supervisory boards of 10 companies which are mandatorily required to install such a board may not become a member of the supervisory board of a company subject to the One Third Employee Participation Act.[55] Additionally, a person who is the legal representative of another corporation in whose supervisory board a managing director of the GmbH has a seat may not become a member of the supervisory board of the GmbH.[56] The aim is to avoid a cross-controlling of corporations which would potentially lead to a reduction in diligence where the control is concerned. Employee representatives on the board must be at least 18 years of age and have been employed by the company for at least one year.[57]

Also, a managing director may not be a member of the supervisory board, and vice versa.[58]

---

53 *Drittelbeteiligungsgesetz* (DrittelbG) (One Third Employee Participation Act) 2004, s1, para. 1, no. 3; *Aktiengesetz* (AktG) (Stock Corporation Act) 1965, s95, sentences 1 to 3 (FRG).

54 For details see Section 130; *Aktiengesetz* (AktG) (Stock Corporation Act) 1965, s100 (FRG).

55 *Drittelbeteiligungsgesetz* (DrittelbG) (One Third Employee Participation Act) 2004, s1, para. 1, no. 3 (FRG); *Aktiengesetz* (AktG) (Stock Corporation Act) 1965, s100, para. 2, no. 1 (FRG).

56 *Drittelbeteiligungsgesetz* (DrittelbG) (One Third Employee Participation Act) 2004, s1, para. 1, no. 3 (FRG); *Aktiengesetz* (AktG) (Stock Corporation Act) 1965, s100, para. 2, no. 3 (FRG).

57 *Drittelbeteiligungsgesetz* (DrittelbG) (One Third Employee Participation Act) 2004, s4, para. 3 (FRG).

58 *Drittelbeteiligungsgesetz* (DrittelbG) (One Third Employee Participation Act) 2004, s1, para. 1, no. 3 (FRG); *Aktiengesetz* (AktG) (Stock Corporation Act) 1965, s105 (FRG).

143. Nomination, term in office and revocation

The representatives of the employees (one third of the members of the supervisory board) are elected by the employees themselves based on a general, secret, equal and direct election. The One Third Employee Participation Act sets out detailed rules for the formal requirements pertaining to such an election.[59] The shareholders' representatives on the supervisory board (two thirds of the members) are either elected by the shareholders' meeting or are delegated by certain individuals if the articles of association provide so. The right to delegate people to join the supervisory board may only be granted to shareholders of the company and only with regard to a maximum of one third of the total number of members of the board.[60]

The term in office of the members of the supervisory board may not extend beyond the date of the shareholders' meeting in which a resolution is passed on the discharge of the supervisory board for the fourth business year following the commencement of their term in office. The business year in which their term of office begins will not be taken into account.[61] In other words, the term of office of a member of the supervisory board, irrespective of whether he or she is a shareholder or employee representative, is usually limited to a maximum of approximately five years. A re-election or re-nomination for additional terms is possible. The articles of association may provide for a shorter term if the regulation to this effect applies to all members (employee and shareholders' representatives) equally.

A shareholders' representative may be removed from the supervisory board based on a shareholders' resolution obtained with three quarters of the votes cast.[62] The articles of association may provide for different majority requirements (also a lower majority) and may stipulate further requirements for removal. If a member of the supervisory board has been delegated, the person entitled to delegate such a member of the board may also remove the delegated

---

59 *Drittelbeteiligungsgesetz* (DrittelbG) (One Third Employee Participation Act) 2004, s5 *et seq*. (FRG).

60 *Drittelbeteiligungsgesetz* (DrittelbG) (One Third Employee Participation Act) 2004, s1, para. 1, no. 3 (FRG); *Aktiengesetz* (AktG) (Stock Corporation Act) 1965, s101, para. 2, sentences 1 and 4 (FRG).

61 *Drittelbeteiligungsgesetz* (DrittelbG) (One Third Employee Participation Act) 2004, s1, para. 1, no. 3 (FRG); *Aktiengesetz* (AktG) (Stock Corporation Act) 1965, s102, para. 1 (FRG).

62 *Drittelbeteiligungsgesetz* (DrittelbG) (One Third Employee Participation Act) 2004, s1, para. 1, no. 3 (FRG); *Aktiengesetz* (AktG) (Stock Corporation Act) 1965, s103, para. 1 (FRG).

member at any time without cause and replace them with another person.[63]

With regard to employee representatives on the supervisory board, there is a particular option for their removal. These representatives may be removed by way of a resolution to be reached by the employees either at the request of the works council or upon the request of at least one fifth of the employees entitled to vote for the employees on the supervisory board.[64] The resolution of the employees must be obtained with a majority of three quarters of the votes cast.

Aside from these options for removing members of the board who are representatives of a particular group, both shareholder and employee representatives may be removed by the court for cause based on a request of the supervisory board to do so. The supervisory board must reach a resolution on the filing of such a request with a simple majority of the votes cast. In the event that the member has been delegated based on the articles of association, shareholders holding 10% of the stated share capital may file such a request.[65]

144. Internal regulations and passing of resolutions

With regard to internal regulations and the requirements for the passing of resolutions, most of the provisions regarding the optional supervisory board apply accordingly.[66] In a company which is subject to the One Third Employee Participation Act, however, most of the outlined applicable regulations are mandatory law, wherein the supervisory board must have a chairman and at least one deputy chairman, both of which must be registered with the commercial register by the managing directors.[67]

The supervisory board can only pass resolutions if at least half of the members required by applicable law or the articles of association participate in the resolution. The articles of association may stipulate additional requirements regarding the ability of the

---

63 *Drittelbeteiligungsgesetz* (DrittelbG) (One Third Employee Participation Act) 2004, s1, para. 1, no. 3 (FRG); *Aktiengesetz* (AktG) (Stock Corporation Act) 1965, s103, para. 2, sentence 1 (FRG).

64 *Drittelbeteiligungsgesetz* (DrittelbG) (One Third Employee Participation Act) 2004, s12, para. 1 (FRG).

65 *Drittelbeteiligungsgesetz* (DrittelbG) (One Third Employee Participation Act) 2004, s1, para. 1, no. 3 (FRG); *Aktiengesetz* (AktG) (Stock Corporation Act) 1965, s103, para. 3 (FRG).

66 For details see Section 132 *et seq.*

67 *Drittelbeteiligungsgesetz* (DrittelbG) (One Third Employee Participation Act) 2004, s1, para. 1, no. 3 (FRG); *Aktiengesetz* (AktG) (Stock Corporation Act) 1965, s107, para. 1 (FRG).

supervisory board to pass resolutions.[68] In any case, at least three members must participate in the resolution, irrespective of whether they are representatives of the employees or of the shareholders.

Members of the supervisory board who are not present when a board resolution is being passed may participate in the voting by submitting a written vote. If the articles do not provide otherwise, resolutions of the supervisory board may also be passed in written form, by phone or in other comparable forms if no member of the supervisory board objects to this proceeding.[69]

Each member of the supervisory board and the managing directors may request that the chairman of the supervisory board calls a board meeting. The meeting must take place within a two-week period after the chairman has notified the board thereof.[70] If the chairman does not comply with such a request, each board member or director may convene the meeting themselves. The supervisory board must record the minutes of each of these meetings, and the respective minutes be signed by the chairman of the supervisory board.[71]

145. Rights and obligations

Regarding its rights and obligations, under the One Third Employee Participation Act, the mandatory supervisory board basically has the same rights and obligations as an optional supervisory board.[72] However, unlike an optional supervisory board, the regulations which apply to a mandatory supervisory board constitute mandatory law to a much greater degree and may not be amended by the articles of association.

The mandatory supervisory board remains responsible for the supervision of the managing directors with the right to inspect the books and records of the company and to request reports from

---

68 *Drittelbeteiligungsgesetz* (DrittelbG) (One Third Employee Participation Act) 2004, s1, para. 1, no. 3 (FRG); *Aktiengesetz* (AktG) (Stock Corporation Act) 1965, s108, para. 2 (FRG).

69 *Drittelbeteiligungsgesetz* (DrittelbG) (One Third Employee Participation Act) 2004, s1, para. 1, no. 3 (FRG); *Aktiengesetz* (AktG) (Stock Corporation Act) 1965, s108, paras. 3 and 4 (FRG).

70 *Drittelbeteiligungsgesetz* (DrittelbG) (One Third Employee Participation Act) 2004, s1, para. 1, no. 3 (FRG); *Aktiengesetz* (AktG) (Stock Corporation Act), 1965, s110, para. 1 (FRG).

71 *Drittelbeteiligungsgesetz* (DrittelbG) (One Third Employee Participation Act) 2004, s1, para. 1, no. 3 (FRG); *Aktiengesetz* (AktG) (Stock Corporation Act) 1965, s107, para. 2, sentence 1 (FRG).

72 See Section 133 *et seq.* for details.

the managing directors.[73] It must also examine the annual financial statement, the annual report, and the proposal of the managing directors regarding the use of the balance sheet profits. After doing so it must report to the shareholders' meeting regarding the outcome of its assessment.[74] The supervisory board is also entitled to set out a list of actions on the part of the managing directors which require its prior consent.[75] In this regard there is considerable dispute as to the extent to which the articles of association may amend such a right, in particular by way of the requirement of a certain quorum in order to establish such a list of actions. Again, if the supervisory board refuses to give its approval for a certain action, the managing directors may request a shareholders' resolution on the issue. In the case of an affirmative shareholders' resolution, the managing directors are entitled to pursue the measure.[76] Here (again) it is disputed whether a three-quarter majority of the votes cast (as stipulated by statutory law) or a simple majority of the votes cast (which is more in line with the corporate structure of the GmbH) is required for such a resolution. The stronger arguments in this regard speak in favour of a simple majority.

146. Compensation

With respect to compensation, the same principles as those outlined regarding an optional supervisory board apply in the case of a mandatory supervisory board.[77]

147. Liability

The standards as regards liability for members of a mandatory supervisory board are the same as those which apply to the members of an optional supervisory board (the due care and diligence of a prudent and proper business person).[78] In this context, however, it is

---

73 *Drittelbeteiligungsgesetz* (DrittelbG) (One Third Employee Participation Act) 2004, s1, para. 1, no. 3 (FRG); *Aktiengesetz* (AktG) (Stock Corporation Act) 1965, s90, paras. 3–5, 111, paras. 1 and 2 (FRG).

74 *Drittelbeteiligungsgesetz* (DrittelbG) (One Third Employee Participation Act) 2004, s1, para. 1, no. 3 (FRG); *Aktiengesetz* (AktG) (Stock Corporation Act) 1965, ss170, 171 (FRG).

75 *Drittelbeteiligungsgesetz* (DrittelbG) (One Third Employee Participation Act) 2004, s1, para. 1, no. 3 (FRG); *Aktiengesetz* (AktG) (Stock Corporation Act) 1965, s111, para. 4 (FRG).

76 *Drittelbeteiligungsgesetz* (DrittelbG) (One Third Employee Participation Act) 2004, s1, para. 1, no. 3 (FRG); *Aktiengesetz* (AktG) (Stock Corporation Act) 1965, s111, para. 4, sentences 3 and 4 (FRG).

77 For details see Section 139.

78 For details see Section 140.

undisputed that the standards pertaining to liability may not be amended by the articles of association.

C. Mandatory supervisory board under the Co-Determination Act

148. Requirements and ramifications

A GmbH is subject to the 1976 Co-Determination Act (*Mitbestimmungsgesetz* – MitbestG 1976) if it generally employs more than 2,000 people.[79] The employees of group companies are considered employees of the parent company (*herrschendes Unternehmen*) for the purposes of calculating the relevant number of employees under the Co-Determination Act.[80] Companies directly and predominantly pursuing a political, religious, charitable, educational, scientific or artistic purpose, or the purpose of which is reporting or activities relating to freedom of speech, are exempted from the Co-Determination Act.[81] Companies which are subject to the Co-Determination Act are mandatorily required to establish a supervisory board.[82] Half of the members of this supervisory board must be delegates of the employees, with the other half being delegates of the shareholders (Co-Determination on a parity basis – *Paritätische Mitbestimmung*).

149. Number of members and eligibility

The size of the supervisory board is determined in particular by the number of employees in the GmbH and its group companies (if applicable). The Co-Determination Act provides that a supervisory board in a company which generally has no more than 10,000 employees consists of 12 members in total, wherein the membership is equally distributed between the representatives of the employees and the shareholders. In companies which generally have more than 10,000 but not more than 20,000 employees, the supervisory board has a total size of 16 members, again with equal distribution of membership. If a company regularly has more than 20,000 employees, the supervisory board consists of 10 representatives for the employees and 10 representatives for the shareholders.[83]

---

79 *Mitbestimmungsgesetz* (MitbestG) (Co-Determination Act) 1976, s1, para. 1 (FRG).

80 *Mitbestimmungsgesetz* (MitbestG) (Co-Determination Act) 1976, s5, para. 1 (FRG); *Aktiengesetz* (AktG) (Stock Corporation Act) 1965, s18 (FRG).

81 *Mitbestimmungsgesetz* (MitbestG) (Co-Determination Act) 1976, s1, para. 4 (FRG).

82 *Mitbestimmungsgesetz* (MitbestG) (Co-Determination Act) 1976, s6, para. 1, 7 para. 1 (FRG).

83 *Mitbestimmungsgesetz* (MitbestG) (Co-Determination Act) 1976, s7, para. 1 (FRG).

The Co-Determination Act provides that certain representatives of the employees (either two or three, depending on the size of the supervisory board) are to be nominated by the trade unions represented in the GmbH. Such representatives of the employees must be at least 18 years of age and have been employed in the company for at least one year.[84] Apart from these particular rules, the rules of eligibility as set forth above with regard to the supervisory board which must be established in companies subject to the One Third Employee Participation Act[85] apply accordingly. Again, the articles of association may only stipulate (additional) personal requirements with regard to the shareholders' representatives in the supervisory board, but not for the members to be nominated by the employees.[86]

150. Nomination, term in office and removal from office

The representatives of the shareholders are nominated either by way of an election of the shareholders' meeting or by means of delegation by an individual or an entity entitled to do so in the articles of association.[87] Again, the right to delegate members of the supervisory board may only be granted to shareholders of the company and for a maximum of one third of the total members of the board. In this regard, the same rules apply for the nomination of the shareholders' representatives as would apply under the One Third Employee Participation Act.

The representatives of the employees, on the other hand, are elected. In companies which generally have no more than 8,000 employees, the members of the supervisory board representing the employees are elected directly by all employees. If the company on average employs more than 8,000 employees, the employees' representatives are elected by delegates who themselves are elected by the employees. In this regard, the Co-Determination Act sets out detailed regulations for both kinds of election.[88]

Regarding the term in office, the same regulations apply under the Co-Determination Act as those which apply under the One Third

84 *Mitbestimmungsgesetz* (MitbestG) (Co-Determination Act) 1976, s7, paras. 2 and 3 (FRG).

85 For details see Section 142.

86 *Mitbestimmungsgesetz* (MitbestG) (Co-Determination Act) 1976, s6, para. 2 (FRG); *Aktiengesetz* (AktG) (Stock Corporation Act) 1965, s100, para. 4 (FRG).

87 *Mitbestimmungsgesetz* (MitbestG) (Co-Determination Act) 1976, s6, para. 2, 8, para. 2 (FRG); *Aktiengesetz* (AktG) (Stock Corporation Act) 1965, s101 (FRG).

88 *Mitbestimmungsgesetz* (MitbestG) (Co-Determination Act) 1976, s9 *et seq*. (FRG).

Employee Participation Act.[89] The term of office of the members of the supervisory board may thus not be longer than a maximum of five years. Re-election or re-nomination is possible.

The shareholders' representatives on the supervisory board may be removed on the basis of a shareholders' resolution requiring three quarters of the votes cast, unless the articles of association provide for another majority requirement or set forth certain other conditions (eg, removal solely for cause).[90] If a shareholders' representative has been delegated based on the articles of association, the person entitled to delegate such a member may also remove this member at any time without cause and replace them with another member.[91] An employees' representative may only be removed upon request. Those entitled to file such a request include three quarters of the employees or a trade union (if the representative has been nominated by a trade union). If the employees' representative has been elected by delegates, a resolution of the delegates with three quarters of the votes cast is required in order for the removal to become effective. If the employees' representative has been elected by the employees directly, a resolution reached by all employees of the company with three quarters of the votes cast is required in order for the removal to become effective.[92]

In addition, irrespective of whether this person is a representative of the employees or of the shareholders, a member of the supervisory board may be removed by a court decision for cause. The court decision requires a request to this effect from the supervisory board, wherein the resolution on this request must be reached with a simple majority of the votes cast.[93] Finally, a member of the supervisory board is also entitled to resign from his or her office at any time in so far as the resignation is not submitted at an inappropriate time (*zur Unzeit*).

---

89 *Mitbestimmungsgesetz* (MitbestG) (Co-Determination Act) 1976, s6, para. 2 (FRG); *Aktiengesetz* (AktG) (Stock Corporation Act) 1965, s102 (FRG).

90 *Mitbestimmungsgesetz* (MitbestG) (Co-Determination Act) 1976, s6, para. 2 (FRG); *Aktiengesetz* (AktG) (Stock Corporation Act) 1965, s103, para. 1 (FRG).

91 *Mitbestimmungsgesetz* (MitbestG) (Co-Determination Act) 1976, s6, para. 2 (FRG); *Aktiengesetz* (AktG) (Stock Corporation Act) 1965, s103, para. 2 (FRG).

92 *Mitbestimmungsgesetz* (MitbestG) (Co-Determination Act) 1976, s23 (FRG).

93 *Mitbestimmungsgesetz* (MitbestG) (Co-Determination Act) 1976, s6, para. 2 (FRG); *Aktiengesetz* (AktG) (Stock Corporation Act) 1965, s103, para. 3 (FRG).

151. Internal regulations and passing of resolutions

As regards internal regulations and the requirements for passing resolutions, the principles as set out in Section 144 for supervisory boards under the One Third Employee Participation Act apply accordingly.[94] However, there are a few exceptions to be observed. Under the Co-Determination Act, the election of the chairman of the supervisory board requires a two-thirds majority of the members of the supervisory board; a simple majority of the votes cast is not sufficient.[95] If the members fail to reach agreement on the chairman, the chairman will be elected by the shareholders' representatives with only a simple majority of the votes cast, whereas the deputy chairman is elected by the representatives of the employees.[96] The supervisory board may afterwards only pass resolutions if at least half of its total statutory members participate in the passing of a resolution.[97] However, it is not necessary for a certain number of employer's or employees' representatives to participate in the meeting. Finally, since the supervisory board has an even number of members, it is possible that a draw may occur during resolutions. In order to resolve such situations, the Co-Determination Act stipulates that if a draw occurs, the vote of the chairman of the supervisory board counts as two votes in the next vote on the same issue.[98] This 'double vote' entitlement does not apply to the deputy chairman. Thus, it is ensured by these means that the representatives of the shareholders are always able to pass a resolution, even against the will of the employees' representatives.

152. Rights and obligations: appointment and removal of the managing directors

Being subject to the Co-Determination Act, the managing directors of a GmbH with mandatory Co-Determination are appointed and removed by the supervisory board and not by the shareholders' meeting.[99] The managing directors are also not appointed for an indefinite period of time, but for a term of a maximum of five

94 *Mitbestimmungsgesetz* (MitbestG) (Co-Determination Act) 1976, s25 (FRG).
95 *Mitbestimmungsgesetz* (MitbestG) (Co-Determination Act) 1976, s27, para. 1 (FRG).
96 *Mitbestimmungsgesetz* (MitbestG) (Co-Determination Act) 1976, s27, para. 2 (FRG).
97 *Mitbestimmungsgesetz* (MitbestG) (Co-Determination Act) 1976, s28 (FRG).
98 *Mitbestimmungsgesetz* (MitbestG) (Co-Determination Act) 1976, s29, para. 2, sentence 1 (FRG).
99 *Mitbestimmungsgesetz* (MitbestG) (Co-Determination Act) 1976, s31 (FRG); *Aktiengesetz* (AktG) (Stock Corporation Act) 1965, ss84, 85 (FRG).

years, with the possibility of re-nomination. The appointment and removal of the managing directors calls for the passing of a resolution by the supervisory board, wherein two thirds of the votes of all of its members are required.[100] The removal of a managing director, however, is only possible for cause, and not at the free discretion of the supervisory board.[101] In addition, the Co-Determination Act stipulates that a labour relations director (*Arbeitsdirektor*), responsible for employee and labour law-related issues, is nominated as an additional managing director, with rights equal to those of the other managing director(s).[102] The formal requirements pertaining to his or her appointment and removal are the same as those which apply to the managing directors.

In addition to the authority to appoint and remove the managing directors and the labour relations director, the Federal Supreme Court has ruled that the supervisory board of a GmbH, being subject to the Co-Determination Act, is also responsible for entering into, amending and terminating service agreements with the managing directors and the labour relations director.[103] Thus, the responsibility regarding the service agreement is no longer with the shareholders' meeting. The authority to appoint and remove these directors from office is inherently linked to the authority to enter into the underlying service agreement.

Finally, the supervisory board represents the GmbH *vis-à-vis* the managing directors.[104] Given the fact that the supervisory board is also entitled to enter into the service agreements with the managing directors, this is a logical prerequisite.

153. Rights and obligations: exercise of ownership rights

A particular regulation applies if the co-determined GmbH holds an interest of at least 25% in another company which itself is subject to the Co-Determination Act. Normally, voting rights of a parent company in a subsidiary are exercised by the managing directors at their own discretion or, in important situations or if the articles

100 *Mitbestimmungsgesetz* (MitbestG) (Co-Determination Act) 1976, s31, para. 2, para. 5 (FRG).

101 *Mitbestimmungsgesetz* (MitbestG) (Co-Determination Act) 1976, s31, para.1 (FRG); *Aktiengesetz* (AktG) (Stock Corporation Act) 1965, s84, para. 3 (FRG).

102 *Mitbestimmungsgesetz* (MitbestG) (Co-Determination Act) 1976, s33 (FRG).

103 14 November 1983, *Bundesgerichtshof* (German Federal Supreme Court) (II ZR 33/83) – BGHZ 89, 48 *et seq.*

104 *Mitbestimmungsgesetz* (MitbestG) (Co-Determination Act) 1976, s25, para. 1, no. 2 (FRG); *Aktiengesetz* (AktG) (Stock Corporation Act) 1965, s112 (FRG).

provide so, on the basis of a corresponding shareholders' resolution. In contrast, the Co-Determination Act stipulates that in a subsidiary which itself is subject to the Co-Determination Act, the managing directors of the GmbH are bound to exercise their voting rights in the subsidiary based on the instructions given by the supervisory board of the GmbH if the voting in the subsidiary relates to the appointment, removal or laying-off of the management in the subsidiary, resolutions on the liquidation or transformation of the subsidiary, entering into corporate agreements (eg, domination and profit and loss transfer agreements) or to a transfer of its assets. It should be noted that such instructions given by the supervisory board only require the majority of the votes of the representatives of the shareholders. The votes of the employees' representatives will not be taken into account.[105]

154. Rights and obligations: other rights and obligations

Aside from the particular rights and obligations described above, the supervisory board of a GmbH subject to the Co-Determination Act has the same rights and obligations as a supervisory board in a GmbH which is subject to the One Third Employee Participation Act.[106] In particular, the supervisory board is entitled to supervise the managing directors and to review the annual financial statements and the annual reports.

155. Compensation

Regarding compensation, the same rules and standards apply as those which apply with regard to the supervisory board under the One Third Employee Participation Act.[107]

156. Liability

Under the Co-Determination Act, the members of the supervisory board are subject to the same standards of duty and care (diligence of a prudent and proper business person) as the members of the supervisory board under the One Third Employee Participation Act.[108]

---

105 *Mitbestimmungsgesetz* (MitbestG) (Co-Determination Act) 1976, s32, para. 1 (FRG).

106 For details see Section 145.

107 *Mitbestimmungsgesetz* (MitbestG) (Co-Determination Act) 1976, s25, para. 1, no. 2 (FRG); *Aktiengesetz* (AktG) (Stock Corporation Act) 1965, ss113, 114 (FRG).

108 *Mitbestimmungsgesetz* (MitbestG) (Co-Determination Act) 1976, s25, para. 1, no. 2 (FRG); *Aktiengesetz* (AktG) (Stock Corporation Act) 1965, s116, 93 (FRG).

D. Mandatory supervisory board under the Co-Determination Act for the Coal and Steel Industry

156a. General overview

A GmbH is subject to the rules of the Co-Determination Act for the Coal and Steel Industry if it: (i) regularly employs more than 1,000 employees, and (ii) is engaged in particular industry sectors, namely coal and iron ore mining and the production of iron and steel goods.[109] Such a GmbH must mandatorily establish a supervisory board. The supervisory board is comprised of 11 members.[110] The shareholders and the employees have five board members each. The eleventh member is a neutral member to be elected by the other members of the board.[111] The rights and obligations of the members of such supervisory boards are identical to those of a supervisory board under the 1976 Co-Determination Act. In the event of a potential conflict of applicable law, the rules of the One Third Employee Participation Act and the 1976 Co-Determination Act will not apply if the Co-Determination Act for the Coal and Steel Industry applies.[112]

In Germany, at the current point in time, there is apparently no GmbH which is subject to the Co-Determination Act for the Coal and Steel Industry, which is why further notes are omitted here.

E. Mandatory supervisory board under the Capital Investment Act

156b. General overview

If the purpose of a GmbH is the administration of certain domestic and EU investment funds (in particular of so-called Undertakings for Collective Investments in transferable securities – UCITS (*Organismen für gemeinsame Anlagen in Wertpapiere* – OGAW), Alternative Investment Funds (AIF) and Public Investment Funds (*Publikumsinvestmentvermögen*) it must mandatorily establish a supervisory board according to the Capital Investment

---

109 *Montanmitbestimmungsgesetz* (MontanMitbestG) (Co-Determination Act for the Coal and Steel Industry) 1951, s1, paras. 1 and 2 (FRG).

110 *Montanmitbestimmungsgesetz* (MontanMitbestG) (Co-Determination Act for the Coal and Steel Industry) 1951, s4 (FRG).

111 *Montanmitbestimmungsgesetz* (MontanMitbestG) (Co-Determination Act for the Coal and Steel Industry) 1951, s8 (FRG).

112 *Drittelbeteiligungsgesetz* (DrittelbG) (One Third Employee Participation Act) 2004, s1, para. 2 (FRG); *Mitbestimmungsgesetz* (MitbestG) (Co-Determination Act) 1976, s1, para. 2 (FRG).

Act (*Kapitalanlagegesetzbuch*), even if its number of employees is below the threshold of the One Third Employee Participation Act (500 employees) or of the 1976 Co-Determination Act (2,000 employees).[113] If any such Co-Determination Acts (including that for the coal and steel industry) apply, they would prevail the Capital Investment Act.

For a supervisory board under the Capital Investment Act, basically the same rules as for the board members to be nominated by the shareholders (not the employees) of a GmbH subject to the One Third Employee Participation Act apply. According to publicly available information, there are some 100 capital investment companies with the legal form of a GmbH requiring a supervisory board under the Capital Investment Act.[114]

Regarding the number of board members, the same rules apply as those pertaining to a GmbH subject to the One Third Employee Participation Act (minimum of three members and maximum of between nine and 21 members).[115]

As regards the question of eligibility, basically the same rules apply as those outlined for the members to be nominated by the shareholders (not the employees) of a GmbH subject to the One Third Employee Participation Act.[116] The Act, however, provides that the board must have at least one member which is (economically) independent of the shareholders, its affiliates and of the business partners of the company.[117] In addition, the board members must ensure the protection of the interests of the investors based on their personality and their expertise.[118] The German Federal Financial Supervisory Authority (*Bundesanstalt für Finanzdienstleistungsaufsicht* – BaFin) must be informed of any nomination and change in the members of the supervisory board. The BaFin is authorised to reject the nomination of a person it deems

---

113 *Kapitalanlagegesetzbuch* (KAGB) (Capital Investment Act) 2013, s18, para. 2 (FRG). The Act replaces the Investment Act (*Investmentgesetz*) with effect as of 22 July 2013 by thus implementing, *inter alia*, Directive 2009/65 EC on the coordination of laws, regulations and administrative provisions relating to undertakings for collective investment in transferable securities (UCITS) and Directive 2011/61/EC on Alternative Investment Fund Managers and amending Directives 2003/41/EC and 2009/65/EC and Regulations (EC) No 1060/2009 and (EU) No 1095/2010.

114 See the German Financial Supervision Authority (BaFin) website for details: www.bafin.de.

115 See Section 142 for details.

116 See Section 142 for details.

117 *Kapitalanlagegesetzbuch* (KAGB) (Capital Investment Act) 2013, s18, para. 3, sentence 2 (FRG).

118 *Kapitalanlagegesetzbuch* (KAGB) (Capital Investment Act) 2013, s18, para. 4 (FRG).

unqualified and may request the nomination of another person. In the event that a company is not only subject to the Capital Investment Act, but also to a Co-Determination Act due to having more than 500 or 2,000 employees on a regular basis, the aforementioned qualifications regarding personality and expertise are not applicable to the members of the board which are to be nominated by the employees (although this is actually desirable anyway).[119]

The members are either elected by the shareholders' meeting or, if the articles of association provide so, are delegated by one shareholder or certain shareholders entitled to do so.[120] If no Co-Determination Act applies, the employees of the company have no right to elect or delegate a member of the board. The delegation right may only be granted for a maximum of one third of the total members of the board. The term of office of the members of the supervisory board may not extend beyond the date of the shareholders' meeting in which a resolution is reached on the discharge of the supervisory board for the fourth business year following the date on which they were appointed.[121] The business year in which they were appointed is not taken into account. Re-election or re-nomination is possible. Members which are elected by the shareholders' meeting may be removed during their term in office by a shareholders' resolution with three quarters of the votes cast. The articles may stipulate a different majority requirement and/or further requirements for removal.[122] Delegated members may be removed and replaced by another person at any time and without cause by the person who delegated them.[123] Removal is also possible by way of court decision. See Section 143 for details.

With regard to the internal regulations, rights and obligations and liability of the supervisory board, basically the same principles apply as those which apply in the case of a board which is subject to the One Third Employee Participation Act.[124]

---

119 *Kapitalanlagegesetzbuch* (KAGB) (Capital Investment Act) 2013, s18, para. 5 (FRG).

120 *Kapitalanlagegesetzbuch* (KAGB) (Capital Investment Act) 2013, s18, para. 2, sentence 3 (FRG); *Aktiengesetz* (AktG) (Stock Corporation Act) 1965, s101 (FRG).

121 *Kapitalanlagegesetzbuch* (KAGB) (Capital Investment Act) 2013, s18, para. 2, sentence 3 (FRG); *Aktiengesetz* (AktG) (Stock Corporation Act) 1965, s102, p. 1 (FRG).

122 *Kapitalanlagegesetzbuch* (KAGB) (Capital Investment Act) 2013, s18, para. 2, sentence 3 (FRG); *Aktiengesetz* (AktG) (Stock Corporation Act) 1965, s103, p. 1 (FRG).

123 *Kapitalanlagegesetzbuch* (KAGB) (Capital Investment Act) 2013, s18, para. 2, sentence 3 (FRG); *Aktiengesetz* (AktG) (Stock Corporation Act) 1965, s103, p. 2 (FRG).

124 *Kapitalanlagegesetzbuch* (KAGB) (Capital Investment Act) 2013, s18, para. 2, sentence 3 (FRG); see Section 144 *et seq*. for details.

VIII. Share capital

A. Payment of share capital

157. General

The stated share capital of a GmbH (minimum: €25,000) may be raised in three different ways: by way of a contribution in cash, by way of a contribution in kind or by a mixture of these two. The particular formal requirements with regard to valid means of raising the share capital will be outlined in the following chapter. The general principle underlying the raising of the share capital is that it must be raised 'effectively', that is, the company must actually receive the sums the shareholders have subscribed for to be placed at the irrevocable and free disposition of its managing directors and these sums may not be repaid during the lifetime of the company.

Where the *Unternehmergesellschaft* (UG) is concerned, its share capital may be as low as €1.00. The capital may only be raised in cash and not by contributions in kind.[1] The following details on contributions in cash also apply to the *Unternehmergesellschaft*.

158. Contributions in cash

The most simple and practical way to raise the share capital of a GmbH is to pay the share capital in cash. Cash in this context means a payment in euros as the national currency. Foreign currencies must be converted into euros before they are available as a means of raising the stated share capital. The payments may either be made in cash, transferred to the managing director and the bank account of the pre-GmbH (subsequent to the notarisation of the articles and the deed of establishment), or to a trustee account of a lawyer or notary. Payment to an account of the pre-GmbH is the customary approach here. Only once this payment has been made is it possible to register the pre-GmbH with the commercial register.[2]

What is decisive here is that the shareholders make their payments with the intention of satisfying their obligation towards

1 For details see Section 34.
2 For details see Section 31.

the GmbH to pay in the share capital. Alternatively, rather than transferring money via wireless bank transfer, a shareholder may also submit a certified cheque issued by the German Federal Bank (*Bundesbank*). Thus, the submission of the certified cheque is in itself deemed to be the effecting of the payment rather than only when the latter is cashed.[3] Since the payment of the share capital must be effected towards the GmbH, a shareholder may not satisfy his or her obligation to pay the contribution towards the GmbH by paying a debt on behalf of the company.

As the law of the GmbH is governed by the principle of effectively raising the stated share capital, a shareholder may not be relieved from his or her obligation to satisfy his or her contribution towards the company.[4] Shareholders may also not offset their obligation to pay the contribution towards the company against a claim of their own against the GmbH, unless: (i) the claim of the shareholder is based on the leasing of assets to the company, and (ii) the offsetting has been agreed upon as a contribution in kind.[5] The GmbH, on the other hand, may offset a claim thereof against a claim of a shareholder in two cases. The first case is where the shareholder is in an economic crisis and the GmbH is in danger of having to fully satisfy the claim of the shareholder towards the GmbH whereas the GmbH will only receive some of its outstanding contribution claim. Under these conditions, jurisprudence and scholars allow the GmbH (not the shareholder!) to offset the respective claims against each other in order to at least avoid the GmbH having to pay more towards the shareholder than it receives from the latter. Secondly, a GmbH may also offset a claim it has towards its shareholder in the event that the claim of the shareholder towards the GmbH is liquid, adequate (*vollwertig*) and due (*fällig*). A claim is liquid if the managing directors, after due examination, come to the conclusion that the claim of the shareholder exists without any doubt. The claim is considered adequate if the company disposes of sufficient liquidity to satisfy any and all outstanding liabilities of the GmbH, including the counterclaim of the shareholder, the moment it offsets a claim against such counterclaim. If these two conditions are satisfied and the claim of the shareholder becomes due, merely a payment from

---

3 *Aktiengesetz* (AktG) (Stock Corporation Act) 1965, s54, para. 3 (FRG) accordingly.

4 *Gesetz betreffend die Gesellschaft mit beschränkter Haftung* (GmbHG) (Act on Limited Liability Companies) 1892, s19, para. 2, sentence 1 (FRG).

5 *Gesetz betreffend die Gesellschaft mit beschränkter Haftung* (GmbHG) (Act on Limited Liability Companies) 1892, s19, para. 2, sentence 2 (FRG).

the shareholder to the company and in turn by the company to the shareholder would be necessary in order for the two corresponding claims to be satisfied. In order to speed up the payment process, the courts allow the company to exonerate itself from the claim of the shareholder. Apart from these two aforementioned exceptions, the GmbH may not offset claims against those of a shareholder.

The raising of the share capital must be registered with the competent commercial register. The respective filing must be carried out by all managing directors jointly.[6] It may only be made after each shareholder has paid in at least one quarter of the acquired contribution towards the stated share capital.[7] Additionally, the total amount of the paid-in contributions in cash and any contributions in kind, if applicable, must amount to at least half of the stated share capital.[8]

When filing the confirmation that the share capital has been raised together with all other documents which must be filed when registering the GmbH,[9] the managing directors must affirm that the contributions towards the stated share capital have been effected and are irrevocably at their free disposal.[10] The court maintaining the respective commercial register has the right and obligation to verify whether the contributions towards the stated share capital have been properly effected.[11] Since the Act to Modernise the Law Governing GmbHs and Combat Abuses came into force, the court may only request additional documentation regarding the due satisfaction of the obligation to pay in the stated share capital if it has serious doubts (*erhebliche Zweifel*) regarding the correctness of the affirmation of the managing directors that the contributions have been properly made.[12] The intention behind this provision is to accelerate the registration process. If proper documentation

---

6 *Gesetz betreffend die Gesellschaft mit beschränkter Haftung* (GmbHG) (Act on Limited Liability Companies) 1892, s78 (FRG).

7 *Gesetz betreffend die Gesellschaft mit beschränkter Haftung* (GmbHG) (Act on Limited Liability Companies) 1892, s7, para. 2, sentence 1 (FRG).

8 *Gesetz betreffend die Gesellschaft mit beschränkter Haftung* (GmbHG) (Act on Limited Liability Companies) 1892, s7, para. 2, sentence 2 (FRG).

9 For further details see Sections 31–33.

10 *Gesetz betreffend die Gesellschaft mit beschränkter Haftung* (GmbHG) (Act on Limited Liability Companies) 1892, s8, para. 2, sentence 1 (FRG).

11 *Gesetz betreffend die Gesellschaft mit beschränkter Haftung* (GmbHG) (Act on Limited Liability Companies) 1892, s9c, para. 1 (FRG).

12 *Gesetz betreffend die Gesellschaft mit beschränkter Haftung* (GmbHG) (Act on Limited Liability Companies) 1892, s8, para. 2, sentence 2 (FRG).

to this effect is not submitted, the court may refuse to register the company.

If the payment of the share capital is not effected when due, the shareholder is obliged to pay interest on the outstanding payment.[13] The company's claim for the payment of the share capital becomes subject to the statute of limitations 10 years after the date on which the payment becomes due.[14]

159. Contributions in kind

Another way of raising the stated share capital is by way of a contribution in kind. Contributions in kind are all contributions towards the share capital which are not made in cash in so far as such contributions have a determinable economic value. The commercial register must be able to determine whether the value of the contribution is at least equal to the contribution subscribed for by the individual shareholder. A contribution in kind may consist of, for example, tangible assets (machines, real estate, goods etc), intangible assets (know-how etc), rights (shares, stock, intellectual property rights, concessions, licences etc), claims towards third parties or towards the GmbH itself, and a mixture of tangible assets and rights such as enterprises, plants, companies, businesses and even goodwill. On the other hand, the mere obligation of a shareholder to provide certain services to the company is not an acceptable contribution in kind.[15] The reasons for excluding services are that their value (for the GmbH) is difficult to determine and no one can actually verify whether the services have been properly provided or provided at all.

As with contributions in cash, the shareholders may not be relieved of their duty to satisfy their obligation to contribute the assets to the share capital of the company. Furthermore, the shareholder may not exercise a retention right regarding the assets to be contributed based on claims he or she has towards the company if they are not related to the assets to be contributed.[16]

---

13 *Gesetz betreffend die Gesellschaft mit beschränkter Haftung* (GmbHG) (Act on Limited Liability Companies) 1892, s20 (FRG).

14 *Gesetz betreffend die Gesellschaft mit beschränkter Haftung* (GmbHG) (Act on Limited Liability Companies) 1892, s19, para. 6, sentence 1 (FRG).

15 *Aktiengesetz* (AktG) (Stock Corporation Act) 1965, s27, para. 2 (FRG) accordingly.

16 *Gesetz betreffend die Gesellschaft mit beschränkter Haftung* (GmbHG) (Act on Limited Liability Companies) 1892, s19, para. 2, sentence 3 (FRG).

Even though a contribution in kind is generally possible, some particular requirements must be fulfilled in order for a contribution towards the share capital to be deemed effectively (validly) provided. In this context, please note that contributions in kind are excluded as a means of raising share capital for a so-called '*Unterne hmergesellschaft*'.[17]

First, the articles of association must state the name of the shareholder making a contribution in kind, that a contribution in kind will be made, the specific asset(s) to be contributed and the amount of the share capital the shareholder intends to raise by transferring the asset to the company.[18] Secondly, the shareholder or the company must prepare a special report (*Sachgründungsbericht*), which should outline the pertinent facts, enabling the commercial register to properly determine the value of the contribution in kind.[19] In practice, the report is almost always prepared by an accounting firm, even though this is not required by law. If this is not the case, and the commercial register comes to the conclusion that the value of the assets falls short of the acquired contribution, the shareholder must pay in the difference to the company in cash.[20] If the value of the contributed assets falls significantly short of the subscribed contribution of the shareholder, the court maintaining the commercial register may even refuse to register the company therein.[21] In practice, a registration will not occur until the last outstanding contributions have been properly made. In the event that an operational company is to be transferred by way of a contribution in kind, the annual financial statements for the last two business years must also be provided.

The transfer of the assets must be effected irrevocably, in full and for placing at the free disposal of the managing directors prior to filing the formation of the GmbH with the commercial register.[22]

---

17 *Gesetz betreffend die Gesellschaft mit beschränkter Haftung* (GmbHG) (Act on Limited Liability Companies) 1892, s5a, para. 2, sentence 2 (FRG). See further Section 34.

18 *Gesetz betreffend die Gesellschaft mit beschränkter Haftung* (GmbHG) (Act on Limited Liability Companies) 1892, s5, para. 4, sentence 1 (FRG).

19 *Gesetz betreffend die Gesellschaft mit beschränkter Haftung* (GmbHG) (Act on Limited Liability Companies) 1892, s5, para. 4, sentence 2 (FRG).

20 *Gesetz betreffend die Gesellschaft mit beschränkter Haftung* (GmbHG) (Act on Limited Liability Companies) 1892, s9, para. 1 (FRG).

21 *Gesetz betreffend die Gesellschaft mit beschränkter Haftung* (GmbHG) (Act on Limited Liability Companies) 1892, s9c, para. 1, sentence 2 (FRG).

22 *Gesetz betreffend die Gesellschaft mit beschränkter Haftung* (GmbHG) (Act on Limited Liability Companies) 1892, s7, para. 3 (FRG).

A partial contribution as in the case of a contribution in cash is not allowed. When filing for registration, the managing director must declare that the transfer of the asset to the company has been properly effected.[23] The claim of the company for the payment of the share capital by contributions in kind also becomes time-barred 10 years after the payment becomes due.[24]

160. Mixed contributions

Mixed contributions towards the stated share capital consisting partly of a contribution in kind and a contribution in cash are subject to the respective rules as set out above for the respective type of contribution. Ultimately, the commercial register must be convinced that the share capital has been raised effectively.

The specific provisions regarding the prohibition of offsetting a claim of the shareholders against the company as a means of paying in the share capital apply accordingly where a contribution in kind is to be made. However, a shareholder may offset a claim he or she has against the company as a means of paying in the share capital based on the permission to use or otherwise lease (*Überlassung*) assets, if this offsetting was already agreed in the articles of association.[25] In addition, the shareholder may not exercise a retention right regarding the assets to be contributed based on claims he or she has towards the company if they are not related to the assets to be contributed.[26]

The claim on the part of the company for the payment of the share capital is also time-barred 10 years after the payment becomes due.[27] If the payment for the cash part of the share capital is not provided when due, the shareholder is obliged to pay interest on the outstanding amount.[28]

---

23 *Gesetz betreffend die Gesellschaft mit beschränkter Haftung* (GmbHG) (Act on Limited Liability Companies) 1892, s8, para. 2, sentence 1 (FRG).

24 *Gesetz betreffend die Gesellschaft mit beschränkter Haftung* (GmbHG) (Act on Limited Liability Companies) 1892, s19, para. 6, sentence 1 (FRG).

25 *Gesetz betreffend die Gesellschaft mit beschränkter Haftung* (GmbHG) (Act on Limited Liability Companies) 1892, s19, para. 2, sentence 2 (FRG).

26 *Gesetz betreffend die Gesellschaft mit beschränkter Haftung* (GmbHG) (Act on Limited Liability Companies) 1892, s19, para. 2, sentence 3 (FRG).

27 *Gesetz betreffend die Gesellschaft mit beschränkter Haftung* (GmbHG) (Act on Limited Liability Companies) 1892, s19, para. 6, sentence 1 (FRG).

28 *Gesetz betreffend die Gesellschaft mit beschränkter Haftung* (GmbHG) (Act on Limited Liability Companies) 1892, s20 (FRG).

B. Disguised contributions in kind

161. Transfer of assets disguised as cash contributions

Since the regulations on the payment of the share capital by way of contributions in kind are rather technical and complicated, attempts are often made to circumvent them. Measures taken in an attempt to circumvent the regulations pertaining to the raising of the share capital by way of a contribution in kind are called disguised contributions in kind (*verschleierte Sacheinlage* or *verdeckte Sacheinlage*). With the enacting of the Act to Modernise the Law Governing GmbHs and Combat Abuses, a new section has been introduced into the Act on Limited Liability Companies which provides a legal definition of disguised contributions in kind.[29] According hereto, a disguised contribution in kind is a contribution in cash by a shareholder which, from an economic point of view and on the basis of an agreement in connection with the subscription for a contribution in cash, must be qualified completely or partly as a contribution in kind. Usually, in such situations, the paid-in cash is repaid in exchange for the transfer of the asset. As regards the temporal aspect here, some courts have ruled that a transfer of assets to the company by the shareholder who made the contribution in cash within a time period of up to six months after the contribution in cash was made is presumed to be effected on the basis of an agreement between the shareholder and the GmbH 'in connection' with the subscription for the cash contribution. It is up to the shareholder to prove that no such connection exists and that the transfer of the assets was not already intended at the point in time when the contribution in cash was made.

If a disguised contribution in kind is made, the agreements in connection therewith and the legal transactions executed for the satisfaction thereof remain valid, in contrast to the legal situation prior to the enacting of the Act to Modernise the Law Governing GmbHs and Combat Abuses. At that time, such agreements were considered void. The shareholder is also not exempted from duly providing his or her contribution towards the share capital. His or her obligation remains unaffected, but is transformed into an obligation to pay in the subscribed amount of the stated share capital in cash, wherein the actual value of the assets transferred to the GmbH

---

29 *Gesetz betreffend die Gesellschaft mit beschränkter Haftung* (GmbHG) (Act on Limited Liability Companies) 1892, s19, para. 4 (FRG).

will be deducted from this (converted) cash obligation. This deduction, however, may not be made to the detriment of the other assets of the company. Therefore, prior to deducting the actual value of the transferred assets, the amount surpassing the nominal value of the cash contribution and paid as a consideration for the assets from the company assets must be deducted from the actual value of the transferred assets.[30] In other words, if the value of the contributed assets exceeds the subscribed contribution to the share capital, the shareholder has duly fulfilled his or her (converted) obligation to provide payment for his or her share capital in cash. The relevant point in time for the determination of the value of the contributed assets is the date of the registration of the company (or the capital increase, as applicable) with the commercial register. If the assets are transferred to the company only after the registration with the commercial register has been filed, this later point in time shall be decisive.[31] The burden of proof for the (full) value of the transferred asset lies with the shareholder.

Typically, a disguised contribution in kind becomes relevant in the case of the insolvency of the GmbH, when the liquidator attempts to collect money on behalf of the GmbH. A customary measure in this regard is to request the shareholders to pay their outstanding contributions in to the share capital (if applicable) for which they have subscribed. Due to this amendment to the Act on Limited Liability Companies, this possibility will likely be excluded in the future to a large extent.

In the case of the *Unternehmergesellschaft*, contributions in kind are not possible at all and are excluded by law.[32] Only cash contributions to the share capital are allowed. The Act on Limited Liability Companies makes no reference to the respective provisions outlined in this paragraph. It is thus questionable whether, in the case of a disguised contribution in kind, the new or the old regulations will apply. The old regulations led to the invalidity of any legal transactions made in connection with the disguised contribution in kind, that is, the obligation to pay in the share capital

---

30 22 March 2010, *Bundesgerichtshof* (German Federal Supreme Court) (II ZR 12/08), NRW 2010, 1948 *et seq.*

31 *Gesetz betreffend die Gesellschaft mit beschränkter Haftung* (GmbHG) (Act on Limited Liability Companies) 1892, s19, para. 4, sentence 3 (FRG).

32 *Gesetz betreffend die Gesellschaft mit beschränkter Haftung* (GmbHG) (Act on Limited Liability Companies) 1892, s5a, para. 2, sentence 2 (FRG).

in cash remained unfulfilled and the whole transaction had to be unwound.

Since this new regulation on disguised contributions in kind leaves many questions open, the Federal Supreme Court has soon had to deal with various cases in connection with the issue. In an early decision of 19 February 2009,[33] the Federal Supreme Court ruled that services (for money – in the case at hand media and marketing services) may not be valid disguised contributions in kind by a shareholder and that their value may not be deducted from the continuing cash obligation. The decision is in line with the previously outlined rule that services are not suitable contributions in kind.[34] The court asserts that an asset which is not suitable as a contribution in kind in the event that such a contribution in kind is intended, is also and in particular not a suitable asset if the transfer of the asset in question is effected in the form of a disguised contribution in kind.[35]

The principles set out above may also bear relevance in the case of a cash pooling system. In a case in which the Federal Supreme Court had to issue a decision,[36] a GmbH was set up by three shareholders by way of contributions in cash. They agreed to install a cash pool including the company with one of the shareholders being responsible for the cash account and being the only person with access to the account. At the end of each day, the amounts paid to the account of the GmbH were automatically transferred to the cash pooling account. After the GmbH became insolvent, the insolvency administrator requested payment of the subscribed contributions from the shareholders. The Federal Supreme Court ruled that, if the balance on the cash pooling account is negative for the GmbH at the point in time at which the amounts on the company account are transferred to the cash pooling account, such a transfer is to be regarded as a disguised contribution in kind. After all, the GmbH is relieved of a liability towards the cash pooling account and will not receive the contribution to be placed at the free disposal of its managing directors. If, on the other hand, the balance on the cash pooling

---

33 16 February 2009, *Bundesgerichtshof* (German Federal Supreme Court) (II ZR 120/07) – BGH NJW 2009, 2375 *et seq.*

34 See Section 159.

35 This view was confirmed by a decision of 1 February 2010, *Bundesgerichtshof* (German Federal Supreme Court) (II ZR 173/08), NRW 2010, 1747 *et seq.*

36 20 July 2009, *Bundesgerichtshof* (German Federal Supreme Court) (II ZR 273/07) – BGH NJW 2009, 3091 *et seq.*

account is even or positive in favour of the company, the transfer of money from the company account to the cash pooling account is to be qualified as a loan from the GmbH to the shareholder holding the account. Such a scenario is subject to the rules pertaining to a repayment of paid-in share capital as set out immediately below (see Section 162). The court also ruled that the shareholders who were neither holders of the cash pooling account nor had access to this account had duly provided their contributions by paying in to the account of the GmbH. These shareholders never retrieved any of their contributions when the amounts on the company account were transferred to the cash pooling account; only the holder of the account in question did so.

In a further recent decision, the Federal Supreme Court upheld earlier rulings on payments of shareholders made to the company in connection with a capital increase, but made prior to the passing of the shareholders' resolution to increase the stated capital. It confirmed that such payments do not generally constitute the proper satisfaction of the contribution obligation of the shareholder.[37] Only in very limited and exceptional cases, for example, the transfer being necessary and there being no alternative way to protect the company from insolvency, is an early payment regarded as the shareholder fulfilling the obligation to pay in his or her contribution in connection with the capital increase. As the contribution is not legally paid, the paying shareholder has a claim against the company for the repayment of his or her contribution. The company, however, has a claim for the payment of the subscribed part of the capital increase once the resolution on the increase has been passed. If the company and the shareholder now agree that, instead of repaying the amount already paid by the shareholder and then paying it in again to satisfy his or her obligation in accordance with the capital increase, no payment shall be made in either direction, the shareholder is actually deemed to contribute his or her claim for repayment to the company. The court has ruled that such an agreement must be qualified as a disguised contribution in kind and must be in compliance with the rules outlined above. The contribution of the repayment claim will thus only result in a fulfilment of the shareholder's payment obligation if his or her repayment claim is fully valid, that is, the repayment claim is fully covered by the assets of the company.

37 10 July 2012, *Bundesgerichtshof* (German Federal Supreme Court) (II ZR 212/10).

162. Repayment of paid-in share capital

Another specific scenario which generates much discussion in connection with contributions in kind has now been settled with the introduction of the Act to Modernise the Law Governing GmbHs and Combat Abuses. The situation in question occurs when a shareholder pays in his or her share capital in cash and the shareholder and the GmbH have already agreed prior to the payment of the share capital by the shareholder that the respective amount shall be repaid to the shareholder (*Hin- und Herzahlen*). Prior to 1 November 2008 (when the Act to Modernise the Law Governing GmbHs and Combat Abuses came into force) the obligation of the shareholder to pay in the subscribed share capital was considered unfulfilled.

The new regulation now provides that if: (i) the shareholder and the GmbH agree prior to the paying in of the subscribed share capital, or at the latest before the paid-in contribution is repaid to the shareholder, that the amount in question should be repaid to the shareholder, or that any other measure should be taken which from an economic point of view equals a repayment of this paid-in share capital, and (ii) this repayment is not considered to be a contribution in kind according to the principles outlined in the previous section (Section 161), the obligation of the shareholder to pay in the share capital shall be considered fulfilled under the condition that (iii) the repayment is covered by an adequate (*vollwertig*) claim for repayment, which is either due at any time or which may become due by a termination without cause by the GmbH.[38] Whether or not a claim is to be considered 'adequate' is to be determined by the managing directors applying the diligence of a prudent business person from an ex-ante perspective. It is not required that the repayment occurs beyond reasonable doubt (*mit an Sicherheit grenzender Wahrscheinlichkeit*), but only that the non-payment of the shareholder is unlikely.[39] According to the new legislation, the obligation to pay in the subscribed share capital is thus considered fulfilled if the company has a 'liquid' and valid claim against its shareholder, for example, in a cash pooling system (see below), which is typically its parent company. The Act on Limited Liability Companies therefore also no longer prescribes that the amount of the (adequate) cash contribution is physically 'available' within the company. It is

38 *Gesetz betreffend die Gesellschaft mit beschränkter Haftung* (GmbHG) (Act on Limited Liability Companies) 1892, s19, para. 5 (FRG).

39 1 December 2008, *Bundesgerichtshof* (German Federal Supreme Court) (II ZR 102/07).

sufficient that the balance sheet of the company shows a respective liquid and valid claim (*Bilanzbetrachtung*) against its shareholder.

In its decision of 1 February 2010,[40] the Federal Supreme Court gave additional guidance on the 'pay in/pay out' (*Hin- und Herzahlen*) requirements in situations where the company has entered into a service agreement with one of its shareholders. It ruled that paying for consultancy services prior to a capital increase will not be considered a case of pay in/pay out if: (i) the services have actually been rendered, (ii) the compensation is arm's-length compensation, and (iii) the services were useful and therefore of value to the company.

Further, the courts deem a cash pooling agreement between the shareholders and the company to sufficiently constitute an agreement to repay the contribution, since this is the logical consequence of the agreement. Regarding the requirement that the claim for repayment be either due at any time or due via termination without cause, this criterion must also be met in a cash pooling agreement.

The repayment arrangement or the repayment itself must be filed with the commercial register together with the other documents to be filed when establishing the company or raising the share capital.[41] The above scenario may typically be found in cases in which the shareholder paying in the share capital and the GmbH are parties in the same cash pooling system (in particular where the parent company pays in the share capital for its subsidiary). In such cases, the paid-in cash often has to be repaid to the shareholder based on the cash pooling agreement. According to the old legislation, it was not recognised in the case law that the obligation to pay in the share capital was satisfied by the shareholder.

The regulations set out above also apply to contributions effected before the Act to Modernise the Law Governing GmbHs and Combat Abuses came into force, unless a final decision has been issued by a court in this regard, or the GmbH and the shareholders have agreed on a settlement. In its decision of 19 February 2009,[42] the Federal Supreme Court confirmed that if a shareholder duly provides his or her contribution in cash and the company thereafter

---

40 *Bundesgerichtshof* (German Federal Supreme Court) (II ZR 173/08).

41 *Gesetz betreffend die Gesellschaft mit beschränkter Haftung* (GmbHG) (Act on Limited Liability Companies) 1892, s19, para. 5, sentence 2 (FRG).

42 16 February 2009, *Bundesgerichtshof* (German Federal Supreme Court) (II ZR 120/07) – BGH NJW 2009, 2375 *et seq*; see also Section 161.

requests services from the said shareholder against payment of a certain consideration, the principles set out above for the repayment of the paid-in share capital will only apply if the GmbH and the shareholder have agreed that his or her cash contribution shall be 'reserved' by the GmbH for the payment of his or her services. If no such arrangement has been agreed upon between the GmbH and its shareholder, the contribution in cash is deemed to have been duly provided and no repayment has occurred. The request for the performance of services by the shareholder must then be qualified as if it were a request for the performance of services by any other third party.

C. Maintenance of share capital

163. General prohibition of repaying share capital

Once the stated share capital has been paid in (also taking into account the situations outlined under Sections 161 and 162), the assets necessary to maintaining the stated share capital of the GmbH may not be repaid to the shareholders.[43] The amount of the stated share capital as set out in the articles of association and as registered with the commercial register must at all times be maintained for the benefit of the creditors. The amount of the registered share capital does not necessarily have to be available at all times in cash on a separate account or in the same form in which it has been contributed if the share capital has been raised by way of a contribution in kind. The Act on Limited Liability Companies requires that the stated share capital is still available in the GmbH from a balance sheet perspective and not used up to settle the liabilities of the company. The assets of the GmbH minus all liabilities and reserves (*Rückstellungen*) must amount to at least the stated share capital figure. Otherwise, the GmbH has an adverse balance (*Unterbilanz*) which prohibits it from making any payments towards its shareholders. In other words, the managing directors must ensure that this minimum amount of the stated share capital is available at the company at any time based on a current balance sheet, and that any assets required to maintain this stated share capital may not be repaid to the shareholders. As regards the drawing up of the

43 *Gesetz betreffend die Gesellschaft mit beschränkter Haftung* (GmbHG) (Act on Limited Liability Companies) 1892, s30, para. 1 (FRG).

respective balance sheet, the German GAAP, and in particular the rules of the German Commercial Code, apply.

The Act on Limited Liability Companies itself only prohibits the 'repayment' of assets to the shareholders. However, it is generally recognised that not only repayments of or in cash, but also other measures by which assets and values from the GmbH are transferred to the shareholders are prohibited under this provision. The prohibition also covers the provision of services, the transfer of tangible and intangible assets, the transfer of use, the provision of security for liabilities of the shareholder, the assumption of joint liability, and the waiving of rights of the company against the shareholder etc. The question of whether a prohibited repayment of this nature has been effected typically arises when the GmbH and the shareholder enter into a legal transaction or business which is not conducted on normal arm's-length terms (see Section 164 below). Additionally, it is not only repayments towards shareholders which are prohibited, but also repayments to third parties if the third party in question has a close relationship with the shareholder. This close relationship with the shareholder may be established by family bonds (eg, spouse, children, grandchildren, grandparents etc) or by way of business ties (eg, payment to a company under the control of a shareholder, trustees, etc).

164. Exceptions from the prohibition of repaying share capital: transactions at arm's length

Any legal transaction which the shareholders and the GmbH enter into on normal arm's-length terms is generally not a violation of the prohibition of repaying the share capital. In such cases, the company receives a consideration which is equal to or higher than the value of the assets it transfers or services it provides to the shareholder. The Federal Supreme Court, however, ruled in a recent case (prior to the Act to Modernise the Law Governing GmbHs and Combat Abuses) that loans granted to shareholders out of the assets bound by the registered share capital not only violate the repayment prohibition where the loan is granted without any interest or at a lower interest rate than is customary in the market, but also if the loan is granted on arm's-length terms. The court argued that the claim of the GmbH for repayment was subordinate to the loan actually granted to the shareholder.[44] However, it remains doubtful whether

44 24 November 2003, *Bundesgerichtshof* (German Federal Supreme Court) (II ZR 171 / 01) – BGHZ 157, 72 *et seq.*

the Federal Supreme Court will continue to uphold this ruling following the recent amendments to the Act on Limited Liability Companies. Since the Act to Modernise the Law Governing GmbHs and Combat Abuses came into force, it is no longer a requirement that the share capital should be 'physically' maintained within the company. It is sufficient if the share capital is maintained from a balance sheet point of view and the company has a liquid and valid claim against the third party.

165. Exceptions from the prohibition of repaying share capital: payments made under an existing domination or profit and loss transfer agreement

In the event that the GmbH is a party to a domination or profit and loss transfer agreement (section 291 Stock Corporation Act), payments issued by the GmbH are also allowed if they are necessary to maintain the registered share capital.[45] This exception not only allows payments directly made between the parties to such agreements, but also payments to another shareholder or to a third party, in particular corporate groups. The reason for this exception is that the GmbH has a compensation claim (section 302, paragraph 1 Stock Corporation Act) against the other party of the domination or profit and loss transfer agreement for any annual shortfall (*Jahresfehlbetrag*) as long as such an agreement is in place.

166. Exceptions from the prohibition of repaying share capital: adequate repayment claim

Furthermore, the GmbH does not violate the prohibition of repaying the stated share capital if the GmbH has an adequate (*vollwertig*) claim for repayment against the shareholder.[46] The question as to whether or not a repayment claim is 'adequate' can be answered with the help of the information outlined under Section 162. With the introduction of this new regulation, the principle of the physical maintenance of the stated share capital (*Substanzschutz*) in a GmbH has largely been abandoned in favour of a balance sheet point of view (*bilanzielle Betrachtungsweise*). The situation covered by this exception usually relates to upstream loans, in particular

45 *Gesetz betreffend die Gesellschaft mit beschränkter Haftung* (GmbHG) (Act on Limited Liability Companies) 1892, s30, para. 1, sentence 2, or, alternatively, 1 (FRG).

46 *Gesetz betreffend die Gesellschaft mit beschränkter Haftung* (GmbHG) (Act on Limited Liability Companies) 1892, s30, para. 1, sentence 2, or, alternatively, 2 (FRG).

within a cash pooling system, wherein the subsidiary must transfer its cash to the parent company. From now on, this kind of transfer is permitted if the GmbH has an adequate claim towards its parent company. It is the task of the managing director to assess whether the claim towards the shareholder is adequate and has full value. It is not necessary that the repayment claim towards the shareholder is due or can be declared due at any given moment without notice. Given the fact that the law now favours the balance sheet point of view, there are good arguments to suggest that the granting of a security of the GmbH on behalf of one of its shareholders does not violate the prohibition of repaying the stated share capital as long as the GmbH has an adequate compensation claim against its shareholder in the event that the security is drawn upon.

167. Exceptions from the prohibition of repaying share capital: repayment of shareholder loans

Finally, the Act on Limited Liability Companies permits a GmbH to repay loans granted by the shareholders to the company, or satisfy claims based on an economically equivalent transaction, at any time.[47] The distinction which needed to be made prior to the enacting of the Act to Modernise the Law Governing GmbHs and Combat Abuses as regards whether or not a shareholder loan was replacing equity and whether it was given during a crisis of the company, however, continues to bear relevance. The issue of whether or not the repayment of such a shareholder loan is contestable shall be dealt with in Section 170.

168. Consequences of a violation

Payments which are made in violation of the prohibition of repaying the stated share capital are to be repaid to the company by the respective recipient.[48] If the recipient is a third party with close ties to the shareholder, the third party is obliged to make such a repayment. If the recipient acted in good faith when receiving the payments, the GmbH may only reclaim the respective payments to the extent that they are required to satisfy the creditors of the

47 *Gesetz betreffend die Gesellschaft mit beschränkter Haftung* (GmbHG) (Act on Limited Liability Companies) 1892, s30, para. 1, sentence 3 (FRG).

48 *Gesetz betreffend die Gesellschaft mit beschränkter Haftung* (GmbHG) (Act on Limited Liability Companies) 1892, s31, para. 1 (FRG).

company.[49] A recipient acts in bad faith if, at the point in time at which he or she receives the payment, he or she has positive knowledge that the payment is required to maintain the stated share capital, or is not aware of this due to gross negligence. Should the recipient not be able to repay the received amount, the other shareholders of the GmbH are liable to an extent commensurate with their participation in the GmbH and to the extent to which the repayment is required to satisfy the creditors of the company.[50]

The company's repayment claim is subject to the statute of limitations 10 years after the prohibited payment to the shareholder or a third party has been made.[51] However, a shareholder is not obliged to repay profits received in good faith if such profits have not been distributed under violation of the regulations for the maintenance of the share capital.[52]

D. Loans

169. Loans to shareholders

A GmbH is not prohibited from granting a loan to a shareholder. However, when doing so, it must ensure that the terms and conditions of the loan in question meet the market standards (arm's-length terms). If the GmbH grants a loan not on ordinary market terms, this could be considered a disguised distribution of profits (*verdeckte Gewinnausschüttung*).[53] Before the Act to Modernise the Law Governing GmbHs and Combat Abuses came into force, the Federal Supreme Court ruled that, despite being granted on ordinary market terms, a loan may violate the rules on the maintenance of the share capital because a claim for repayment does not have the same value as the granted loan itself.[54] It remains to be seen whether the Federal Supreme Court will uphold this opinion now that the Act on Limited Liability Companies has been amended. Payments and loans granted to a shareholder are generally acceptable if they

---

49 *Gesetz betreffend die Gesellschaft mit beschränkter Haftung* (GmbHG) (Act on Limited Liability Companies) 1892, s31, para. 2 (FRG).

50 *Gesetz betreffend die Gesellschaft mit beschränkter Haftung* (GmbHG) (Act on Limited Liability Companies) 1892, s31, para. 3 (FRG).

51 *Gesetz betreffend die Gesellschaft mit beschränkter Haftung* (GmbHG) (Act on Limited Liability Companies) 1892, s31, para. 5 (FRG).

52 *Gesetz betreffend die Gesellschaft mit beschränkter Haftung* (GmbHG) (Act on Limited Liability Companies) 1892, s32 (FRG).

53 For further details on disguised distributions of profits, see Section 200.

54 See Section 164 for details.

are backed up by an adequate claim for repayment, that is, if the shareholder has sufficient liquidity to repay the granted loan when necessary.[55] In particular, this regulation permits cash pooling between a parent company and its subsidiary.

170. Shareholder loans

A GmbH and a shareholder may agree at any time on the granting of a loan from the shareholder to the GmbH. In principle, the terms and conditions may be freely negotiated between the parties within the limits prescribed by law and the duty of loyalty. Such a duty, however, does not oblige the shareholder to grant the company loans on more favourable conditions than those it would extend towards a third party. The GmbH, on the other hand, must ensure that the loan is given on arm's-length terms.

Since the enacting of the Act to Modernise the Law Governing GmbHs and Combat Abuses, the GmbH is also entitled to repay a shareholder loan at any time, even if the company has an adverse balance at the time of repayment or is otherwise in distress.[56] Prior to the amendment of the Act on Limited Liability Companies, a repayment of the shareholder loan was not possible if the GmbH was in a state of 'crisis' at the time of repayment of the loan, that is, if the company was in a situation in which a third party would not have granted a loan on ordinary market terms, but only subject to the provision of additional security and/or a higher interest rate. As soon as an insolvency proceeding was opened following a crisis of a GmbH, it was possible to repay the shareholder loan without restriction. However, the creditors of the GmbH were able to challenge such a repayment if they had obtained an enforceable judgment against the GmbH and if they were not satisfied by the company and the repayment of the shareholder loan was effected in the year prior to or following the filing of the opening of the insolvency proceedings. If the insolvency proceeding was opened, the shareholder loan was only satisfied as a subordinate insolvency claim compared to other claims against the GmbH, that is, the shareholder did not generally have his or her loan repaid, at least not in

55 *Gesetz betreffend die Gesellschaft mit beschränkter Haftung* (GmbHG) (Act on Limited Liability Companies) 1892, s30, para. 1, sentence 2, or, alternatively, 2 (FRG).

56 *Gesetz betreffend die Gesellschaft mit beschränkter Haftung* (GmbHG) (Act on Limited Liability Companies) 1892, s30, para. 1, sentence 3 (FRG).

full. The same applied to measures which were equal in economic terms to the granting of a loan to the company by a shareholder.

Regarding the ramifications of the generally permitted repayment of a shareholder loan by the GmbH (see Section 167), a distinction must be drawn between the rules which must be applied outside of an insolvency proceeding and the rules which must be applied after an insolvency proceeding has been opened.

Outside of an insolvency proceeding, a legal transaction in which either a security for a shareholder loan has been granted by the GmbH within the last 10 years prior to the obtaining of an enforceable judgment (*Schuldtitel*) against the company or thereafter, or a shareholder loan has been repaid in the last year prior to or after the obtaining of an enforceable judgment, is contestable in court.[57] As a consequence, the shareholder or the third party must repay the sums received from the GmbH. Parties entitled to challenge such legal transactions include all debtors of the company which have obtained an enforceable judgment against the company and whose claims against the company are due in so far as the foreclosure with regard to the assets has failed to provide or it may be assumed that it will fail to provide satisfaction for the creditor.[58] The challenging of the legal transaction in this regard is time-barred if three years have passed commencing from the end of the year in which the creditor obtained the enforceable judgment.[59] The above also applies if the GmbH repays a loan granted by a third party where a shareholder has provided a security for such a third-party claim.[60]

If an insolvency proceeding has been opened in connection with the assets of the GmbH, the situation is slightly different. An insolvency proceeding must be opened when the GmbH is either insolvent (*zahlungsunfähig*) or over-indebted, that is, if the assets of the company have a lower value than the liabilities of the company.[61] In the event that the company files for insolvency itself, the insolvency proceeding may already be opened on the grounds of

---

57 *Anfechtungsgesetz* (AnfG) (German Act on the challenging of legal actions taken by a debtor outside of the insolvency proceedings) 1994, s6, para. 1 (FRG).

58 *Anfechtungsgesetz* (AnfG) (German Act on the challenging of legal actions taken by a debtor outside of the insolvency proceedings) 1994, s2 (FRG).

59 *Anfechtungsgesetz* (AnfG) (German Act on the challenging of legal actions taken by a debtor outside of the insolvency proceedings) 1994, s6, para. 2 (FRG).

60 *Anfechtungsgesetz* (AnfG) (German Act on the challenging of legal actions taken by a debtor outside of the insolvency proceedings) 1994, s6a (FRG).

61 *Insolvenzordnung* (InsO) (Insolvency Ordinance) 1994, ss17 and 19, paras. 1 and 2 (FRG).

imminent illiquidity (*drohende Zahlungsunfähigkeit*).[62] Shareholder loans or legal transactions of a similar nature are not taken into account for the purpose of assessing whether or not a GmbH is over-indebted only in so far as the GmbH and the respective shareholder have entered into a subordination agreement (*Rangrücktritt*) with respect to the shareholder loan.[63] In other words, if the GmbH and the shareholder have not explicitly agreed that the shareholder loan shall be satisfied after any other claims of third-party debtors (see next paragraph), the shareholder loan is treated as if it were any other third-party liability and must be recorded as a liability when the balance sheet is drawn up to establish whether the GmbH is over-indebted.

Once the insolvency proceedings have been opened, the Insolvency Ordinance (*Insolvenzordnung*) prescribes the order in which the claims of the creditors of the GmbH must be satisfied. Any shareholder claims are automatically considered to be junior to any other claims of the creditors (which is not to be confused with a subordination outlined in the previous paragraph). Shareholder loans will only be satisfied if the claims of all other third-party creditors of the GmbH have been satisfied beforehand.[64] A shareholder may also be a third-party creditor to the company if he or she has entered into a transaction with the company – other than a shareholders' loan – on arm's-length terms just like any other third party would do (eg, provision of goods or services). However, the subordinate ranking of the shareholder loan does not occur in two important cases: first, if a creditor acquires shares in the GmbH at a point in time at which the GmbH is already insolvent, at which insolvency is impending or the GmbH is over-indebted, or for the purpose of a restructuring of the company. In this case, shareholder claims resulting out of already existing or newly granted loans shall not be subordinated to the claims of other creditors of the company until the restructuring measures are finished.[65] This regulation aims to adequately account for the risk associated with investing in an insolvent company for the purpose of its restructuring. Secondly, shareholder loans granted by a shareholder holding less than 10% of the share capital who is not a managing director of the GmbH are

---

62 *Insolvenzordnung* (InsO) (Insolvency Ordinance) 1994, s18 (FRG).

63 *Insolvenzordnung* (InsO) (Insolvency Ordinance) 1994, s19, para. 2, sentence 3 (FRG).

64 *Insolvenzordnung* (InsO) (Insolvency Ordinance) 1994, s39, para. 1, no. 5 (FRG).

65 *Insolvenzordnung* (InsO) (Insolvency Ordinance) 1994, s39, para. 4 (FRG).

also not considered subordinated loans and are to be satisfied like any other loans.[66]

With the opening of the insolvency proceedings, basically the same mechanisms for challenging legal transactions undertaken in a certain temporal context in connection with the opening of the insolvency proceedings apply as those which apply outside of a pending insolvency proceeding. Legal transactions which either grant security for a shareholder loan or a similar claim are contestable if the security in question has been granted in the last 10 years prior to the filing of the opening of the insolvency proceedings or after this filing has been undertaken.[67] Additionally, if a shareholder loan or comparable claim has been repaid in the last year prior to the filing for the opening of insolvency proceedings or after this filing, the repayment is also contestable in court.[68] Similarly, a repayment of a loan to a third party is contestable if a shareholder has granted a security for such a third-party claim and the repayment has occurred within the aforementioned one-year period.[69] The right to challenge such transactions does not apply in the cases previously outlined in this section in which the shareholder loans do not have junior ranking.[70] The exclusion of the right to challenge these particular shareholder loans is the logical consequence of the fact that they do not rank subordinate to other third party claims.

The insolvency administrator is entitled to challenge such transactions, but not the creditors themselves.[71]

Furthermore, the Act to Modernise the Law Governing GmbHs and Combat Abuses introduces a new principle into the Insolvency Ordinance in cases where a shareholder has not granted a loan to the GmbH, but has left the company an asset for use without transferring title. This typically gives the shareholder, and any other creditor, the right to request the re-transfer of the corresponding asset prior to the assets of the debtor (GmbH) being sold and the revenues being distributed between its creditors. After all, the respective asset does not belong to the company, but to the shareholder. The law now excludes such a right of re-transfer regarding the asset of the shareholder for the duration of the insolvency

66 *Insolvenzordnung* (InsO) (Insolvency Ordinance) 1994, s39, para. 5 (FRG).
67 *Insolvenzordnung* (InsO) (Insolvency Ordinance) 1994, s135, para. 1, no. 1 (FRG).
68 *Insolvenzordnung* (InsO) (Insolvency Ordinance) 1994, s135, para. 1, no. 2 (FRG).
69 *Insolvenzordnung* (InsO) (Insolvency Ordinance) 1994, s135, para. 2 (FRG).
70 *Insolvenzordnung* (InsO) (Insolvency Ordinance) 1994, s135, para. 4 (FRG).
71 *Insolvenzordnung* (InsO) (Insolvency Ordinance) 1994, s129, para. 1 (FRG).

proceedings, however, only for a maximum of one year after the opening of the proceedings. Furthermore, it is required that the respective asset is of direct significance where the maintenance of the business of the GmbH is concerned. The shareholder is entitled to receive remuneration for leasing the asset to the company in the amount of the average remuneration granted during the last year prior to the opening of the insolvency proceedings.[72]

171. Loans to managing directors

The managing directors, proxies, agents and other legal representatives of the company may receive a loan from the GmbH unless it is granted out of assets which are required to maintain the registered share capital.[73] A loan granted contrary to this provision (and the underlying legal documents) is valid, but must be repaid to the GmbH immediately. It is unclear in this situation whether the amendments to the rules on the maintenance of the stated share capital as outlined in Sections 163 to 168 apply accordingly or whether the rules prior to the enacting of the Act to Modernise the Law Governing GmbHs and Combat Abuses would apply here. This will have to be clarified in the future by scholars and the courts, since the provision pertaining to loans to officers in a GmbH does not make reference to the respective section in the Act on Limited Liability Companies which permits exceptions from the general provision prescribing the repayment of the stated share capital.

E. Additional contributions

172. Call for additional contributions

The articles of association may provide that the shareholders are obliged to make additional contributions to the GmbH beyond the amount of the stated share capital (*Nachschusspflicht*).[74] The obligation to make additional contributions may either be unlimited or limited as regards the amount.

If the additional contributions are not limited to a certain amount, each shareholder who is not willing or able to pay in the

72 *Insolvenzordnung* (InsO) (Insolvency Ordinance) 1994, s135, para. 3 (FRG).

73 *Gesetz betreffend die Gesellschaft mit beschränkter Haftung* (GmbHG) (Act on Limited Liability Companies) 1892, s43a, sentence 1 (FRG).

74 *Gesetz betreffend die Gesellschaft mit beschränkter Haftung* (GmbHG) (Act on Limited Liability Companies) 1892, s26, para. 1 (FRG).

additional contribution has the right to relieve him- or herself of the obligation to pay in the additional contribution by leaving his or her share at the disposal of the GmbH within a period of one month after being requested to pay in such a contribution. The GmbH itself is also entitled to declare *vis-à-vis* the shareholder that it considers the latter's share to have been left at the disposal of the company if the additional contribution is not paid in within one month after the GmbH has issued a request to this effect.[75] In both cases, the GmbH has the right to sell the share by way of a public auction in order to collect the outstanding amount. The auction must take place within one month after the declaration of the shareholder or the GmbH, respectively. If the public auction should yield a profit which exceeds the amount of the additional contribution and the costs of the auction, the shareholder is entitled to receive this additional profit. A sale of the share by private contract is only possible with the consent of the shareholder.[76] In the event that the claim of the GmbH is not satisfied by way of selling the share, the share will from then on be owned and held by the GmbH itself.[77] The articles of association may provide that the aforementioned rules only apply when the additional contributions exceed a particular amount.[78]

The articles may also provide for a limited obligation to pay in an additional contribution. If this additional contribution is not paid in when due, the regulations regarding the forfeiture of shares as specified in detail under Section 185 will apply. In short, this means that if the shareholder fails to pay in his or her additional contribution when due, the GmbH may set a deadline for paying in the contribution. If this deadline is not met, the company may declare that the share of the respective shareholder is forfeited and the GmbH is the new owner of the respective share.[79]

---

75 *Gesetz betreffend die Gesellschaft mit beschränkter Haftung* (GmbHG) (Act on Limited Liability Companies) 1892, s27, para. 1 (FRG).

76 *Gesetz betreffend die Gesellschaft mit beschränkter Haftung* (GmbHG) (Act on Limited Liability Companies) 1892, s27, para. 2 (FRG).

77 *Gesetz betreffend die Gesellschaft mit beschränkter Haftung* (GmbHG) (Act on Limited Liability Companies) 1892, s27, para. 3 (FRG).

78 *Gesetz betreffend die Gesellschaft mit beschränkter Haftung* (GmbHG) (Act on Limited Liability Companies) 1892, s27, para. 4 (FRG).

79 *Gesetz betreffend die Gesellschaft mit beschränkter Haftung* (GmbHG) (Act on Limited Liability Companies) 1892, s28, para. 1; 21 *et seq.* (FRG).

F. Changes in terms of share capital

173. Increase in share capital

A capital increase may be effected either by introducing fresh equity into the company (effective capital increase) or by converting reserves (*Rücklagen*) into share capital (nominal capital increase).

174. Increase in share capital: effective capital increase

An effective capital increase may be effected by way of contributions in cash or by contributions in kind. Any capital increase necessarily leads to a change in the articles and therefore requires a shareholders' resolution on the amendment of the articles, stipulating the amount by which the share capital is to be increased and the new amount of the stated share capital. The resolution requires a majority of three quarters of the votes cast and must be notarised.[80] The articles of association may stipulate additional requirements. In the event that the capital increase is not made by way of a contribution in cash but by way of a contribution in kind, the object of the contribution in kind and the amount of the stated share capital to be covered by such a contribution must be stipulated in the resolution on the capital increase.[81]

Furthermore, the resolution on the capital increase must state whether the new shares will be acquired by the existing shareholders or if (only) third parties under the exclusion of the shareholders may (also) participate in the capital increase.[82] Unlike the Stock Corporation Act (*Aktiengesetz* – AktG), the Act on Limited Liability Companies does not explicitly provide for a subscription right on the part of the current shareholders of the GmbH in the event of a capital increase. Nevertheless, it is generally recognised in the case law and by legal scholars that an exclusion of the subscription right on the part of the shareholders in a GmbH is only possible under exceptional circumstances. Such exceptional circumstances are recognised as being present if: (i) the GmbH has an urgent economic interest in excluding the current shareholders from participating in the capital increase, (ii) the intended aim can only be achieved

---

80 *Gesetz betreffend die Gesellschaft mit beschränkter Haftung* (GmbHG) (Act on Limited Liability Companies) 1892, s53, para. 2 (FRG).

81 *Gesetz betreffend die Gesellschaft mit beschränkter Haftung* (GmbHG) (Act on Limited Liability Companies) 1892, s56, para. 1 (FRG).

82 *Gesetz betreffend die Gesellschaft mit beschränkter Haftung* (GmbHG) (Act on Limited Liability Companies) 1892, s55, para. 2 (FRG).

by excluding the current shareholders, and (iii) the benefits arising from having a new shareholder providing fresh capital prevail over the dilution of the existing shares, that is, a loss of participation and voting rights on the part of the current shareholders. The typical case in which the shareholders' subscription rights are excluded would be the contribution of a company as a whole into the GmbH in return for the granting of new shares.

In a subsequent step, the (new) shareholders must subscribe for the share which is to be newly created. A declaration to this effect must either be set out in a notarial deed (which is usually combined with the deed pertaining to the increase in the share capital) or must be notarised.[83] By way of such a declaration, the subscriber enters into a subscription agreement with the company, obliging him or her to pay in the contribution as set out in the resolution on the capital increase. The GmbH, on the other hand, declares that it will allocate the newly created share(s) to the (new) shareholder(s) against payment of the agreed contribution. If a shareholder acquires an additional share during a capital increase, his or her existing (old) share and the new share remain separate shares and are not combined into one single share.[84]

Any newly created share must have a nominal value in full euros of at least €1.00. The paying in of the contributions during a capital increase is subject to the same principles which apply in connection with the formation of the GmbH. Contributions in kind must be paid in in full as a prerequisite for the registration of the share capital. With regard to contributions in cash, however, it is only necessary to pay in at least 50% thereof.[85] However, if the capital increase is effected by way of contributions in kind, a special report on the value of the contributed goods is not required by law here (in contrast to the situation when founding the GmbH; see Section 10 for details). Notwithstanding the above, the court maintaining the respective commercial register may request additional documentation to prove that the contributions in kind are not significantly overvalued.[86] This is why in practice almost every capital increase

83 *Gesetz betreffend die Gesellschaft mit beschränkter Haftung* (GmbHG) (Act on Limited Liability Companies) 1892, s55, para. 1 (FRG).

84 *Gesetz betreffend die Gesellschaft mit beschränkter Haftung* (GmbHG) (Act on Limited Liability Companies) 1892, s55, para. 3 (FRG).

85 *Gesetz betreffend die Gesellschaft mit beschränkter Haftung* (GmbHG) (Act on Limited Liability Companies) 1892, s57, para. 2 (FRG).

86 *Gesetz betreffend die Gesellschaft mit beschränkter Haftung* (GmbHG) (Act on Limited Liability Companies) 1892, s57a, 9c, para. 1 (FRG).

by way of contributions in kind is accompanied by an external report confirming the value of the contributed assets.

Since a change in the share capital signifies an amendment to the articles of association, this change needs to be registered. Only upon registration of the capital increase does the capital increase become legally effective.[87] The filing may only take place once the resolved capital increase is covered by respective subscriptions of the (new) shareholders. The documents to be filed must include: (i) the declarations of the subscribers, (ii) a list of the persons acquiring the newly created shares, and (iii) – in the case of a capital increase in kind – any agreements underlying the contribution in kind.[88] When registering the capital increase, the managing directors must also confirm that the contributions have been made unconditionally and placed at their free disposal.[89]

175. Increase in share capital: capital increase by way of the conversion of capital reserves

Another way of increasing the stated share capital of the company is via the conversion of all or part of the capital reserves (*Rücklagen*) of the GmbH into equity.[90] The first step in this regard necessitates a resolution by means of which the articles of association are amended and the share capital increased accordingly. The resolution also requires three quarters of the votes cast and must be notarised. A resolution to this effect may only be passed after the annual financial statement for the last business year prior to the resolution on the capital increase has been drawn up and the GmbH has passed a resolution on the use of the results.[91] The resolution itself must be based on a balance sheet.[92] The balance sheet may either be a particular balance of accounts to be drawn up during the year, or may be the last annual balance sheet if this was audited

---

87 *Gesetz betreffend die Gesellschaft mit beschränkter Haftung* (GmbHG) (Act on Limited Liability Companies) 1892, s54, para. 3 (FRG).

88 *Gesetz betreffend die Gesellschaft mit beschränkter Haftung* (GmbHG) (Act on Limited Liability Companies) 1892, s57, para. 3 (FRG).

89 *Gesetz betreffend die Gesellschaft mit beschränkter Haftung* (GmbHG) (Act on Limited Liability Companies) 1892, s57, para. 2 (FRG).

90 *Gesetz betreffend die Gesellschaft mit beschränkter Haftung* (GmbHG) (Act on Limited Liability Companies) 1892, s57c (FRG).

91 *Gesetz betreffend die Gesellschaft mit beschränkter Haftung* (GmbHG) (Act on Limited Liability Companies) 1892, s57c, para. 2 (FRG).

92 *Gesetz betreffend die Gesellschaft mit beschränkter Haftung* (GmbHG) (Act on Limited Liability Companies) 1892, s57c, para. 3 (FRG).

and certified by an auditor and the effective date of the balance of accounts in question was not earlier than eight months prior to the registering of the capital increase with the commercial register.[93] If a particular balance sheet is drawn up for the purpose of the capital increase, this balance sheet must also be audited and certified by an auditor.[94] Its effective date may also be not older than eight months prior to the registering of the capital increase.

The capital increase may be effected by either issuing new shares or by an increase in the nominal value of the existing shares of the current shareholders. The increase in the value of the existing shares or the distribution of the newly created shares amongst the shareholders must be effected according to their respective current shareholdings in the GmbH.[95] The capital increase must be registered together with the underlying certified balance sheet.[96] Here too, the capital increase only becomes valid once the registration in the commercial register has been completed.[97]

176. Increase in share capital: authorised capital

The Act to Modernise the Law Governing GmbHs and Combat Abuses has introduced a new way of increasing the share capital of a GmbH. The articles of association may now authorise the managing directors for a maximum period of five years either following the registration of the company in the commercial register or a corresponding amendment of the articles of association to increase the share capital up to a certain amount by issuing new shares against contributions.[98] The nominal value of the authorised capital may not be higher than half of the stated share capital. Unless the authorisation in the articles explicitly states otherwise, the authorised capital may only be used to increase the stated share

---

93 *Gesetz betreffend die Gesellschaft mit beschränkter Haftung* (GmbHG) (Act on Limited Liability Companies) 1892, s57e, para. 1 (FRG).

94 *Gesetz betreffend die Gesellschaft mit beschränkter Haftung* (GmbHG) (Act on Limited Liability Companies) 1892, s57f, para. 2 (FRG).

95 *Gesetz betreffend die Gesellschaft mit beschränkter Haftung* (GmbHG) (Act on Limited Liability Companies) 1892, s57j, (FRG).

96 *Gesetz betreffend die Gesellschaft mit beschränkter Haftung* (GmbHG) (Act on Limited Liability Companies) 1892, s57i, (FRG).

97 *Gesetz betreffend die Gesellschaft mit beschränkter Haftung* (GmbHG) (Act on Limited Liability Companies) 1892, s54, para. 3 (FRG).

98 *Gesetz betreffend die Gesellschaft mit beschränkter Haftung* (GmbHG) (Act on Limited Liability Companies) 1892, s55a, (FRG).

capital in the form of cash. An increase by way of a contribution in kind is only allowed if the authorisation explicitly indicates this.[99]

If the articles do not provide otherwise, the managing directors decide upon the point in time at which they wish to make use of the authorised capital to increase the share capital. It is also up to the managing directors to decide upon the conditions for the issuing of the new shares, for example, the nominal value of the capital increase, the nominal value of each new share, the issue price etc. The decision regarding the exclusion of the subscription right of the current shareholders, however, is solely at the discretion of the directors if the articles of association explicitly authorise this. Even if the directors do have authorisation in this respect, they must respect the limits pertaining to the exclusion of subscription rights as outlined under Section 174. The further steps in connection with the capital increase (agreement between the shareholder and the company on the acquisition and issuing of newly created shares, minimum contributions towards newly created share capital, filing and registration with the commercial register etc) are subject to the same principles as those outlined above for capital increases in cash or in kind respectively.

177. Decrease in share capital

The share capital in a GmbH may, of course, also be reduced. A decrease in the share capital of a GmbH may be effected by an ordinary or a simplified capital reduction. Both procedures require an amendment of the articles of association based on a shareholders' resolution passed with a majority of three quarters of the votes cast and the amendment must be notarised.[100]

An ordinary decrease in the stated share capital is only possible after the respective resolution of the shareholders has been published in the company's designated publications (*Gesellschaftsblätter*) and may only be registered with the commercial register one year after the public announcement of the decrease has been published.[101] In this public announcement, the creditors of the GmbH must be invited to contact the company. If the creditors are known to the

---

99 *Gesetz betreffend die Gesellschaft mit beschränkter Haftung* (GmbHG) (Act on Limited Liability Companies) 1892, s55a, para. 3 (FRG).

100 *Gesetz betreffend die Gesellschaft mit beschränkter Haftung* (GmbHG) (Act on Limited Liability Companies) 1892, s53, para. 1 (FRG).

101 *Gesetz betreffend die Gesellschaft mit beschränkter Haftung* (GmbHG) (Act on Limited Liability Companies) 1892, s58, para. 1 (FRG).

company, it must contact them itself. Creditors who contact the GmbH after the publication of the capital decrease and do not give their consent thereto must be satisfied or provided with security for their claims against the GmbH. As a consequence of the capital decrease, the nominal amounts of the shares are usually reduced accordingly or shares are confiscated by the company.

Since the requirements for an ordinary decrease in the share capital are rather complicated and technical, the law also provides for a simplified reduction in the share capital if the purpose of the decrease in the share capital is to balance a loss or other reductions in the assets of the GmbH.[102] In order to compensate for the fact that the public, in particular the creditors, are not to be informed about such a simplified reduction in the stated share capital, the capital gained by the decrease in the share capital may only be used to equalise losses of the company or for activation as a capital reserve of the GmbH.[103]

Each capital decrease, whether ordinary or simplified, must be registered with the commercial register and only becomes effective once it has been registered.[104]

102 *Gesetz betreffend die Gesellschaft mit beschränkter Haftung* (GmbHG) (Act on Limited Liability Companies) 1892, s58a (FRG).

103 *Gesetz betreffend die Gesellschaft mit beschränkter Haftung* (GmbHG) (Act on Limited Liability Companies) 1892, s58b (FRG).

104 *Gesetz betreffend die Gesellschaft mit beschränkter Haftung* (GmbHG) (Act on Limited Liability Companies) 1892, s54, para. 3 (FRG).

IX. Changes in shareholding and related transactions

178. General

This chapter addresses the different ways in which a share in a GmbH may be transferred to a third party along with the specific rights which may be granted in relation to a share.

A. Transfer of shares by agreement

179. Freedom of transferability

The shareholders in a GmbH may freely transfer their shares in a GmbH to a third party.[1] The transfer of a share in a GmbH means the transfer of the share 'as is', that is, with any and all rights and obligations pertaining thereto.[2]

Nevertheless, applicable law and the articles of association provide or may provide for certain restrictions on the transfer of shares in a GmbH which make the transfer more complicated in technical terms than the transfer of, for example, stock traded on a stock exchange. The shares in a GmbH are not traded on a stock exchange or another regulated market. This means that there are no share certificates issued either physically or electronically. The current status as regards the shareholders and their respective shareholdings is reflected in the shareholders' list, which is filed with the commercial register. The transfer requires the conclusion of an individual agreement with the acquiring party. By excluding the possibility of the shares in a GmbH being traded on the stock market, the law makes it clear that an interest in a GmbH is not intended to be a short-term investment, but rather a long-term commitment. Shareholder profits are to be achieved by way of the distribution of the profits of the GmbH itself, not by trading its shares.

1 *Gesetz betreffend die Gesellschaft mit beschränkter Haftung* (GmbHG) (Act on Limited Liability Companies) 1892, s15, para. 1 (FRG).

2 *Bürgerliches Gesetzbuch* (BGB) (Civil Code) 1900, ss413, 401 (FRG).

The shareholders may also just transfer parts of their shares to a third party. This kind of transfer of a part of a share requires the prior consent of the shareholders.[3] The consent may be granted on a case-by-case basis or generally in advance in the articles of association. The authorisation to grant consent in this regard may be transferred to another corporate body or be entirely excluded by the articles.

180. Restrictions on transfer

The articles of association may provide various restrictions on the transfer of the shares.[4] This allowing of the shareholders to stipulate such restrictions means that the number of shareholders and the individuals or entities who may become shareholders can be kept (relatively) low. Again, this concept differs markedly from that underlying a freely traded stock corporation.

The most common restriction on the transferability of shares is the requirement that consent is obtained from the other shareholders for the transfer of the shares (*Vinkulierung*). In the event that this consent is denied, the shareholder may not validly transfer his or her shares to a third party. The articles of association may freely determine the criteria that must be fulfilled in order to obtain the consent of the shareholders or the cases in which consent is not required in the first place, unless such conditions constitute an abuse of the law. A typical restriction in practice is that the shares may only be transferred to third parties which satisfy certain requirements, for example, professional knowledge or financial criteria. However, it is also possible that the articles do not contain any statement on the criteria for the transfer of shares, merely stating instead that the transfer requires the consent of the other shareholders without setting forth specific details. The granting of consent is generally at the free discretion of the shareholders, taking into account their respective duties of loyalty towards each other. Consent may therefore not be unreasonably denied. The shareholders must weigh the interests of the company in not having the third party as a new shareholder against the interests of the shareholder who is willing to sell in good faith. In case of doubt, the shareholders are entitled to

---

3 *Gesetz betreffend die Gesellschaft mit beschränkter Haftung* (GmbHG) (Act on Limited Liability Companies) 1892, s46, no. 4 (FRG).

4 *Gesetz betreffend die Gesellschaft mit beschränkter Haftung* (GmbHG) (Act on Limited Liability Companies) 1892, s15, para. 5 (FRG).

refuse approval. The shareholder requesting consent may challenge the resolution in accordance with the general principles pertaining to the challenging of shareholder resolutions. The articles may also provide that the respective consent is not given by the shareholders but by another corporate body, for example, the supervisory board or another administrative body.

Another restriction of transfer which is frequently seen in the articles of a GmbH is a pre-emptive right on the part of the other shareholders. A transfer of the share to a third party is then only possible if the shareholder has first offered his or her share to the other shareholders for acquisition under the same conditions which have been agreed upon with the third party. If the other shareholders do not make use of or waive their pre-emptive right, the shareholder may sell and transfer his or her share to the third party (subject to a potential requirement of the consent of the shareholders as outlined above). The shareholder is under the obligation to inform the third party prior to selling and transferring the share that such a pre-emptive right exists. Otherwise, the shareholder would be acting in bad faith.

Aside from these two typical restrictions of transfer (which can be and are often combined), the articles may also provide for any other kind of restriction on the transfer of shares, as long as such restrictions do not violate the fiduciary duties of the shareholders between themselves and are not abusive in nature. In the event that the articles even exclude the transfer of the shares to a third party in general, the shareholders must be granted a right to leave the company if further membership thereof has become unacceptable.

181. Notarial form

The most important restriction prescribed by law on the free transferability of shares in a GmbH is the requirement that these may only be sold and transferred on the basis of a notarial deed. The Act on Limited Liability Companies prescribes the notarial form for both the agreement in which the shareholder establishes the obligation to sell the share and the document pertaining to the legal transfer itself.[5] If the sale and the transfer are covered by the same notarial deed, it is sufficient if one deed is issued. In practice, the sale of the share (the signing of share purchase agreement) and the

5 *Gesetz betreffend die Gesellschaft mit beschränkter Haftung* (GmbHG) (Act on Limited Liability Companies) 1892, s15, para. 4, sentence 1, para. 3 (FRG).

transfer of the share (closing of the transaction) are usually undertaken in two steps once certain conditions have been fulfilled. Both documents must be notarised. The principles regarding notarisation by a foreign notary[6] apply accordingly in the case of a transfer of the shares in a GmbH. It has been recognised in the case law that notarisation undertaken by a notary in certain Swiss cantons (eg, Basel-Stadt and Zurich) is an acceptable equivalent to notarisation within Germany.

If the agreement on the sale of the shares has not been notarised, this results in the invalidity of the agreement in question. However, if (at the point in time of its conclusion) the transfer agreement is effectively notarised at a later date, the lack of notarisation with regard to the sale agreement is considered to have been remedied and the sale agreement then becomes valid with retroactive effect.[7]

182. Acquisition in good faith

Prior to the enacting of the Act to Modernise the Law Governing GmbHs and Combat Abuses, an acquisition of shares in a GmbH from a non-shareholder, even in good faith, was not possible. Now that the new law has come into force, an acquisition in good faith has become possible.[8] It is required that the seller of the share was registered as the owner thereof in the shareholders' list published in the commercial register.[9] The shareholders' list has become the legal basis for a good faith acquisition and thus of imminent importance.

There are, however, certain (further) restrictions and exemptions in the case of an acquisition in good faith. First, an acquisition in good faith is not possible if the share which is to be transferred does not exist, that is, has never been legally created. It is, though, unclear what happens if the share exists but not in the way indicated in the shareholders' list, in particular if the share has a nominal amount which differs from the amount indicated in the list. This issue is still unresolved and will have to be clarified by the courts.

Secondly, an acquisition in good faith is not possible if an objection is registered in the shareholders' list against the ownership of

---

6 For details see Section 28.

7 *Gesetz betreffend die Gesellschaft mit beschränkter Haftung* (GmbHG) (Act on Limited Liability Companies) 1892, s15, para. 4, sentence 2 (FRG).

8 *Gesetz betreffend die Gesellschaft mit beschränkter Haftung* (GmbHG) (Act on Limited Liability Companies) 1892, s16, para. 3 (FRG).

9 For details on the shareholders' list, see Section 183.

the respective seller.[10] An objection to this effect may be registered in the shareholders' list on the basis of an injunction or based on the consent of the person registered therein.

Furthermore, an acquisition in good faith is excluded if the acquiring party knows that the seller is not the owner of the share or if the acquiring party is not aware of this fact due to gross negligence.[11] Finally, an acquisition in good faith is not possible if the person selling the share was not registered as the owner of the share in the shareholders' list for a period of at least three years.[12] An error in this regard must not necessarily be attributable to the real owner of the share. The question as to the cases in which such an error is attributable to the real owner of the share and the cases in which this does not apply remains an issue of contention between legal scholars and the courts.

Given these facts, a party acquiring a share should strive to have the shareholders' list amended as soon as possible after he or she has acquired the share in question in order to avoid a third party acquiring it in good faith. Also, any current shareholders in a GmbH should monitor and update the shareholders' lists where necessary.

It should be pointed out here that the good faith only relates to the seller's ownership of the share; the share is not necessarily free of and unburdened by any lien or pledge. The shareholders' list also does not offer good faith purchasers protection as regards the unrestricted ability of the seller to transfer the share.[13] Even if it is possible to acquire ownership in good faith, if the acquired share is encumbered with a lien or pledge, such an encumbrance continues to exist.

183. Amendment of shareholders' list

After any change occurs in terms of the people who are shareholders, in particular following the transfer of a share, the list of shareholders must be updated. These changes in terms of the people who are shareholders must have actually occurred. This means that it is not

10 *Gesetz betreffend die Gesellschaft mit beschränkter Haftung* (GmbHG) (Act on Limited Liability Companies) 1892, s16, para. 3, sentence 3, or, alternatively, 3 (FRG).

11 *Gesetz betreffend die Gesellschaft mit beschränkter Haftung* (GmbHG) (Act on Limited Liability Companies) 1892, s16, para. 3, sentence 3, or, alternatively, 1 and, alternatively 2 (FRG).

12 *Gesetz betreffend die Gesellschaft mit beschränkter Haftung* (GmbHG) (Act on Limited Liability Companies) 1892, s16, para. 3, sentence 2 (FRG).

13 See, eg, 11 March 2010, *Oberlandesgericht München* (Munich Court of Appeals) (23 U 2814/09).

acceptable to file an amended shareholders' list where the transfer of the share is subject to certain conditions and these conditions have not yet been fulfilled. The commercial register may reject such a shareholder's list.[14] Updating the shareholders' list is of paramount importance, since the only persons considered to be owners of a share *vis-à-vis* the GmbH are those who are registered as the owners of the shares in the shareholders' list which is to be published in the commercial register.[15] People who are included in the shareholders' list are not entitled to exercise any rights *vis-à-vis* the company. Prior to the enacting of the Act to Modernise the Law Governing GmbHs and Combat Abuses, a simple notification submitted to the GmbH either by the old or the new shareholder was deemed sufficient. The point in time from which onwards an acquiring party was considered the new owner with all rights and obligations *vis-à-vis* the company was thus pushed forward to the date of the filing of the list of shareholders with the commercial register. This gave rise to certain potential problems in the event that the person acquiring the shares wished to immediately undertake certain corporate acts directly after acquiring them, for example, a change in terms of the managing directors or amendments to the articles of association. In order to address this problem adequately, the Act on Limited Liability Companies provides that all measures taken by an acquiring party and relating to the GmbH are considered valid with retroactive effect in so far as the shareholders' list is published in the commercial register without undue delay after such a corporate act has been undertaken.[16]

Nevertheless, a certain degree of uncertainty remains, as it is unclear when exactly the shareholders' list is deemed to have been published in the commercial register 'without undue delay'. It would therefore be recommendable for an acquiring party not to take any measures relating to the GmbH until the list of shareholders has been updated and registered with the commercial register. In practice, however, it is often not possible to wait until the updated list has been registered in order to take such corporate measures, which must often be taken at the time of or immediately after the closing of a share deal. Usually, the notaries involved in a share transaction

---

14 20 September 2011, *Bundesgerichtshof* (German Federal Supreme Court) (II ZB 17/10).

15 *Gesetz betreffend die Gesellschaft mit beschränkter Haftung* (GmbHG) (Act on Limited Liability Companies) 1892, s16, para. 1, sentence 1 (FRG).

16 *Gesetz betreffend die Gesellschaft mit beschränkter Haftung* (GmbHG) (Act on Limited Liability Companies) 1892, s16, para. 1, sentence 2 (FRG).

will not object to measures taken prior to the registration of the amended list which would themselves have required notarisation. Furthermore, a power of attorney on the part of the seller of the share for the intended post-closing measure, or the taking of the respective measure with the consent or even with the participation of the seller, are ways of minimising legal uncertainty in practice. It remains to be seen how this uncertainty will be dealt with in the future case law.

The responsibility for updating and registering the shareholders' list, after a change in terms of the people who are shareholders has occurred, lies principally with the managing directors.[17] If they fail to do this, they may be held personally liable by the parties affected by the change or the creditors of the company.[18] However, if a notary has participated (*mitwirken*) in any measures leading to a change in the shareholder structure (eg, notarisation of a share purchase or transfer agreement, merger agreement, capital increase etc), the notary rather than the managing director is responsible for updating the list of shareholders and must register it with the commercial register.[19] There is still some residual uncertainty regarding what 'participate' really means, that is, when does the filing lie within the realm of responsibility of the notary and when does the responsibility lie with the directors? In practice, when the situation is unclear, the amended shareholders' list is sometimes signed by both the notary and the managing directors. However, this approach remains disputed, and a final decision of the Federal Supreme Court is still outstanding in this regard.

The GmbH will receive a copy of the amended list of shareholders from the notary. In cases where a (German) notary has not participated in a measure relating to the corporate structure (eg, transfer of share by way of succession etc), the responsibility for updating the list of shareholders remains with the managing director. The standard situation in which this issue is relevant is when a notarisation is performed by a foreign notary. The Düsseldorf Court of Appeal (*Oberlandesgericht*),[20] however, has

17 *Gesetz betreffend die Gesellschaft mit beschränkter Haftung* (GmbHG) (Act on Limited Liability Companies) 1892, s40, para. 1 (FRG).

18 *Gesetz betreffend die Gesellschaft mit beschränkter Haftung* (GmbHG) (Act on Limited Liability Companies) 1892, s40, para. 3 (FRG) (see also Sections 109 and 126).

19 *Gesetz betreffend die Gesellschaft mit beschränkter Haftung* (GmbHG) (Act on Limited Liability Companies) 1892, s40, para. 2 (FRG).

20 Decision as of 2 March 2011 (I – 3 Wx 236/10).

ruled that if the notarisation was performed by a foreign notary and the resulting notarisation is valid as it complies with the standards under German law, the notary in question is also legally entitled to legitimately submit an amended shareholders' list to the commercial register. In the case in question, a Swiss notary (in the canton of Basel-Stadt) notarised a share transfer agreement and submitted the amended shareholders' list. Nevertheless, it remains unclear which notary is responsible for updating the list of shareholders in the event that several notaries have participated in the measure leading to the change in the shareholder structure. Similarly, it is unclear what happens in cases in which the task of filing an updated list of shareholders is undertaken by the managing director of the GmbH, but the law prescribes that the notary is responsible for undertaking the filing in question. All these questions are yet to be resolved in the case law and by legal scholars in the future.

It may, nonetheless, be noted that the selling shareholder being registered on the list is not a prerequisite for the validity of a transfer of a share in a GmbH. Being on the list of shareholders is only one way to indicate the entitlement to a right to sell the share, but this is not a requirement under statutory law.

184. Self-acquisition of shares by the GmbH

The GmbH may, under certain circumstances, acquire its own shares or accept them as a pledge. The first condition is that the shares the company intends to acquire are fully paid in.[21] If the share capital relating to an acquired share has not been fully paid in, the underlying legal transactions are void. In addition, fully paid-in shares may only be acquired if the acquisition can be financed out of the free assets which are not required to maintain the stated share capital and the GmbH would thus be able to establish reserves in the amount of the consideration for these shares without the need to reduce the stated share capital.[22]

Furthermore, the self-acquisition of shares is also allowed if the acquisition is required to compensate shareholders for certain measures under the Law Regulating the Transformation of

21 *Gesetz betreffend die Gesellschaft mit beschränkter Haftung* (GmbHG) (Act on Limited Liability Companies) 1892, s33, para. 1 (FRG).

22 *Gesetz betreffend die Gesellschaft mit beschränkter Haftung* (GmbHG) (Act on Limited Liability Companies) 1892, s33, para. 2, sentence 1 (FRG).

Companies. By way of exception, in such cases, according to the prevailing view, the self-acquisition of shares is allowed even if they are not fully paid in. In this regard, however, it is required that the acquisition is effected six months after the measure under the Law Regulating the Transformation of Companies has become valid and that the GmbH is able to establish the reserves as prescribed by the German Commercial Code (*Handelsgesetzbuch*) for its own shares without reducing the stated share capital.[23]

B. Forfeiture (*Kaduzierung*) of shares

185. General

The shareholders are obliged to pay in the contribution to the share capital they subscribed for by the due date and as stipulated in the articles of association. If no specific date has been stipulated, the contributions must be paid in immediately. If this payment obligation is not fulfilled by the due date, the GmbH may claim interest on the contribution of the shareholder (if the contribution is to be made in cash).[24]

Additionally, the GmbH may stipulate a specific date by way of registered letter by which the shareholder must finally pay in his or her contribution. This additional period (*Nachfrist*) may not be less than one month.[25] After the additional period has elapsed, the GmbH may declare the share of the respective shareholder to have been forfeited including any partial contributions already paid. Such a declaration of forfeiture must also be made via registered letter addressed to the shareholder.[26] The shareholder nevertheless remains liable for paying in the contribution he or she has subscribed for. Moreover, any predecessor of the forfeited shareholder remains liable for paying in the share capital relating to the forfeited share with regard to contributions for which a claim for payment has been made within a period of five years from the point

---

23 *Gesetz betreffend die Gesellschaft mit beschränkter Haftung* (GmbHG) (Act on Limited Liability Companies) 1892, s33, para. 3 (FRG).

24 *Gesetz betreffend die Gesellschaft mit beschränkter Haftung* (GmbHG) (Act on Limited Liability Companies) 1892, s20 (FRG).

25 *Gesetz betreffend die Gesellschaft mit beschränkter Haftung* (GmbHG) (Act on Limited Liability Companies) 1892, s21, para. 1 (FRG).

26 *Gesetz betreffend die Gesellschaft mit beschränkter Haftung* (GmbHG) (Act on Limited Liability Companies) 1892, s21, para. 2 (FRG).

in time onwards at which the shareholder is considered the owner of the share in relation to the company.[27]

If the predecessors are also not able to raise the required share capital relating to the forfeited share, the GmbH may auction or, with the consent of the excluded shareholder, otherwise sell the share to collect the necessary contribution.[28] If the potential predecessors are not able to raise the outstanding contribution and the public auctioning of the share fails to yield the necessary amount required to provide payment for the outstanding share capital, the other (existing) shareholders of the GmbH are severally liable for the contribution to the forfeited share to the extent proportionate to their respective shareholding in the GmbH.[29] The regulations on the forfeiture of shares are mandatory law and may not be waived or amended in the articles of association.[30]

C. Redemption (*Einziehung*) of shares

186. Redemption with the consent of the shareholder

The Act on Limited Liability Companies recognises that shares in a GmbH may also be redeemed. Redemption requires a provision to this effect in the articles of association. If the redemption is only permitted with the consent of the shareholder, a simple provision stating that the redemption is possible is sufficient to allow a redemption of the shares.[31]

Redeeming the shares with the consent of the shareholder requires a shareholders' resolution[32] if the articles of association do not provide otherwise. Given the fact that in this situation a redemption is not possible against the will of the shareholder, the shareholder whose share is to be redeemed is entitled to vote at the shareholders' resolution.

---

27 *Gesetz betreffend die Gesellschaft mit beschränkter Haftung* (GmbHG) (Act on Limited Liability Companies) 1892, s22, para. 1 and para. 2 (FRG).

28 *Gesetz betreffend die Gesellschaft mit beschränkter Haftung* (GmbHG) (Act on Limited Liability Companies) 1892, s23 (FRG).

29 *Gesetz betreffend die Gesellschaft mit beschränkter Haftung* (GmbHG) (Act on Limited Liability Companies) 1892, s24 (FRG).

30 *Gesetz betreffend die Gesellschaft mit beschränkter Haftung* (GmbHG) (Act on Limited Liability Companies) 1892, s25 (FRG).

31 *Gesetz betreffend die Gesellschaft mit beschränkter Haftung* (GmbHG) (Act on Limited Liability Companies) 1892, s34, para. 1 (FRG).

32 *Gesetz betreffend die Gesellschaft mit beschränkter Haftung* (GmbHG) (Act on Limited Liability Companies) 1892, s46, no. 4 (FRG).

187. Redemption without the consent of the shareholder

In the event that shares are supposed to be redeemed against the will of the shareholder, the articles of association must explicitly state the conditions under which a redemption to this effect should be possible. The shareholder has a right to be informed of the circumstances under which his or her membership rights in a GmbH may be terminated against his or her will prior to the acquisition of the share.[33] Typical reasons for redemption are the seizure of the share, the insolvency of the shareholder and the transfer of the share to a third person with the requisite consent of the other shareholders or the failure of a third person to satisfy certain requirements. Apart from these specific grounds for redemption, the articles may provide that the redemption of a share is possible for cause (*wichtiger Grund*) in connection with the personality of a certain shareholder making it unacceptable for the other shareholders to continue operating the GmbH with the respective shareholder.

The redemption of a shareholder's share requires a prior shareholders' resolution[34] if the articles of association do not provide otherwise. In the event of redemption against the will of the shareholder, the shareholder is not entitled to vote on the respective shareholder resolution.[35]

188. Compensation claim

The shareholder whose shares are redeemed is entitled by law to receive compensation for the redeemed share, irrespective of whether the redemption was pursued with the consent or against the will of the shareholder.

If the articles of association do not provide otherwise, the shareholder is entitled to receive the full market value of the share as compensation. Usually, however, the articles provide that if a shareholder exits (or has to leave) the company other than by way of the sale of his or her share, the amount of compensation is limited. The company and the other shareholders endeavour by these means to keep the maximum possible funds in the company in order to

---

33 *Gesetz betreffend die Gesellschaft mit beschränkter Haftung* (GmbHG) (Act on Limited Liability Companies) 1892, s34, para. 2 (FRG).

34 *Gesetz betreffend die Gesellschaft mit beschränkter Haftung* (GmbHG) (Act on Limited Liability Companies) 1892, s46, no. 4 (FRG).

35 *Gesetz betreffend die Gesellschaft mit beschränkter Haftung* (GmbHG) (Act on Limited Liability Companies) 1892, s47, para. 4 (FRG).

keep it operational. It is often the case that the compensation is limited to the book value or the nominal value of the share. A limitation to the book value is generally accepted by the courts. A limitation of this kind, however, is not entirely free of restrictions. If the difference between the current market value and the compensation provided in the articles of association becomes too high (the courts refer to a 'severe disproportion' – *grobes Mißverhältniss*), the courts will no longer recognise the limitation of the compensation claim of the shareholder. No exact factor is specified in the case law in connection with situations where the difference between the current market value and the value provided in the articles is found to be inadequate and not acceptable to the shareholder. There have been court decisions which show a tendency to consider a value of 60% or less of the market value to be inappropriate. Yet the courts also take into account circumstances aside from the purely mathematical issue such as, for example, the period of time for which the shareholder was a member of the GmbH, the way the shareholder contributed to the development of the GmbH, the circumstances leading to his or her leaving the company and the payment conditions relating to the compensation claim (instalments, interest etc). The courts will weigh and balance all of these circumstances against each other.

If a court finds the compensation claim to be too low based on the above criteria, in most cases it will not grant the shareholder the full market value but an 'adequate amount' for his or her share. The compensation clause itself remains valid and will not be amended by the court decision. An exception is only made in cases where at the point in time at which the compensation clause was introduced in the articles, the latter already provided for a severe disproportion between the market value of a share in the GmbH and the amount of the compensation claim. In such cases the clause is considered invalid and the shareholder is entitled to a compensation based on the full market value of the share. In practice, most compensation clauses are valid to begin with and become disproportionate as the value of the company grows.

The case law does not indicate an exact amount as regards what is considered 'adequate' compensation for a share compared with the full market value. In view of this, there is a great deal of uncertainty surrounding the amount a shareholder will receive as compensation for his or her share when this is redeemed and when the compensation provisions in the articles are invalid. The same principles for calculating the compensation also apply when a shareholder has to leave the company by other means than redemption, in particular if he or she is excluded for cause or when the shareholder terminates the membership him- or herself.[36]

188a. Effectiveness of redemption

Prior to the decision of the German Federal Supreme Court of 24 January 2012,[37] the prevailing, but highly disputed, opinion was that the redemption of shares in a GmbH only becomes valid after the compensation has been paid in full to the shareholder from whom the shares have been redeemed. This has often created and continues to create problems in practice when the amount of the compensation is disputed and/or to be paid in instalments. In more recent cases, the redemption of a share or the exclusion of a shareholder prior to the payment of the (full) compensation has been found to be acceptable, but only if the articles of association explicitly confirm this.[38] This situation often led to legal uncertainty between the old and the excluded shareholders and in many cases resulted in shareholder resolutions being challenged by shareholders from whom the shares had been redeemed, who were claiming that they had not yet been finally excluded from the GmbH and that they had the right to participate in the voting process. In the aforementioned decision, the Federal Supreme Court put an end to this uncertainty by ruling that the redemption of shares in a GmbH becomes immediately valid the moment the fact that a shareholders' resolution on the redemption has been passed is communicated to the shareholder in question, in so far as the resolution on the redemption is not void itself (see immediately below for details). In other words, if the respective shareholder is present when the corresponding resolution is passed, the redemption of his or her shares is valid the moment the resolution is passed. The court explicitly ruled that the (full) payment of the compensation claim is no longer a criterion for the redemption becoming valid. It is also not necessary for the articles of association to contain a provision setting forth this legal consequence. To safeguard the interests of the excluded shareholder, however, the court ruled that the (remaining) shareholders should be personally liable towards the excluded shareholder for the payment of his or her compensation

36 For details see Sections 189–190.
37 *Bundesgerichtshof* (German Federal Supreme Court) (II ZR 109/11).
38 8 December 2008, *Bundesgerichtshof* (German Federal Supreme Court) (II ZR 263/07).

claim in the event that the company itself is not able to satisfy the respective (instalment) claim when due.

Irrespective of the exact amount of the compensation the shareholder is entitled to, however, the GmbH must in any case be able to pay the compensation without resorting to the assets necessary to maintain the stated share capital.[39] If the GmbH lacks the necessary assets to maintain its stated share capital and satisfy the compensation claim of the shareholder, the GmbH is entitled to refuse the payment of the compensation claim until the financial situation has improved. According to the Federal Supreme Court, the respective shareholders' resolution on the redemption of the share is void if, at the time the resolution is passed, it is clear or foreseeable that the compensation claim cannot be paid from the available assets of the company.[40] In such cases, by way of exception, the redemption does not become valid with the passing of the resolution and its communication to the shareholder, but only after the compensation claim of the shareholder has been satisfied. In order to avoid this situation from the outset, the articles of association often provide that a compensation claim is not to be paid at once but in several instalments. These instalments, however, may not represent a disproportionate deviation from the law. This could render a compensation clause which is otherwise acceptable as far as the level thereof is concerned invalid (see above). If the articles do not provide otherwise, a compensation claim is due immediately after the shareholders' resolution leading to the redemption of the share. The same applies to the exclusion of the shareholder after it has been passed. Nevertheless, the courts consider it acceptable if the compensation claim is paid in up to five (equal) yearly instalments and against adequate interest. Any arrangement which goes beyond five yearly instalments must be evaluated on a case-by-case basis.

188b. Consequence of redemption; maintenance of stated share capital

Another legal consequence of a valid redemption of a share is that the respective share ceases to exist. If the shareholders have not yet reached a resolution on the distribution of the profits from the

---

39 *Gesetz betreffend die Gesellschaft mit beschränkter Haftung* (GmbHG) (Act on Limited Liability Companies) 1892, s34, para. 3; s30, para. 1 (FRG).

40 5 April 2011, *Bundesgerichtshof* (German Federal Supreme Court) (II ZR 263/08).

previous business year(s), the shareholder whose share is redeemed forfeits any claim to receive such profits.

Furthermore, the nominal amount of the stated share capital and the nominal amount of each (remaining, non-redeemed) share remain unaffected, meaning that the value of the stated share capital and the aggregate nominal value of the remaining shares are distinct from each other. This is not permissible according to the amended section 5, paragraph 3, sentence 2 of the Act to Modernise the Law Governing GmbHs and Combat Abuses. According to this provision, the nominal value of the stated share capital and the aggregate nominal value of the shares in the company must be identical at any time during the whole life cycle of the GmbH. This issue can be resolved in three ways, by either: (i) reducing the share capital, (ii) creating a new share with a corresponding nominal value, or (iii) by increasing the nominal value of the remaining shares (*Aufstockung*). As a consequence, a shareholders' resolution on the redemption of a share which at the same time does not provide for any of the measures outlined above to balance the nominal value of the stated share capital and the (remaining) shares is considered not only challengeable, but void.

D. Exclusion of shareholders

189. Legal grounds for an exclusion

Irrespective of the presence of a provision in this respect in the articles of association, it is recognised that a shareholder may be excluded from the GmbH for cause (*wichtiger Grund*) if such cause is related to his or her person. The continued membership of the shareholder in question must be unacceptable to the other shareholders and there must be no other means available to remedy the existing problems between the shareholders which are less severe but equally effective. In other words, the exclusion of the shareholder is to be considered the *ultima ratio* (last resort). Examples in which an exclusion for cause has been recognised are the lack of personal qualifications as set out as a requirement in the articles of association, criminal activities, severe breaches of obligations, and competitive or other activities detrimental to the GmbH. In each case, the behaviour of the other shareholders who wish to exclude a shareholder must be taken into account, in particular the way in which they have contributed to the development of the situation in which they now wish to exclude the particular shareholder.

189a. Legal proceedings

According to the jurisprudence in this regard, an exclusion of a shareholder requires that a shareholders' resolution is passed with a majority of three quarters of the votes cast.[41] The managing directors are obliged to inform the shareholder that he or she is to be excluded from the GmbH. In addition, due to its wide-ranging effects, the Federal Supreme Court requires not only a shareholders' resolution to this effect, but also a motion for expulsion (*Ausschlussklage*) filed with the court in order to prevent the shareholder from having the grounds for his or her exclusion examined by a court.[42] The motion must be filed by the shareholders requesting the exclusion of the shareholder. The exclusion is ultimately based on a final judgment of a court which declares the exclusion for cause to be valid. The articles of association may, however, also provide that a motion for expulsion is not required. In this case, the shareholder must challenge the shareholders' resolution on his or her exclusion by way of an action of opposition (*Anfechtungsklage*).

189b. Legal consequences and compensation

The articles of association should also provide for a clear regulation on what happens with the share of an excluded shareholder. Usually it is stipulated that the share is either redeemed (see Section 186 *et seq.*) or that the excluded shareholder must transfer the share to another shareholder or a third party.

If the exclusion is considered valid, the shareholder is entitled to receive compensation for his or her exclusion. The principles outlined in Section 188 with regard to compensation in the event of a redemption of the shares of a shareholder apply accordingly.

E. Termination of a shareholding by a shareholder

190. General

Each shareholder is entitled to terminate his or her shareholding in a GmbH by declaring that he or she will no longer be a shareholder in the company. It is always possible to make such a declaration *vis-à-vis* the company for cause. Aside from this termination of the

---

41 *Gesetz betreffend die Gesellschaft mit beschränkter Haftung* (GmbHG) (Act on Limited Liability Companies) 1892, s60, para. 1, no. 2 (FRG) accordingly.

42 *Gesetz betreffend die Gesellschaft mit beschränkter Haftung* (GmbHG) (Act on Limited Liability Companies) 1892, s61 (FRG); *Handelsgesetzbuch* (HGB) (Commercial Code) 1897, ss117, 127, 133, 140 (FRG) accordingly.

membership for cause, it is disputed whether a general termination right exists on the part of a shareholder in a GmbH.

Irrespective of the above, the articles of association may set out other criteria entitling shareholders to terminate their membership in the GmbH other than for cause. Again, a prerequisite condition for a right to terminate the shareholding for cause is that it must be unacceptable if the shareholder who is willing to leave remains a shareholder in the GmbH. Furthermore, it is recognised that the shareholder must have paid in his or her share in full in order to be entitled to terminate membership. The termination is to be declared *vis-à-vis* the managing director of the GmbH.

Upon termination, shareholders are entitled to receive compensation for their share. Regarding the value of such compensation claims, the principles outlined above in connection with the redemption of the share[43] apply accordingly. When determining the amount of compensation, the circumstances which led to the shareholder quitting the company will need to be given special consideration. The claim for compensation must again be satisfied without using the assets required to maintain the share capital.

F. Transfer by way of succession

191. General

The shares in a GmbH are subject to transfer by way of succession (*Erbfolge*).[44] In cases where a shareholder has several successors, these become joint new owners of the share (community of heirs – *Erbengemeinschaft*). The several owners of the share may only exercise the rights relating to the share jointly and are jointly liable *vis-à-vis* the GmbH for any obligation relating thereto.[45] Therefore, the death of a shareholder does not lead to a liquidation or termination of the GmbH unless the articles of association provide otherwise. The settlement (*Auseinandersetzung*) between the co-heirs may either be achieved by dividing the share amongst them which requires a prior shareholders' resolution,[46] or the share may be sold

---

43 For further details see Section 188.

44 *Gesetz betreffend die Gesellschaft mit beschränkter Haftung* (GmbHG) (Act on Limited Liability Companies) 1892, s15, para. 1 (FRG).

45 *Gesetz betreffend die Gesellschaft mit beschränkter Haftung* (GmbHG) (Act on Limited Liability Companies) 1892, s18, paras. 1 and 2 (FRG).

46 *Gesetz betreffend die Gesellschaft mit beschränkter Haftung* (GmbHG) (Act on Limited Liability Companies) 1892, s46, no. 4 (FRG).

to one of the co-heirs, the other shareholders or to a third party, wherein the proceeds are distributed between the (other) co-heirs. In both cases, the transfer requires a notarised share purchase and transfer agreement.[47] If the transfer of the share requires the prior consent of the GmbH and/or the shareholders, this consent must also be obtained prior to the transfer.[48]

In most cases, however, the shareholders have an interest in the number of shareholders not being uncontrollably increased, for instance by way of succession. There are basically two ways of keeping the number of shareholders low and excluding unwanted persons from the GmbH. First, the articles of association may provide that in the event of the death of a shareholder, his or her shares will be redeemed.[49] The compensation received will be distributed amongst the successors of the deceased shareholder. The articles may provide that redemption will not occur if the share is passed on to family members or other persons which fulfil certain criteria. Secondly, the articles may also stipulate that the heir(s) of a share in a GmbH is/are obliged to transfer the share to a person already named in the articles or to be determined by the remaining shareholders. The third person nominated or to be nominated acquires a right (but not an obligation) that the share be transferred thereto. This transfer would then be effected by means of a notarial deed.

The right of a shareholder to dispose of his or her share by way of a testament remains unaffected by the above.

G. Pledging (*Verpfändung*) of shares

192. General

The pledging of shares in a GmbH is subject to the same rules as the transfer of shares, that is, this requires the issuing of a notarial deed in which the shares are pledged.[50] However, the agreement by which the obligation to grant a pledge in a share is created does not require any particular form. Only the act of pledging itself demands the notarial form. A pledge, once established, may be terminated

47 *Gesetz betreffend die Gesellschaft mit beschränkter Haftung* (GmbHG) (Act on Limited Liability Companies) 1892, s15, para. 1 (FRG).

48 *Gesetz betreffend die Gesellschaft mit beschränkter Haftung* (GmbHG) (Act on Limited Liability Companies) 1892, s15, para. 5 (FRG).

49 For details see Sections 186–188a.

50 *Gesetz betreffend die Gesellschaft mit beschränkter Haftung* (GmbHG) (Act on Limited Liability Companies) 1892, s15, para. 3 (FRG).

without observing any special requirements in terms of form, unless the agreement between the pledgee and the pledgor provides otherwise. If a pledged share is transferred to a third party, the pledge continues to exist in connection with the share.[51]

The pledgor remains a shareholder of the company. The pledging of the share in itself does not comprise the right to profits related to the share which must be agreed upon separately. The pledge in itself also does not grant a voting right to the pledgee nor other administrative rights related to the pledged shares. The pledge thus has no influence on the rights and obligations of the shareholder towards the company. By way of a pledge agreement it is therefore usual to address these issues by, for example, giving the pledgee a right to receive the profits from the shareholder or giving him or her an instruction right on how the pledgor must make use of his or her rights as a shareholder.

In the event that the GmbH is liquidated while the pledge exists or the shareholder for whatever reason is excluded from or terminates his or her membership in the GmbH, the pledge continues to apply to the liquidation and compensation profits. The pledge is finally realised after it becomes due via public auction or by a freehand sale of the pledged share. The latter is only possible if this has been agreed between the pledgor and the pledgee. The pledge agreement usually also provides for further details on the exploitation (*Verwertung*) of the pledged share.

H. Beneficial interest (*Nießbrauch*) in shares

193. General

In addition to the pledging of a share itself, a notarial deed must also be issued in order for a beneficial interest to be granted.[52] The agreement by which the obligation to grant a beneficial interest is created, on the other hand, does not require any particular form. The same is true where the beneficial right is to be terminated. Before the Act to Modernise the Law Governing GmbHs and Combat Abuses came into force it was generally recognised that a prerequisite for the granting of a beneficial interest was the

---

51 *Bürgerliches Gesetzbuch* (BGB) (Civil Code) 1900, ss401, 413 (FRG).

52 *Bürgerliches Gesetzbuch* (BGB) (Civil Code) 1900, s1069, p. 1 (FRG); *Gesetz betreffend die Gesellschaft mit beschränkter Haftung* (GmbHG) (Act on Limited Liability Companies) 1892, s15, para. 3 (FRG).

notification of the GmbH in order to make it aware that such an interest existed. The same regulation applied in the case of a transfer of the share in a GmbH. With the enacting of the new law, the regulations pertaining to the notification were amended and, when a share is transferred to a third party, the transfer itself now requires the publication of an amended shareholders' list in the commercial register.[53] The notification of the GmbH is no longer deemed sufficient nor is it required. However, since under German law there is no public register for beneficial interests or pledges, there are good reasons to believe that such notification will still be sufficient after the enacting of the Act to Modernise the Law Governing GmbHs and Combat Abuses.

The beneficial interest grants the beneficiary the right to the profits related to the encumbered share without the beneficiary becoming a shareholder in the GmbH. Thus, an amendment of the shareholders' list is not required. The beneficial right continues automatically as regards share substitutes such as, for example, a claim for compensation or liquidation profits. If a share thus encumbered is transferred, the beneficial interest continues to exist.[54]

53 *Gesetz betreffend die Gesellschaft mit beschränkter Haftung* (GmbHG) (Act on Limited Liability Companies) 1892, s16, paras. 1, 40 (FRG).

54 *Bürgerliches Gesetzbuch* (BGB) (Civil Code) 1900, ss401, 413 (FRG).

X. Financial statements and distribution of profits

A. Financial statements

194. General

The following section shall offer a brief overview of the mechanisms which apply when preparing financial statements and the principles underlying the drawing up of the balance sheet of a GmbH. The German Commercial Code, in which most of the principles pertaining to the preparation of the financial statements are set forth, distinguishes between small, medium-sized and large companies. Depending on the size of the GmbH, the obligations regarding the preparation and publication of the respective financial statement may differ. As a rule of thumb, the smaller the company, the more it may profit from certain forms of relief in connection with the preparation of financial statements.

In this context, small corporations (including GmbHs) are those whose figures do not exceed at least two of the three criteria listed below:

(i) €4,840,000 in total assets;
(ii) €9,680,000 in revenues (last 12 months prior to balance sheet cut-off date);
(iii) an annual average of 50 employees.

Medium-sized corporations are those whose figures exceed at least two of the three criteria listed above for smaller companies and whose figures do not exceed at least two of the three following criteria:

(i) €19,250,000 in total assets;
(ii) €38,500,000 in revenues (last 12 months prior to balance sheet cut-off date);
(iii) an annual average of 250 employees.

Large corporations are those whose figures exceed at least two of the three criteria named in the previous list for medium-sized companies.[1] The respective criteria must be satisfied on the balance sheet cut-off dates for two consecutive business years.[2]

195. Annual financial statement

All corporations (including any GmbH) must prepare an annual financial statement consisting of a balance sheet and a profit and loss statement plus an annex thereto which must in turn be prepared by the managing directors (see details under Section 196).[3] Additionally, any corporation – except small corporations – must prepare an annual report (*Lagebericht*). The annual report must describe the development of the business (*Geschäftsverlauf*) during the previous year and the overall situation of the company in a way which fairly represents the state of the company.[4] The annual report must also set forth the potential further development of the company including the risks and opportunities. The annual financial statement and the annual report are to be prepared in the first three months of a business year for the previous business year. For small companies, it is sufficient if they prepare and present their annual financial statements at the latest six months after the end of the respective business year, if this six-month period is consistent with the ordinary business practice of the company in question.[5] The law further stipulates certain forms of relief for small and medium-sized companies with regard to the content of the balance sheet and of the annual financial statement.

196. Competent corporate bodies and proceedings

The managing directors of the GmbH are responsible for proper bookkeeping and for the preparation and presentation of the annual financial statement.[6] If an annual report must be prepared, this is also the responsibility of the managing directors. As soon as the annual financial statement and the annual report are prepared, the

---

1 *Handelsgesetzbuch* (HGB) (Commercial Code) 1897, s267, paras. 1–3 (FRG).
2 *Handelsgesetzbuch* (HGB) (Commercial Code) 1897, s267, para. 4 (FRG).
3 *Handelsgesetzbuch* (HGB) (Commercial Code) 1897, s264, paras. 1, 242 (FRG); *Gesetz betreffend die Gesellschaft mit beschränkter Haftung* (GmbHG) (Act on Limited Liability Companies) 1892, s42 (FRG).
4 *Handelsgesetzbuch* (HGB) (Commercial Code) 1897, s289, para. 1 (FRG).
5 *Handelsgesetzbuch* (HGB) (Commercial Code) 1897, s264, para. 1 (FRG).
6 *Gesetz betreffend die Gesellschaft mit beschränkter Haftung* (GmbHG) (Act on Limited Liability Companies) 1892, s41 (FRG).

managing directors must submit these documents to an auditor for review, unless the company is a small company, in which case such an audit is not required.[7] After the auditor has examined the annual financial statement and the annual report, he must submit an examination report to the managing directors of the GmbH.[8] If the GmbH has a supervisory board, irrespective of whether this is mandatory or obligatory, the annual financial statement and the annual report must also be submitted to the supervisory board for review.[9] The supervisory board must examine the documents submitted and prepare a corresponding report. The report is to be submitted to the managing directors one month after the documents have been made available.[10] Additionally, the supervisory board must inform the shareholders' meeting in writing about the results of the examination.[11] If the annual financial report and the annual report are to be examined by an auditor, the auditor must submit his or her report not to the managing directors, but to the supervisory board directly.[12] The supervisory board must then also review the report of the auditor and issue a statement as to its content.[13] Once the managing directors have received the report from the supervisory board and the report from the auditor, they must submit these reports without undue delay to the shareholders' meeting.[14] If the GmbH does not have a supervisory board and its annual financial statements or annual report are not subject to audit requirements, the managing directors must submit these documents to the shareholders' meeting immediately after they have been prepared.[15]

197. Publication of the annual financial statement

Immediately after the annual financial statement has been submitted to the shareholders, however, at the latest 12 months after the balance sheet cut-off date, it must be filed with the electronic

---

7 *Handelsgesetzbuch* (HGB) (Commercial Code) 1897, s316, para. 1, s320, para. 1 (FRG).

8 *Handelsgesetzbuch* (HGB) (Commercial Code) 1897, s321, para. 5, sentence 1 (FRG).

9 *Aktiengesetz* (AktG) (Stock Corporation Act) 1965, s170, para. 1 (FRG) accordingly.

10 *Aktiengesetz* (AktG) (Stock Corporation Act) 1965, s171, para. 3, sentence 1 (FRG) accordingly.

11 *Aktiengesetz* (AktG) (Stock Corporation Act) 1965, s171, para. 2, sentence 1 (FRG) accordingly.

12 *Handelsgesetzbuch* (HGB) (Commercial Code) 1897, s321, para. 5, sentence 2 (FRG).

13 *Aktiengesetz* (AktG) (Stock Corporation Act) 1965, s171, para. 2, sentence 3 (FRG).

14 *Gesetz betreffend die Gesellschaft mit beschränkter Haftung* (GmbHG) (Act on Limited Liability Companies) 1892, s42a, para. 1 (FRG).

15 *Gesetz betreffend die Gesellschaft mit beschränkter Haftung* (GmbHG) (Act on Limited Liability Companies) 1892, s42a, para. 1 (FRG).

federal gazette (*elektronischer Bundesanzeiger*) for publication. The annual report and the report of the supervisory board (if applicable) must also be submitted.[16] Small and medium-sized companies, however, may profit from certain forms of relief in connection with the publication obligation. Small corporations are only required to file and publish the balance sheet and the annex thereto in the electronic federal gazette. They do not have to file a profit and loss statement.[17] Since they do not have to prepare an annual report, logically, such a report does not have to be filed.

Medium-sized companies may only file and publish a simplified balance sheet and a simplified annex. However, they do have an obligation to file and publish the annual report in full.

The managing directors of the GmbH are responsible for the filing and publication of the relevant documentation.

198. Approval of the annual financial statement

Within the first eight months, or in the case of a small company, the first 11 months, of a business year, the shareholders must reach a resolution on the approval (*Feststellung*) of the annual financial statement and on the use of the balance sheet profit from the previous business year.[18] For this purpose, the managing directors must submit the annual financial statement and the annual report (if applicable) together with the auditor's report (if applicable) to the shareholders.[19] The report of the supervisory board (if applicable) must also be submitted to the shareholders.[20] If the GmbH has a supervisory board, the managing directors must first submit to the supervisory board the proposal they wish to submit to the shareholders' meeting for the use of the balance sheet profit.[21] The articles of association may provide that the annual financial statement and the use of the profits shall not be approved and determined by the shareholders' meeting, but by another corporate

---

16 *Handelsgesetzbuch* (HGB) (Commercial Code) 1897, s325, para. 1 (FRG).

17 *Handelsgesetzbuch* (HGB) (Commercial Code) 1897, s326 (FRG).

18 *Gesetz betreffend die Gesellschaft mit beschränkter Haftung* (GmbHG) (Act on Limited Liability Companies) 1892, s42a, para. 2 (FRG).

19 *Gesetz betreffend die Gesellschaft mit beschränkter Haftung* (GmbHG) (Act on Limited Liability Companies) 1892, s42a, para. 1, sentences 1 and 2 (FRG).

20 *Gesetz betreffend die Gesellschaft mit beschränkter Haftung* (GmbHG) (Act on Limited Liability Companies) 1892, s42a, para. 1, sentence 3 (FRG).

21 *Gesetz betreffend die Gesellschaft mit beschränkter Haftung* (GmbHG) (Act on Limited Liability Companies) 1892, s52, para. 1 (FRG); *Aktiengesetz* (AktG) (Stock Corporation Act), 1965, s170, para. 2, sentence 1 (FRG).

body such as the supervisory board or a special shareholders' committee. The responsibility for such a resolution may even be transferred to individual shareholders as a particular right. There is also a strong argument in favour of transferring the responsibility for approving the annual financial statement and the use of the profits to the managing directors themselves, despite the fact that an effective instance of control might not take place in this case. In the event that it is left to the shareholders to reach a resolution in this regard, they will reach this resolution by way of a simple majority of the votes cast.

B. Distribution of profits

199. Ordinary distribution of profits

Each shareholder is entitled to receive profits in relation to his or her shareholding in the GmbH and based on the annual financial statement of the company.[22] The articles of association may provide for a different distribution of profits amongst the shareholders.

A claim for the receipt of profits exists if the following criteria are met: (i) the (annual) financial statement must show a balance sheet profit (*Bilanzgewinn*) or an annual net profit (*Jahresüberschuss*), (ii) this profit must be confirmed by way of a shareholders' resolution or otherwise as stipulated by the articles of association, and (iii) the shareholders' meeting or another competent corporate body reaches a resolution on the allocation of the profits to the shareholders (*Ergebnisverwendungsbeschluss*). The claim for profits becomes due after the aforementioned resolution under (iii) on the allocation of the profits has been passed, unless the articles provide otherwise. Usually, the claim for profits is satisfied by way of payments in cash, wherein the articles of association or a shareholders' resolution may also provide that the distribution of profits is made in kind. If the articles of association do not provide otherwise, the claim to receive the annual profit is subject to the statute of limitations after three years commencing with the end of the year in which the claim came into existence, that is, in which the resolution on the distribution of profits was passed.[23]

---

22 *Gesetz betreffend die Gesellschaft mit beschränkter Haftung* (GmbHG) (Act on Limited Liability Companies) 1892, s29, para. 3 (FRG).

23 *Bürgerliches Gesetzbuch* (BGB) (Civil Code) 1900, ss195, 199 (FRG).

However, a shareholder is not entitled to receive profits if the payment of the profits would require assets which are necessary to maintain the stated share capital. Additionally, a shareholder may not receive profits if the shareholders' meeting resolves by a simple majority of the votes cast that no profits will be distributed amongst the shareholders. The shareholders may resolve that profits are to be booked as retained earnings (*Gewinnrücklage*) or that they will be carried forward.[24] This typically creates conflicts with the minority shareholders when the majority shareholders wish to use the profits to fund the company whereas the minority shareholders are interested in receiving profits. Resolutions to this effect, however, are only considered invalid if they violate the principle of equal treatment of the shareholders or if the majority shareholders violate their fiduciary duties towards the minority shareholders. It remains disputed and uncertain under which circumstances these fiduciary duties will be deemed violated and thus a shareholders' resolution to this effect may be challenged before the courts. The articles of association may prevent such problems from arising by providing that a minimum dividend has to be distributed each year.

The shareholders will also not be entitled to receive any profits if the GmbH has entered into a profit and loss transfer agreement under which it must transfer all of its profits to either one or several shareholders or even to a third party. The shareholders who are not party to such an agreement are not entitled to receive any profits. They are, however, entitled to receive compensation from the other party to the agreement.[25] The amount of the compensation corresponds to the previous and expected profits the shareholders would have received if the GmbH had not entered into the profit and loss transfer agreement. Finally, a distribution of profits is also excluded in the case of a loss carry forward from the previous business years which is higher than the profit to be distributed in the current business year.[26]

200. Disguised distribution of profits

Apart from an ordinary distribution of profits based on a shareholders' resolution, the company may grant benefits to its shareholders

24 *Gesetz betreffend die Gesellschaft mit beschränkter Haftung* (GmbHG) (Act on Limited Liability Companies) 1892, s29, para. 2 (FRG).

25 *Aktiengesetz* (AktG) (Stock Corporation Act) 1965, s304 (FRG) accordingly.

26 *Gesetz betreffend die Gesellschaft mit beschränkter Haftung* (GmbHG) (Act on Limited Liability Companies) 1892, s29, para. 1, sentence 1 (FRG).

outside of the formal proceedings as outlined in the previous section and without the GmbH receiving adequate compensation in return. Such measures fall collectively under the term 'disguised distribution of profits'. These disguised distributions (under tax law also referred to as constructive dividends) are primarily significant in terms of tax law. Disguised distributions of profits comprise any and all benefits a shareholder (or a closely related third party) receives from the company based on his or her membership of the GmbH outside of the regular distribution of profits without the company receiving arm's-length compensation. The term is interpreted very broadly by the German courts and even more broadly by the German tax authorities. Typical cases of the disguised distribution of profits would for instance be the provision of goods and services for free or at a value below the market price, the provision of loans without or at a reduced interest rate or the payment of shareholder obligations by the GmbH. The term also covers measures undertaken by a shareholder *vis-à-vis* the company such as providing services and goods at rates above a fair market value or the granting of a shareholder loan at an interest rate which is above market value. In all of these cases, the shareholder receives benefits from the company he or she would not receive from a third party under the same conditions. Therefore, if a diligent managing director acting on the basis of sound economic principles would have entered into the same legal transaction with a non-shareholder (arm's-length transaction), the respective legal transaction is unlikely to be regarded as a disguised distribution of profits.

In contrast to the case where a stock corporation is concerned, where disguised distributions of profits are strictly prohibited, these are acceptable in a GmbH under certain circumstances. One of these acceptable scenarios involves transactions on arm's-lengths terms, which strictly speaking do not even fall into this category of transaction (see definition above). Aside from this, a disguised distribution of profits is legally permissible – at least from a corporate law perspective – if the following criteria are met: first, the distribution of profits may not violate the regulations regarding the maintenance of the stated share capital of the GmbH.[27] In other words, if the benefit granted to the shareholder results in the assets of the GmbH being diminished to a level below the value of the stated

27 *Gesetz betreffend die Gesellschaft mit beschränkter Haftung* (GmbHG) (Act on Limited Liability Companies) 1892, ss30, 31 (FRG).

share capital, the distribution is invalid. Furthermore, the benefits distributed must respect the principle of the equal treatment (*Gleichbehandlungsgrundsatz*) of the shareholders. All shareholders of the GmbH must profit in the same way from the benefits granted by the GmbH. However, the articles of association may provide that certain shareholders are entitled to receive certain benefits from the GmbH which other shareholders will not receive. Similarly, the shareholders who do not benefit from the distributed profits in the same way as the other shareholders may give their consent to not being treated in a manner equal to the other shareholders who do receive this profit. Finally, the same corporate body that is responsible for the resolution on the ordinary distribution of profits must also reach a resolution in a case of the disguised distribution of profits. According to statutory law, it falls within the sphere of responsibility of the shareholders' meeting to approve the annual financial statement and to reach a resolution on the use of the profits. Therefore, if such a distribution of profits is undertaken by another corporate body, that is, typically a managing director or the supervisory board, based on this fact alone, the distribution will already be considered an illegal disguised distribution of profits. Such a distribution is, however, permitted in the case of a single-shareholder GmbH or when the responsibility for reaching a resolution on the distribution of profits has been transferred to another corporate body (ie, a supervisory board).

In the event of a disguised distribution of profits, the respective shareholder receiving the benefit in question is obliged to repay the profit to the GmbH. The company is entitled to claim damages under generally applicable principles. The distribution may, however, be remedied if a respective shareholders' resolution is passed with all shareholders voting to authorise such a distribution of profits or when the transaction with the shareholder is undertaken anew on arm's-length terms.

The principles outlined above also apply if the person benefiting from the distribution is not a shareholder, but a third party closely related to the shareholder (eg, parents, children, husband, wife). The benefits must then be distributed based on the membership of the shareholder in the company.

XI. Company transformations

201. General

The following section offers a brief outline of the most important ways in which a GmbH (or any other entity) may be transformed into another corporate form or in which another corporate form can be transferred into a GmbH. The most important procedures via which a transfer may be effected are listed in the Law Regulating the Transformation of Companies (*Umwandlungsgesetz*) and include merger (*Verschmelzung*), spin-off (*Abspaltung*) and conversion (*Formwechsel*). These three types of company transformation will be described below.

A. Merger

202. Types of merger

The Law Regulating the Transformation of Companies provides for two different types of merger. In the first type of merger, the assets of the transferring company are transferred by way of universal succession (usually by way of up-stream or downstream merger) in their entirety to another already existing company (receiving company – *Verschmelzung zur Aufnahme*).[1] The second possible form of merger is the transfer of the assets of the transferring companies by way of universal succession in their entirety to a newly formed company (receiving company – *Verschmelzung durch Neugründung*). This new entity is only formed for the purpose of receiving the assets of the transferring companies.[2] In both cases, the shareholders of the transferring entity will receive shares in the receiving company as compensation for the transfer of the assets. The merger will, ultimately, lead to the termination of the transferring company/companies.

---

1 *Umwandlungsgesetz* (UmwG) (Law Regulating the Transformation of Companies) 1994, s2, no. 1, 4 *et seq*. (FRG).

2 *Umwandlungsgesetz* (UmwG) (Law Regulating the Transformation of Companies) 1994, s2, no. 2, 36 *et seq*. (FRG).

A merger is basically possible between any types of legal entity, also between entities with a different legal structure such as corporations (GmbH, AG), partnerships (GbR, OHG, KG) and other entities existing under German law.[3]

203. Prerequisites: merger agreement

Any type of merger requires the companies which are to be merged to enter into a merger agreement.[4] Such an agreement is negotiated between the management of the merging entities. The minimum content of this merger agreement is outlined below:[5]

- the company names and the places of business of the companies to be merged;
- the agreement on the transfer of the assets of each transferring entity in their respective entirety in return for the granting of shares or other membership rights in the receiving entity;
- the share exchange ratio and, if required, the amount of the extra payments in cash, or information on the membership rights in the receiving entity; in the event that the companies to be merged have different legal forms (eg, when an AG is merged with a GmbH), the receiving entity not only has to propose its own shares as a consideration towards the shareholders of the transferring company, but must also offer to acquire the shares in the transferring company in return for compensation in cash;[6]
- specific details on the transfer of the shares of the receiving entity or on the acquisition of the membership rights in the receiving entity;
- the date from which onwards the parties owning these shares or membership rights shall be entitled to participate in the balance sheet profit, along with all of the particular details relating to this claim;
- the date from which onwards all measures of the transferring entity shall be deemed to have been made on behalf of the receiving entity and the effective date of merger;

---

3 *Umwandlungsgesetz* (UmwG) (Law Regulating the Transformation of Companies) 1994, s3 (FRG).

4 *Umwandlungsgesetz* (UmwG) (Law Regulating the Transformation of Companies) 1994, s4, para. 1, 36 (FRG).

5 *Umwandlungsgesetz* (UmwG) (Law Regulating the Transformation of Companies) 1994, s5, para. 1 (FRG).

6 *Umwandlungsgesetz* (UmwG) (Law Regulating the Transformation of Companies) 1994, s29, paras. 1, 36 (FRG).

- the rights which the receiving entity grants to individual shareholders as well as the persons with particular rights such as non-voting shares, multiple voting rights shares, debentures and beneficial rights, or the measures stipulated for those persons;
- any particular benefit granted to a member of the management board or of the supervisory board or a managing shareholder, a general partner, an auditor or a merger auditor;
- the consequences of the merger for the employees and their representatives as well as the measures intended in relation thereto.

In the event that the merger is effected by way of the formation of a new company, the merger document must also contain the articles of association of the new entity.[7]

If a wholly owned subsidiary is to be merged with its parent company, the merger agreement does not need to contain the information as set out under nos. 2 to 5 of section 5, paragraph 1 of the Law Regulating the Transformation of Companies (= bullet points 2 to 5 above).[8] The merger agreement must in any case be notarised.[9]

204. Prerequisites: merger report

The managing directors of each of the entities to be merged must prepare a comprehensive written report in which they must describe in detail the legal and economic implications of the merger, the merger agreement or its draft and in particular the share exchange ratio or the information on the membership rights in the receiving entity (merger report).[10] The merger report may also be jointly prepared by the managing directors of the entities involved. The law does not stipulate further details in this regard. The report must be detailed enough to allow the shareholders to inform themselves comprehensively about the intended merger. In particular, this means that the

---

7 *Umwandlungsgesetz* (UmwG) (Law Regulating the Transformation of Companies) 1994, s37 (FRG).

8 *Umwandlungsgesetz* (UmwG) (Law Regulating the Transformation of Companies) 1994, s5, para. 2 (FRG).

9 *Umwandlungsgesetz* (UmwG) (Law Regulating the Transformation of Companies) 1994, s6 (FRG).

10 *Umwandlungsgesetz* (UmwG) (Law Regulating the Transformation of Companies) 1994, s8, para. 1 (FRG).

details on the intended share exchange ratio must be set forth in sufficient detail. The managing directors must set forth specific details on the evaluation and on the methods applied in the evaluation and related sample calculations. In this regard, the managing directors of the involved entities negotiating on the merger agreement and on the merger report are not free to determine the share exchange ratio; rather, the share exchange ratio must be fair and equitable for the shareholders of both the receiving and the transferring company. Otherwise, the shareholders of one of the companies would suffer a loss based on the merger, which is not allowed. If necessary, compensation for fractional amounts (*Spitzenbeträge*) is to be provided in cash, wherein these cash payments may only amount to a maximum of 10% of the value of the shares granted by the receiving company towards the shareholders of the transferring company.[11] In calculating the values of the entities to be merged, the same methods and principles must be applied to both companies in order to receive comparable results.

On the other hand, the merger report does not need to disclose particular information if the disclosure may have a significant negative effect on one of the involved entities or any of their affiliates.[12] Relevant information of this nature could be for instance a business or trade secret of one of the companies. The merger report must set forth the reasons why certain specific information has not been included in the report.

Notwithstanding the above, a merger report is not required if all shareholders of the entities involved in the merger waive the requirement to have the report prepared or if the receiving entity is the sole shareholder in the transferring entity.[13] The respective waivers must be notarised.

205. Prerequisites: merger audit

The merger agreement or its draft, respectively, is to be examined by one or several independent auditors, which are to be nominated by the district court (*Landgericht*) in which the transferring entity has

11 *Umwandlungsgesetz* (UmwG) (Law Regulating the Transformation of Companies) 1994, s5, para. 1, no. 3, 54, para. 4 (FRG).

12 *Umwandlungsgesetz* (UmwG) (Law Regulating the Transformation of Companies) 1994, s8, para. 2 (FRG).

13 *Umwandlungsgesetz* (UmwG) (Law Regulating the Transformation of Companies) 1994, s8, para. 3 (FRG).

its place of business, upon the proposal of the managing directors of the entities to be merged.[14] The audit covers in particular the completeness and correctness of the merger agreement, in particular whether the agreed-upon share exchange ratio is equitable. The auditors must prepare a written report on their audit.[15] The report must also state whether or not the auditors think that the proposed exchange ratio is equitable.[16]

An audit of the merger is again not required in cases where a wholly owned subsidiary is merged with its parent company (upstream merger) or if all shareholders of all entities involved waive the requirement pertaining to the preparation of the merger report.[17]

206. Prerequisites: observance of formation formalities

If the merger is effected by way of transferring the assets of the entities to form a NewCo (*Verschmelzung zur Neugründung*), this entity must be established according to the general regulations prescribed by law for the formation of the respective company.[18] This usually also calls for a special report (*Sachgründungsbericht*) when the entity to be established is to be formed by way of contributions in kind.[19] If, however, the transferring entity is a corporation, irrespective of whether it has been established by contributions in kind or by contributions in cash, this special report is not required.[20]

207. Prerequisites: informing the works council

If the entities involved in the merger have a works council, the merger agreement or a draft thereof must be sent to this/these works council/s, at the latest one month prior to the shareholders'

---

14 *Umwandlungsgesetz* (UmwG) (Law Regulating the Transformation of Companies) 1994, s9, para.1, s10, para. 1 (FRG).

15 *Umwandlungsgesetz* (UmwG) (Law Regulating the Transformation of Companies) 1994, s12, para. 1 (FRG).

16 *Umwandlungsgesetz* (UmwG) (Law Regulating the Transformation of Companies) 1994, s12, para. 2 (FRG).

17 *Umwandlungsgesetz* (UmwG) (Law Regulating the Transformation of Companies) 1994, s9, para. 2 (FRG).

18 *Umwandlungsgesetz* (UmwG) (Law Regulating the Transformation of Companies) 1994, s36, para. 2 (FRG).

19 *Umwandlungsgesetz* (UmwG) (Law Regulating the Transformation of Companies) 1994, s58, para. 1, s75, para. 1 (FRG).

20 *Umwandlungsgesetz* (UmwG) (Law Regulating the Transformation of Companies) 1994, s58, para. 2, s75, para. 2 (FRG).

meeting in which the merger agreement is to be adopted.[21] If the shareholders' meeting occurs earlier than one month after the works council has been informed, the respective resolution will be considered invalid and the merger may not become effective. It is advisable that the works council should confirm the receipt of the merger agreement or the draft thereof because without proof of this a registration of the merger in the commercial register may not be possible.[22] In this regard, the works council solely has a right to be informed; it is not entitled to stop the merger by exercising a veto right or by requesting that certain provisions of the merger agreement are re-negotiated.

208. Prerequisites: informing shareholders

The merger requires a shareholders' resolution on the part of both the transferring entity and the receiving entity to confirm the adoption of the merger agreement.[23] The resolutions must be notarised.[24] The formal requirements for convening a shareholders' meeting in this regard are subject to the applicable statutory law or the articles of association of the respective company. When convening the shareholders' meeting to obtain the consent of the shareholders, the managing directors must specifically indicate that the merger will be a topic of discussion at the shareholders' meeting.[25] In addition, the shareholders are to be provided with the merger agreement or a draft thereof and the merger report at the latest at the point in time of the convening of the shareholders' meeting in which the consent is to be granted with regard to the merger agreement.[26] The general information rights of the shareholders under statutory law or the articles of association remain unaffected.

---

21 *Umwandlungsgesetz* (UmwG) (Law Regulating the Transformation of Companies) 1994, s5, para. 3 (FRG).

22 *Umwandlungsgesetz* (UmwG) (Law Regulating the Transformation of Companies) 1994, s17, para. 1 (FRG).

23 *Umwandlungsgesetz* (UmwG) (Law Regulating the Transformation of Companies) 1994, s13, para. 1 (FRG).

24 *Umwandlungsgesetz* (UmwG) (Law Regulating the Transformation of Companies) 1994, s13, para. 3 (FRG).

25 *Umwandlungsgesetz* (UmwG) (Law Regulating the Transformation of Companies) 1994, s49, para. 1 (FRG).

26 *Umwandlungsgesetz* (UmwG) (Law Regulating the Transformation of Companies) 1994, s47 (FRG).

209. Prerequisites: resolution on the merger

At the shareholders' meeting, the shareholders must give their consent to the merger agreement, which thereby becomes valid. The shareholders' resolution in a GmbH requires a majority of three quarters of the votes cast.[27] Where particular rights of particular shareholders are affected by the resolution, the consent of these shareholders is also required.[28] The shareholders' resolution by way of which the merger agreement becomes effective may only be challenged within one month after it has been passed.[29]

If the shareholders of the transferring entity are of the opinion that the share exchange ratio is too low or that the membership rights granted in the receiving entity are not adequate compensation for the shares in the transferring entity, the shareholders of the transferring entity are not entitled to challenge the shareholders' resolutions to be passed in connection with the merger based on such complaints.[30] Statutory law provides for a particular proceeding in which shareholders may claim compensation in cash if the court comes to the conclusion that the share exchange ratio etc is inadequate.[31]

210. Prerequisites: capital increase

In most cases, a merger requires a capital increase on the part of the receiving company in order to have the necessary shares available to compensate the shareholders of the transferring company. The shares are issued in exchange for the contribution in kind in the form of the transferred assets. A capital increase is not required when the receiving company holds sufficient shares of its own which it may use to compensate the shareholders of the transferring company.[32]

---

27 *Umwandlungsgesetz* (UmwG) (Law Regulating the Transformation of Companies) 1994, s50, para. 1 (FRG).

28 *Umwandlungsgesetz* (UmwG) (Law Regulating the Transformation of Companies) 1994, s50, para. 2 (FRG).

29 *Umwandlungsgesetz* (UmwG) (Law Regulating the Transformation of Companies) 1994, s14, para. 1 (FRG).

30 *Umwandlungsgesetz* (UmwG) (Law Regulating the Transformation of Companies) 1994, s14, para. 2 (FRG).

31 *Umwandlungsgesetz* (UmwG) (Law Regulating the Transformation of Companies) 1994, s15 (FRG); *Spruchverfahrensgesetz* (SpruchG) (Award Proceeding Act) 2003, s1, no. 4 (FRG).

32 *Umwandlungsgesetz* (UmwG) (Law Regulating the Transformation of Companies) 1994, s54, para. 1, sentence 2 (FRG).

In certain situations, the receiving company may not even effect a capital increase. This is the case if either: (i) the receiving company holds shares in the transferring company, or (ii) the transferring company holds its own shares, or (iii) a transferring company holds shares in the receiving company for which the contributions have been fully paid in.[33]

If a capital increase occurs, it is subject to the regulations applicable to the company in question.[34] Furthermore, in the event of a capital increase on the part of the receiving company, the merger may only be registered after the increase of the share capital has been registered.[35]

211. Prerequisites: appointment of managing directors

If the merger is effected in the way of the transferring company transferring its assets to the receiving company wherein only the receiving company survives (*Verschmelzung zur Aufnahme*), the managing directors of the receiving company keep their positions in office. The terms of office of the managing directors of the transferring company, however, will automatically cease upon the merger becoming effective. Notwithstanding the above, their underlying service agreements remain unaffected by the merger.

If the merger is effected by the entities transferring their assets to a newly founded company (*Verschmelzung durch Neugründung*), the managing directors of the new company in question and, if required, of a supervisory board, must be nominated (anew) in accordance with the respective applicable regulations.

212. Prerequisites: other important aspects

In connection with a merger, the issue of whether or not the merger in question requires cartel clearance must also be taken into account. The managing directors of the entities involved in the merger must ensure that clearance of this kind is not required, or, if it is required, must ensure that such clearance is granted prior to the merger becoming effective. From a practical point of view, it only makes sense to enter into negotiations on a merger agreement if merger clearance is likely to be granted or is not required.

---

33 *Umwandlungsgesetz* (UmwG) (Law Regulating the Transformation of Companies) 1994, s54, para. 1, sentence 1 (FRG).

34 For details on capital increase in a GmbH see Section 157 *et seq*.

35 *Umwandlungsgesetz* (UmwG) (Law Regulating the Transformation of Companies) 1994, s53 (FRG).

If the GmbH is to be merged with a stock corporation listed on a stock exchange, the fact of the merger will generally necessitate an *ad hoc* publication on the part of the stock corporation.[36] Since the merger proceedings are comprised of various steps, it is, however, uncertain which step will constitute the right moment to make an *ad hoc* publication. It should be borne in mind that each instance of entering into merger negotiations with another entity may reasonably establish an obligation to initiate such *ad hoc* publication. This would hamper the ability of the managing directors to begin negotiations with various parties or to explore the market opportunities associated with the merger. The latest possible point in time at which the merger should be published would be the point in time at which the merger agreement has been negotiated or at least a final draft has been prepared. This does not, however, exclude the possibility that a publication may be required at an earlier point in time subject to the respective circumstances involved. Ultimately, the issue must be decided upon on a case-by-case basis.

213. Prerequisites: registration of the merger

After the necessary steps for the merger have been taken, and in particular once the consent of the shareholders has been given, the merger must be registered with the competent commercial register for the companies involved (ie, the registers where the companies have their places of business).[37] If the merger is effected by way of transferring assets to a NewCo, the establishment of the NewCo is to be registered by all of the transferring entities with the commercial register where the NewCo shall have its place of business.[38] All of the aforementioned filings are to be made by the responsible corporate body, that is, the managing directors of the GmbH.[39]

The filings must be accompanied by a certified copy of the merger agreement, the minutes of the resolutions of the shareholders, the merger report, the audit report, proof that the merger report has been communicated to the works council (or, if there is no works

---

36 *Wertpapierhandelsgesetz* (WpHG) (Securities Trading Act) 1998, s15 (FRG).

37 *Umwandlungsgesetz* (UmwG) (Law Regulating the Transformation of Companies) 1994, s16, para. 1; s38, para. 1 (FRG).

38 *Umwandlungsgesetz* (UmwG) (Law Regulating the Transformation of Companies) 1994, s38, para. 2 (FRG).

39 *Gesetz betreffend die Gesellschaft mit beschränkter Haftung* (GmbHG) (Act on Limited Liability Companies) 1892, s78 (FRG).

council, a declaration of the managing directors that such a works council does not exist in the respective company) or, where applicable, the waivers of the respective requirement to prepare a merger report and an audit report.[40] Additionally, the filed documents must include a final balance (*Schlussbilanz*) of each transferring entity.[41]

Furthermore, the managing directors responsible for the registration must issue a declaration to the effect that there is no action pending against the validity of a merger resolution or that no such action has been filed within the time limit prescribed by law, or, respectively, that a claim of this kind has been finally dismissed.[42]

If the merger is effected by an upstream or downstream merger (*Verschmelzung durch Aufnahme*), the merger must first be registered in the register for the transferring company, wherein it must be indicated that the merger will only become effective with the registration of the merger in the register for the receiving company.[43] The register for the receiving company may only register the merger on the condition that the capital increase, if applicable, has previously been registered.[44]

If the merger occurs by way of transferring assets to a NewCo (*Verschmelzung zur Neugründung*), the merger must be registered with the commercial register for the NewCo rather than the commercial register for a receiving entity. In other words, the NewCo replaces the receiving entity in the case of an upstream or downstream merger. This registration may only take place after the merger has been registered in the commercial register/s for the transferring entities.[45]

214. Prerequisites: effects of the registration

The registration of the merger in the commercial register for the receiving company, or for the NewCo, as the case may be, has a constitutive effect, that is, the merger will only become effective

40 *Umwandlungsgesetz* (UmwG) (Law Regulating the Transformation of Companies) 1994, s17, para. 1 (FRG).

41 *Umwandlungsgesetz* (UmwG) (Law Regulating the Transformation of Companies) 1994, s17, para. 2 (FRG).

42 *Umwandlungsgesetz* (UmwG) (Law Regulating the Transformation of Companies) 1994, s16, para. 2 (FRG).

43 *Umwandlungsgesetz* (UmwG) (Law Regulating the Transformation of Companies) 1994, s19, para. 1 (FRG).

44 See also Section 211 for details.

45 *Umwandlungsgesetz* (UmwG) (Law Regulating the Transformation of Companies) 1994, s36, para. 1, sentence 2 (FRG).

after the registration has been made. The assets of the transferring company are transferred by law to the receiving company/NewCo via the registration, including all liabilities.[46] The transferring company expires by law, and the shareholders of the transferring entity become shareholders in the receiving company unless specific exceptions apply as outlined in Section 210 (in cases where a capital increase is not required or allowed).[47]

Furthermore, any deficits with regard to the notarial form of the merger agreement and other potential declarations are considered remedied.[48] If there are contractual relationships in place between the transferring and the receiving entity, in particular a domination or a profit and loss transfer agreement, the agreement in question will expire automatically as soon as the merger becomes effective. The termination of a domination or profit and loss transfer agreement must also be registered with the commercial register. Other agreements existing with third parties are automatically transferred to the new entity.

215. Prerequisites: publication

The relevant commercial registers for the respective entities involved in a merger must publish the registration of the merger.[49] From the point of publication onwards, any offers for compensation in cash in exchange for shares may be accepted.[50] This exchange for cash need only be offered in the merger agreement if an upstream or downstream merger is effected between entities with different legal forms.[51]

Within three months after the date of publication of the merger, a proceeding to examine whether the exchange ratio has been equitable may be initiated.[52]

---

46 *Umwandlungsgesetz* (UmwG) (Law Regulating the Transformation of Companies) 1994, s20, para. 1, no. 1 (FRG).

47 *Umwandlungsgesetz* (UmwG) (Law Regulating the Transformation of Companies) 1994, s20, para. 1, nos. 2 and 3 (FRG).

48 *Umwandlungsgesetz* (UmwG) (Law Regulating the Transformation of Companies) 1994, s20, para. 1, no. 4 (FRG).

49 *Umwandlungsgesetz* (UmwG) (Law Regulating the Transformation of Companies) 1994, s19, para. 3 (FRG).

50 *Umwandlungsgesetz* (UmwG) (Law Regulating the Transformation of Companies) 1994, ss29, 31 (FRG).

51 See Section 203 for details.

52 *Spruchverfahrensgesetz* (SpruchG) (Act on Shareholders' Actions) 2003, s4, para. 1, no. 4 (FRG).

216. Protection of creditors

The creditors of an entity involved in a merger are entitled to be provided with security for their claims on the following conditions: (i) at the latest within six months after the merger has been registered in the commercial register, they set forth their claim in writing, unless they may claim fulfilment of their claims (ie, their claim is due); and (ii) they explain in reasonable detail that the merger will endanger the satisfaction of their claim.[53]

216a. Potential tax-neutrality of mergers and other forms of restructuring

Under the German Mergers and Reorganisation Tax Act (*Umwandlungssteuergesetz*), certain forms of corporate restructuring such as a merger may be possible without associated negative tax consequences for the transferring entity and its shareholders. However, certain conditions must be fulfilled in order for this to be the case. In theory, the possibility of a tax-neutral merger may now also apply to certain cross-border restructurings within the EU.

If the prerequisites of the Mergers and Reorganisation Tax Act cannot be satisfied, a merger may be deemed to be a sale of the transferring entity's assets (eg, a GmbH), thus potentially triggering a taxation of any hidden reserves where the transferring GmbH is concerned and/or a capital gains taxation where the GmbH's shareholders are concerned (see also below, D. Tax issues relating to reorganisations).

B. Company splitting

217. Types of company splitting

The law provides for three different types of company splitting, which may themselves be divided into subtypes. The first kind of splitting is the split-up (*Aufspaltung*), in which the assets of an existing entity are split up and transferred to existing entities or entities yet to be founded by way of transferring these assets to the newly founded entity, in each case by way of granting shares or other membership rights in the entities receiving the assets to the shareholders of the transferring entity. The transferring entity

53 *Umwandlungsgesetz* (UmwG) (Law Regulating the Transformation of Companies) 1994, s22 (FRG).

thereby expires and ceases to exist. In other words, its total assets are transferred to other existing or newly founded entities.[54]

The spin-off (*Abspaltung*) as the second type of splitting is characterised by an existing entity spinning off only parts of its assets and transferring them to either one or several existing entities or to one or more newly founded entities in return for the granting of shares or membership rights in these receiving entities to the shareholders of the transferring entity.[55] The transferring entity survives the transaction.

The third type of splitting is the de-merger (*Ausgliederung*). The de-merger and the spin-off have the same characteristics, that is, also in the case of a de-merger, an existing entity transfers parts of its assets to another existing entity or a newly founded entity while the transferring entity 'survives' the transfer of assets. With a de-merger, however, the shares in the receiving or newly founded entity are not granted to the shareholders of the transferring entity, but to the transferring entity itself. This means that the shareholders of the transferring entity only participate indirectly in the transfer of the assets by way of the shares they hold in the transferring entity.[56]

In all of these cases, it is not required that the assets are only transferred either to an existing or a newly founded entity: they may also be transferred to an existing and a newly formed company at the same time.[57] Regarding the particular requirements, the law draws a distinction between whether the splitting is effected by transferring assets to an existing company, which is called splitting for the purposes of absorption (*Spaltung zur Aufnahme*), or whether the assets are transferred to a newly founded entity, which is called splitting for the purposes of new formation (*Spaltung zur Neugründung*).

The basic principles underlying these two types of splitting will be outlined below. The law stipulates that, to a large extent, the rules applicable to a merger also apply to cases of splitting. It only sets out additional rules with regard to a splitting where such rules

---

54 *Umwandlungsgesetz* (UmwG) (Law Regulating the Transformation of Companies) 1994, s123, para. 1 (FRG).

55 *Umwandlungsgesetz* (UmwG) (Law Regulating the Transformation of Companies) 1994, s123, para. 2 (FRG).

56 *Umwandlungsgesetz* (UmwG) (Law Regulating the Transformation of Companies) 1994, s123, para. 3 (FRG).

57 *Umwandlungsgesetz* (UmwG) (Law Regulating the Transformation of Companies) 1994, s123, para. 4 (FRG).

are deemed necessary given the different kind of legal structure compared with a merger. The same entities which may be party to a merger may also be party to a company split, that is, in particular a GmbH.

218. Prerequisites: splitting and takeover agreement or splitting plan

In the case of splitting for absorption it is required that the company transferring its assets and the company receiving the assets enter into a splitting and takeover agreement (*Spaltungs- und Übernahmevertrag*). Such an agreement must include at least the following information and provisions:

- business denomination or company name (*Firma*) and place of business of the legal entities involved in the splitting;
- agreement on the assets to be transferred as a whole from the transferring entity in return for the granting of shares in the receiving entity;
- in the case of a split-up or spin-off, the share exchange ratio and, if required, the amount of the additional cash payments or information on the membership rights in the receiving entity;
- in the case of a split-off and spin-off, details on the transfer of the shares of the receiving entity or on the acquisition of membership rights in the receiving entities;
- the point in time from which onwards the parties owning these shares or membership rights shall be entitled to participate in the balance sheet profits as well as any particular details relating to this claim for profits;
- the point in time from which onwards the measures of the transferring entity are considered undertaken on behalf of each of the receiving entities (effective splitting date);
- the rights which the receiving entity grants to individual shareholders and to persons holding particular rights such as non-voting shares, multiple voting shares, debentures and beneficial rights, or the measures stipulated for those persons;
- any particular benefit or other advantage which is granted to a member of the management or of the supervisory board of the entities involved in the splitting, to each managing shareholder, a general partner, an auditor or a splitting auditor;
- the exact denomination and distribution of the assets to be transferred to the receiving entities and the business or parts

of the business to be transferred and allocated to the receiving entities;
- in the case of a split-up or spin-off, the distribution of the shares of each of the involved entities between the shareholders of the transferring entity and the criteria for the distribution;
- the consequences of the split for the employees and their representatives and the measures relating thereto.[58]

If the splitting is effected by way of a splitting for the purposes of new formation, the splitting and takeover agreement is replaced by a splitting plan which sets forth the steps to be taken by the transferring entity in founding the new entity and transferring the assets thereto.[59] The splitting plan must also contain the articles of association of the newly founded entity.[60] The splitting and transfer agreement and the splitting plan must both be notarised.[61]

If the splitting is done by way of a de-merger, the splitting and takeover agreement does not need to contain the information set forth under nos. 3, 4 and 10 of section 126, paragraph 1 of the Law Regulating the Transformation of Companies (bullet nos. 3, 4 and 10 above). Since then, it is the transferring entity itself which will receive the shares in the newly founded entity and not the shareholders of the transferring entity.

One of the most important provisions in the splitting and takeover agreement is the precise denomination of the assets to be transferred. Each individual item to be transferred must be specifically denominated (*Bestimmtheitsgrundsatz*). This is particularly important in connection with the transfer of real estate.[62] In such cases, the splitting and transfer agreement must specify the respective land register district in which the real estate is registered, the land register folio number and further details to facilitate the clear identification of the piece of land to be transferred. With regard to other assets which are to be transferred, documents such

58 *Umwandlungsgesetz* (UmwG) (Law Regulating the Transformation of Companies) 1994, s126, para. 1 (FRG).

59 *Umwandlungsgesetz* (UmwG) (Law Regulating the Transformation of Companies) 1994, s136 (FRG).

60 *Umwandlungsgesetz* (UmwG) (Law Regulating the Transformation of Companies) 1994, s135, 37 (FRG).

61 *Umwandlungsgesetz* (UmwG) (Law Regulating the Transformation of Companies) 1994, s125, 6 (FRG).

62 *Umwandlungsgesetz* (UmwG) (Law Regulating the Transformation of Companies) 1994, s126, para. 2, sentence 1 and 2 (FRG).

as balance sheets or inventory lists may be referred to in order to determine which assets are to be transferred.[63]

Another very important aspect of the splitting and takeover agreement is the determination of the share exchange ratio setting forth how many shares the shareholders of the transferring entity are to receive in the receiving entity. It is not required here that the shareholders of the transferring entity participate in the shares of the receiving entity to the same extent/ratio/percentage as they do in the transferring entity as long as they consent to such an asymmetrical distribution of the shares in the receiving entity.[64]

219. Prerequisites: splitting report

The management board of each entity involved in the split must prepare a written report in which the splitting, the splitting agreement or the plan, respectively, and, where necessary, the share exchange ratio and the criteria for the distribution of the shares in the receiving entity amongst the existing shareholders along with any additional cash payments, if applicable, are to be explained as regards their legal and economic consequences (*Spaltungsbericht*).[65] The managing directors of the involved entities may prepare a joint splitting report. Aside from this, the same regulations apply as those applicable to a merger. This means, in particular, that a splitting report is not required if all of the shareholders of the involved entities waive the requirement to prepare it.[66]

220. Prerequisites: splitting audit

As with a merger, the splitting and takeover agreement and, according to the case in question, the splitting plan must be reviewed by special splitting auditors which are to be appointed by the court upon the request of the managing directors.[67] The auditors must submit their splitting report to the managing directors. In this regard, an audit is only required in the event of a split-up or a spin-off, but not

---

63 *Umwandlungsgesetz* (UmwG) (Law Regulating the Transformation of Companies) 1994, s126, para. 2, sentence 3 (FRG).

64 *Umwandlungsgesetz* (UmwG) (Law Regulating the Transformation of Companies) 1994, s128 (FRG).

65 *Umwandlungsgesetz* (UmwG) (Law Regulating the Transformation of Companies) 1994, s127 (FRG).

66 *Umwandlungsgesetz* (UmwG) (Law Regulating the Transformation of Companies) 1994, s125, 8, para. 3 (FRG).

67 *Umwandlungsgesetz* (UmwG) (Law Regulating the Transformation of Companies) 1994, s125, 9, 10 (FRG).

in the case of a de-merger.[68] Moreover, it is also not required if all the shareholders of the entities involved waive the requirement to prepare such a report or to have it audited.

221. Prerequisites: submission to the works council

As in the case of a merger, the splitting and takeover agreement or the splitting plan must be submitted to the works councils of the entities involved. The submission must be made at the latest one month prior to the date upon which the shareholders of the involved entities reach a resolution on the adoption of the agreement or the plan.[69] The shareholders' meeting(s) consenting to the splitting should not take place prior to the expiration of this one-month period; otherwise the resolution would be considered invalid. As is the case where a merger is concerned, the works council has no right of veto against the splitting and may not request re-negotiations.

222. Prerequisites: consent of shareholders and change in share capital

With regard to the splitting and takeover agreements and the splitting plan, the consent of the shareholders of all entities involved in the splitting must be obtained.[70] The shareholders' resolution must be notarised.[71] If a GmbH or a stock corporation is involved in the splitting, the shareholders' resolution requires a majority of three quarters of the votes cast.[72] Where partnerships are involved in the splitting, a unanimous resolution on the part of all partners is required.[73] As regards giving prior notice to the shareholders in a GmbH, the principles as set forth under Section 208 apply accordingly.

The respective shareholders' resolution may not be passed earlier than one month after the splitting and takeover agreement or

68 *Umwandlungsgesetz* (UmwG) (Law Regulating the Transformation of Companies) 1994, s125, sentence 2 (FRG).

69 *Umwandlungsgesetz* (UmwG) (Law Regulating the Transformation of Companies) 1994, s126, para. 3 (FRG).

70 *Umwandlungsgesetz* (UmwG) (Law Regulating the Transformation of Companies) 1994, ss125, 135, 13 (FRG).

71 *Umwandlungsgesetz* (UmwG) (Law Regulating the Transformation of Companies) 1994, ss125, 135, para. 1, 13, para. 3 (FRG).

72 *Umwandlungsgesetz* (UmwG) (Law Regulating the Transformation of Companies) 1994, s125, 50, 65, para. 1 (FRG).

73 *Umwandlungsgesetz* (UmwG) (Law Regulating the Transformation of Companies) 1994, s125, 43 (FRG).

splitting plan has been submitted to the works councils of the companies involved (see also Section 221).

In the event that the splitting requires a capital increase in the companies involved, typically in the case of the receiving company which must grant shares in return for the receipt of the assets of the transferring entity, the shareholders' resolution of this entity must also pass a resolution on the increase in its share capital in accordance with the respective rules for the increase in the stated share capital of the entity concerned.[74] Additionally, the same principles apply to a capital increase as those outlined above for a merger.[75] Where the splitting is effected by way of a de-merger or spin-off, a decrease in the share capital of the transferring entity may be required.[76] In these cases, the capital decrease is also effected in accordance with the rules of the respective entity.[77]

223. Prerequisites: observance of formation regulations

In cases of splitting for the purposes of new formation, it is required that the regulations concerning the establishment of the new company to be founded are fully complied with.[78] If a limited liability company or stock corporation is founded in the splitting process, a special report (*Sachgründungsbericht*) is required for the establishment of such a company because the stated share capital thereof is raised by way of contributions in kind.[79]

224. Prerequisites: filing and registration in the commercial register

The split must be registered with the commercial register by the management of the entities involved.[80] If a NewCo is established in the process of the splitting (splitting for the purposes of new

74 For details on the increase of the stated share capital in a GmbH, refer to Section 173 *et seq.*

75 For details see Section 210.

76 *Umwandlungsgesetz* (UmwG) (Law Regulating the Transformation of Companies) 1994, ss139, 145 (FRG).

77 For the rules regarding a capital decrease in a GmbH see Section 177.

78 *Umwandlungsgesetz* (UmwG) (Law Regulating the Transformation of Companies) 1994, s135, para. 2 (FRG).

79 *Umwandlungsgesetz* (UmwG) (Law Regulating the Transformation of Companies) 1994, ss138, 144 (FRG); *Gesetz betreffend die Gesellschaft mit beschränkter Haftung* (GmbHG) (Act on Limited Liability Companies) 1892, s5, para. 4 (FRG); *Aktiengesetz* (AktG) (Stock Corporation Act) 1965, ss32, 33 (FRG).

80 *Umwandlungsgesetz* (UmwG) (Law Regulating the Transformation of Companies) 1994, ss125, 16, para. 1; 129; 137, para. 2 (FRG).

formation), the new entity must be registered by the directors of the transferring company.[81]

At the point of filing, the managing directors must declare that there is no action pending against the shareholders' resolution or that such an action has not been dismissed by the court respectively.[82] Additionally, the filing of the split must be accompanied by the same documents as those submitted in connection with a merger, that is, in particular the splitting and takeover agreement or splitting plan, the notarial deeds for the shareholders' resolution on the splitting, the proof that the splitting agreement or splitting plan have been submitted to the works council, the splitting report and the splitting audit (if required), the closing balance sheet for the transferring entity and the documentation regarding measures to increase or decrease the stated share capital of any of the entities involved (if applicable).[83]

In the case of a split for the purposes of absorption, the splitting may only be registered in the commercial register of the transferring company after the splitting has been registered in the commercial register of the receiving entities. Upon registration in the commercial register of the transferring entity, the split becomes legally effective.[84]

In the case of a split for the purposes of new formation, the newly established legal entity must also be registered. The splitting will only be registered with the register of the transferring entity after the register for the newly created entity has informed the register for the transferring entity that the newly founded entity has been registered (and thus has come into existence).[85] Upon registration in the commercial register for the transferring entity, the splitting becomes legally effective.[86]

81 *Umwandlungsgesetz* (UmwG) (Law Regulating the Transformation of Companies) 1994, s137, para. 2 (FRG).

82 *Umwandlungsgesetz* (UmwG) (Law Regulating the Transformation of Companies) 1994, ss125, 135, 16, para. 2 (FRG).

83 *Umwandlungsgesetz* (UmwG) (Law Regulating the Transformation of Companies) 1994, ss125, 135, 17 (FRG).

84 *Umwandlungsgesetz* (UmwG) (Law Regulating the Transformation of Companies) 1994, ss130, 131 (FRG).

85 *Umwandlungsgesetz* (UmwG) (Law Regulating the Transformation of Companies) 1994, s137 (FRG).

86 *Umwandlungsgesetz* (UmwG) (Law Regulating the Transformation of Companies) 1994, s131 (FRG).

Where the splitting calls for a decrease in the stated share capital of the transferring entity, the splitting may only be registered with the commercial register for the said transferring entity (and thus only become effective) after the decrease in the share capital has been registered.[87]

225. Prerequisites: legal effects of splitting

The splitting becomes legally effective as soon as it has been duly registered in the relevant register for the transferring entity. The legal effects of the splitting are as follows: first, the assets to be transferred to the receiving entity including all liabilities pertaining thereto are transferred by way of universal succession to the receiving entity and as set forth in the splitting and takeover agreement or the splitting plan. Secondly, if the splitting is accomplished by way of a split-up, the 'split-up' legal entity ceases to exist by law, wherein no particular liquidation proceedings are required. Thirdly, in the case of a split-up or spin-off, the shareholders of the transferring entity will automatically become shareholders in the receiving entity according to their share exchange ratio as set forth in the splitting and takeover agreement or the splitting plan. In the case of a de-merger, the transferring entity will receive the shares in the receiving entity also based on the splitting and takeover agreement or the splitting plan. Finally, any defects (if applicable) in relation to the notarisation of the splitting and takeover agreement or any required consents or waivers are considered obtained and remedied upon registration in the commercial register.[88]

226. Protection of creditors

The creditors of the transferring entities involved in a splitting enjoy particular protection under statutory law. First, the creditors of any entity involved in a splitting are entitled to be provided with security on the same conditions as those which apply in the case of a merger.[89] However, only the entity against which the claim is directed is obliged to provide security and not any of the other involved entities.[90] Secondly, the entities involved in the splitting

---

87 *Umwandlungsgesetz* (UmwG) (Law Regulating the Transformation of Companies) 1994, s139 (FRG).

88 *Umwandlungsgesetz* (UmwG) (Law Regulating the Transformation of Companies) 1994, s131, para. 1 (FRG).

89 For details see Section 216.

90 *Umwandlungsgesetz* (UmwG) (Law Regulating the Transformation of Companies) 1994, s133, para. 1, sentence 2 (FRG).

are jointly and severally liable for all liabilities of the transferring entity which were established prior to the splitting becoming effective.[91] However, the entities involved in the splitting which are not intended to be the debtors of this particular claim in question according to the splitting and transfer agreement or splitting plan will only be jointly and severally liable for such claims for a period of five years after the split becomes effective.[92] After this period of time, their joint and several liability with the transferring entity expires.

Finally, the splitting may be structured so that after it becomes effective, one of the entities involved is responsible for the administration of the transferred assets (*Anlagegesellschaft*) whereas the other entities (or entity) use these assets for running their business (*Betriebsgesellschaft*). In such cases, the *Anlagegesellschaft* is jointly and severally liable together with the *Betriebsgesellschaft* for all social benefit plans, compensation and settlement claims and for claims arising from company pension plans (*betriebliche Altersvorsorge*) for a period of five years after the split becomes effective.[93]

C. Conversion

227. Types of conversion

Conversion (*Formwechsel*), as the third form of company transformation, allows a company to be converted from one legal form into another (eg, from a GmbH into an AG) whilst retaining the legal identity of the converted company, wherein, amongst other legally available forms, all kinds of partnerships (OHG, KG) and corporations (AG, GmbH) may be converted reciprocally.[94] It is not required that a partnership is converted into another kind of partnership or a corporation into another kind of corporation, for example, a general partnership (OHG) may be converted into a GmbH, or vice versa. The outcome of a conversion may therefore also be a GmbH.

---

91 *Umwandlungsgesetz* (UmwG) (Law Regulating the Transformation of Companies) 1994, s133, para. 1, sentence 1 (FRG).

92 *Umwandlungsgesetz* (UmwG) (Law Regulating the Transformation of Companies) 1994, s133, para. 3 (FRG).

93 *Umwandlungsgesetz* (UmwG) (Law Regulating the Transformation of Companies) 1994, s134 (FRG).

94 *Umwandlungsgesetz* (UmwG) (Law Regulating the Transformation of Companies) 1994, s191 (FRG).

228. Prerequisites: conversion resolution

A conversion requires a resolution on the part of the shareholders of the entity to be converted which may only be passed in a shareholders' meeting.[95] The conversion resolution must include the following information and provisions, these being minimum requirements:

- the legal form of the entity after the conversion;
- the business denomination or company name (*Firma*) of the entity after its conversion;
- the participation/s of the current shareholders in the entity after conversion pursuant to the provisions applicable to the new entity;
- number, nature and scope of the shares or membership interests which the current shareholders shall be granted by the conversion or which shall be granted to a joining general partner (note: a general partner is only possible in a general partnership (OHG) or in a limited partnership (KG), but not in a GmbH);
- the rights granted to individual shareholders as well as the holders of particular rights such as non-voting shares, preferred shares, multiple voting rights shares, debentures and beneficial rights in the converted entity or the measures which are stipulated for those persons;
- offer for compensation according to section 207 of the Law Regulating the Transformation of Companies (cash compensation in return for the transfer of the shares of the converted entity), unless the conversion resolution has to be adopted unanimously by all shareholders or the entity to be converted only has one shareholder;
- the consequences of the conversion for the employees and their representatives as well as the measures stipulated in relation thereto.[96]

The conversion resolution must be notarised.[97] In the case of a conversion of one corporation into another type of corporation and in

95 *Umwandlungsgesetz* (UmwG) (Law Regulating the Transformation of Companies) 1994, s193, para. 1 (FRG).

96 *Umwandlungsgesetz* (UmwG) (Law Regulating the Transformation of Companies) 1994, s194, para. 1 (FRG).

97 *Umwandlungsgesetz* (UmwG) (Law Regulating the Transformation of Companies) 1994, s193, para. 3 (FRG)

cases in which a partnership is converted into a corporation, the conversion resolution must also set out the articles of association of the newly established entity.[98]

The provisions as outlined under bullet nos. 3 and 4 above are particularly relevant here. The quantity, nature and scope of the participation in the newly converted entity may not be determined arbitrarily. Rather, the stated share capital of the new entity must correspond at least to the stated share capital of the existing entity if there is a conversion from one corporation into another corporation.[99] In the case of a conversion from a GmbH into an AG, the stated share capital must be increased if the current stated share capital of the GmbH does not reach the minimum required stated share capital of an AG, namely €50,000. The resolution on the capital increase may be combined with the resolution on the conversion and must comply with the general rules applicable to the respective entity.[100] If the participation of the current shareholders in the converted entity is not intended to be the same as it was prior to the conversion, the consent of the effected shareholders must be obtained in this respect.[101] The law assumes that the conversion does not in itself change the shareholding of the current shareholders in the converted entity.

229. Prerequisites: submission to works council

The draft of the conversion resolution must be submitted to the works council of the entity to be converted at the latest one month prior to the shareholders' meeting in which the shareholders are to adopt the conversion resolution.[102] The works council has no veto or similar rights with regard to the resolution to be passed. If the shareholders' resolution on the conversion is passed earlier, it will be invalid. If the entity does not have a works council, this prerequisite does not apply.

98 *Umwandlungsgesetz* (UmwG) (Law Regulating the Transformation of Companies) 1994, ss218, 243, para. 1 (FRG).

99 *Umwandlungsgesetz* (UmwG) (Law Regulating the Transformation of Companies) 1994, s247, para. 1 (FRG).

100 For the regulations applicable to a capital increase in a GmbH, see Section 173.

101 *Umwandlungsgesetz* (UmwG) (Law Regulating the Transformation of Companies) 1994, ss241, 242 (FRG).

102 *Umwandlungsgesetz* (UmwG) (Law Regulating the Transformation of Companies) 1994, s194, para. 2 (FRG).

230. Prerequisites: conversion report

Unless the entity to be converted only has one shareholder or if, by way of a notarial deed, all shareholders waive the requirement pertaining to having a conversion report prepared,[103] the management of the entity to be converted must prepare a conversion report setting forth in sufficient detail the legal and economic consequences of the conversion, and in particular the future participation of the shareholders in the new entity (*Umwandlungsbericht*).[104] Similarly to the case with a merger or a splitting, the report must be drawn up in sufficient detail to allow the shareholders to reach an informed decision on the granting of consent with regard to the conversion or the denial thereof. The conversion report must be laid out in the shareholders' meeting resolving on the conversion for inspection of the shareholders.[105]

231. Prerequisites: conversion audit

The law does not provide for an audit of the conversion itself. The conversion resolution, however, must include a compensation offer in cash for all those shareholders who refuse to give their consent to the conversion.[106] The appropriateness of such an offer must be assessed by an auditor.[107] The auditor is nominated by the court based on a proposal of the management board of the entity which is to be converted.[108] The audit report must be submitted to the management board of the entity to be converted. It is disputed whether the shareholders are entitled to review the audit report or whether their rights are limited to the right to be informed in the shareholders' meeting.

---

103 *Umwandlungsgesetz* (UmwG) (Law Regulating the Transformation of Companies) 1994, s192, para. 2 (FRG).

104 *Umwandlungsgesetz* (UmwG) (Law Regulating the Transformation of Companies) 1994, s192, para. 1 (FRG).

105 *Umwandlungsgesetz* (UmwG) (Law Regulating the Transformation of Companies) 1994, s239, para. 1 (FRG).

106 *Umwandlungsgesetz* (UmwG) (Law Regulating the Transformation of Companies) 1994, s207, 194, para. 1, no. 6 (FRG).

107 *Umwandlungsgesetz* (UmwG) (Law Regulating the Transformation of Companies) 1994, s208, 30 (FRG).

108 *Umwandlungsgesetz* (UmwG) (Law Regulating the Transformation of Companies) 1994, s208, 30, 10 (FRG).

232. Prerequisites: observing formation regulations

Even though a conversion under the Law Regulating the Transformation of Companies will not have an effect on the identity of the company to be converted, a conversion is nonetheless treated as an establishment of a new entity by way of contributions in kind. Therefore, the regulations on the formation of companies (by way of contributions in kind) apply accordingly to a conversion.[109] The aim of these regulations is to avoid the rules regarding the establishment of a company by way of contributions in kind being circumvented, thus protecting the interests of creditors of a company. As a consequence, if a company is to be converted into a GmbH, a special report on contributions in kind (*Sachgründungsbericht*) must be prepared.[110] The special report must also include details on the business development and the current status of the company to be converted. Furthermore, the outcome of a conversion wherein the converted entity is a corporation may not be that the nominal value of the stated share capital exceeds the assets of the converted company less the liabilities of the company.[111]

233. Prerequisites: shareholders' resolution

When the shareholders' meeting is convened to adopt the resolution on the conversion of the company, the shareholders must be informed in writing about the conversion being the issue of discussion at the meeting. In this regard, the managing directors must provide the shareholders with a copy of the conversion report.[112] The resolution itself by which the conversion is adopted requires a majority of three quarters of the votes cast if the converted entity has the legal form of a corporation (AG, GmbH).[113] Where the converted entity (= GmbH) is to have the legal form of a partnership, the consent of all shareholders of the entity to be converted must be obtained.[114] The articles of association of the converted entity are

---

109 *Umwandlungsgesetz* (UmwG) (Law Regulating the Transformation of Companies) 1994, s197 (FRG).

110 *Umwandlungsgesetz* (UmwG) (Law Regulating the Transformation of Companies) 1994, s220, para. 2 (FRG).

111 *Umwandlungsgesetz* (UmwG) (Law Regulating the Transformation of Companies) 1994, s220, para. 1; s245, paras. 1–3 (FRG).

112 *Umwandlungsgesetz* (UmwG) (Law Regulating the Transformation of Companies) 1994, ss238, 230, para. 1 (FRG).

113 *Umwandlungsgesetz* (UmwG) (Law Regulating the Transformation of Companies) 1994, s240, para. 1 (FRG).

114 *Umwandlungsgesetz* (UmwG) (Law Regulating the Transformation of Companies) 1994, s233, para. 1 (FRG).

also deemed to be adopted along with the resolution by which the conversion is adopted. Furthermore, the shareholders typically also reach a resolution on the increase in the stated share capital during the same meeting, if such an increase is required.

It should be noted here that such a resolution on the conversion may not be passed before a period of one month after the works council has been informed of the conversion and the conversion report has been submitted thereto.

234. Prerequisites: nomination of corporate bodies

The conversion has no effect on the legal identity of the company as such. There is no legal succession as there is in the case of a merger or in the case of splitting. In legal terms, the converted entity is considered to be the same legal entity as it was before the conversion. If the conversion resolution does not provide otherwise, the shareholders in the converted entity are the same as the shareholders in the former entity.[115] Furthermore, in the event that the converted entity has a supervisory board, in principle, the members of the supervisory board retain their office until the end of their regular term in office, unless the conversion resolution provides for the termination of the term in office of the members of the supervisory board.[116] If the company is subject to a Co-Determination Act, only those members who have been elected or delegated by the shareholders may be removed from office in the conversion resolution.

As regards the management, the law does not provide that the managing directors will remain in office after the conversion becomes effective. Therefore, the shareholders must reach a resolution on the nomination of the persons who are to be the managing directors of the converted entity once the conversion becomes effective.

235. Prerequisites: filing and registration of conversion

The conversion must be registered in the relevant commercial register for the entity to be converted.[117] The filing must be made

---

115 *Umwandlungsgesetz* (UmwG) (Law Regulating the Transformation of Companies) 1994, s202, para. 1, no. 2 (FRG).

116 *Umwandlungsgesetz* (UmwG) (Law Regulating the Transformation of Companies) 1994, s203 (FRG).

117 *Umwandlungsgesetz* (UmwG) (Law Regulating the Transformation of Companies) 1994, ss198, 222, 246 (FRG).

by the competent management of the entity to be transferred. When filing for registration, the directors must declare that there are no actions pending against the conversion resolution or that actions to this effect have not been dismissed by a court.[118] The filed documents must include certified copies of, in particular, the minutes of the conversion resolution, the conversion report (or its waiver, as applicable) and proof that the splitting agreement or splitting plan have been submitted to the works council.[119] The new directors of the GmbH as a converted entity must also be filed with the commercial register.[120]

235a. Prerequisites: legal effects of conversion

The conversion will only become effective upon the registration thereof in the relevant commercial register for the converted entity. Once the conversion is registered, the conversion has the following effects: (i) the entity to be converted continues to exist in the legal form it has been given under the conversion resolution, (ii) the shareholders of the entity to be converted will automatically become shareholders of the converted entity according to the same shareholder ratio unless the conversion resolution provides otherwise, and (iii) any defects (if applicable) with regard to the notarisation of the conversion resolution and to waivers or consent to the conversion are considered remedied.[121] Since the conversion has no effect on the identity of the company as such, any and all agreements the converted entity was party to remain unaffected by the conversion. This is also true for domination or profit and loss transfer agreements.

Furthermore, if a GmbH is converted into an AG, the stated share capital of the GmbH will become the stated share capital of the AG. The same applies, vice versa, if an AG is converted into a GmbH.[122]

118 *Umwandlungsgesetz* (UmwG) (Law Regulating the Transformation of Companies) 1994, s198, para. 3, 16, paras. 2 and 3 (FRG).

119 *Umwandlungsgesetz* (UmwG) (Law Regulating the Transformation of Companies) 1994, s199 (FRG).

120 *Umwandlungsgesetz* (UmwG) (Law Regulating the Transformation of Companies) 1994, s246, para. 2 (FRG).

121 *Umwandlungsgesetz* (UmwG) (Law Regulating the Transformation of Companies) 1994, s202, para. 1 (FRG).

122 *Umwandlungsgesetz* (UmwG) (Law Regulating the Transformation of Companies) 1994, s247, para. 1 (FRG).

236. Prerequisites: publication

The relevant commercial register must publish the conversion once it has been registered in accordance with the rules prescribed by the state regulations pertaining to the publication of registrations in the commercial register. Once publication has occurred, the shareholders who are not willing to grant their consent to the conversion may accept the offer to transfer their shares to the company in return for compensation in cash within a period of two months after the publication.[123]

In the event that a shareholder claims that the compensation offer has been calculated at too low a level, he or she may file an action within a period of three months after the publication of the conversion by the public register to have the compensation offer assessed in order to receive additional payment in cash.[124]

237. Rights of creditors

Creditors of a company to be converted enjoy the same protection as creditors of an entity which is to be merged with another entity.[125]

D. Tax issues relating to reorganisations

237a. General overview

In principle, the tax treatment of reorganisations is governed by the general tax provisions under the corporate tax laws and (for shareholders who are individuals) the income tax laws.

However, the Mergers and Reorganisation Tax Act includes provisions which facilitate the tax-neutral implementation of reorganisations. It does not apply to every reorganisation of an enterprise, although it basically covers all forms of transformations under German civil law as well as the contribution in kind in the form of the transferring entity's domestic or foreign separable branch of its business operation in return for interests in the receiving company. It also covers contributions in kind in the form of so-called entrepreneurial partnership interests and contributions in kind in the form of shares in a resident or non-resident corporation in return

---

123 *Umwandlungsgesetz* (UmwG) (Law Regulating the Transformation of Companies) 1994, ss207, 209 (FRG).

124 *Umwandlungsgesetz* (UmwG) (Law Regulating the Transformation of Companies) 1994, ss196, 212 (FRG).

125 For details see Section 216.

for interests in the receiving company (corporation or partnership, deemed co-entrepreneurship under German tax laws).

For German tax purposes, the merger of a corporation into a partnership (or into an individual's business) or the conversion of a corporation into a partnership is generally treated as a (taxable) transfer of assets from the corporation. Assets transferred by the corporation must, as a matter of principle, be valued at a fair market value (potentially resulting in a taxable gain in the amount of the difference between the fair market value and the tax basis of the assets on the tax-effective transfer date). In so far as Germany does not lose the right to tax built-in gains on transferred assets as a result of the deemed transfer (for example, because the assets are retained in the permanent German establishment of a non-resident individual or corporation), provided that the transferring corporation obtains approval from the tax authorities, the transferred assets may be transferred based on their carryover basis.

The shareholder of a transferring GmbH is deemed to have sold the shares in the transferring corporation for a fair market value consideration, and is deemed to have acquired the shares in the transferee corporation for that same consideration. In so far as Germany does not lose the right to tax built-in gains on shares (for example, in a purely domestic corporate-to-corporate reorganisation), the shareholder may – upon application to the tax authorities – roll his or her tax basis in the transferring corporation over to the transferee corporation. This tax neutrality is also possible within an EU context if Germany forfeits the right to tax capital gains on shares (for example when the shareholder is resident in another EU member state). In such a case, however, Germany reserves the right to tax the EU shareholder on a later transfer of the shares in the transferee corporation in the same way as Germany had the right to tax the shareholder on his or her shares in the transferor corporation (and disregarding the attribution of taxation rights under an applicable tax treaty).

The contribution of qualifying assets (that is, an entire trade or business, a separate division, a partnership interest, or a controlling shareholding (more than 50%)) by a shareholder into a German or foreign (EU or non-EU) corporation in exchange for new shares would generally result in a contribution of such assets at a fair market value. In so far as Germany does not lose the right to tax built-in gains on the transferred assets, the transferred assets could (upon application by the transferring corporation) be transferred based on their carryover basis. If the carryover basis is elected, there would be, as is the case under the current rules, a 'duplication of built-in gains' (that is, in the assets of the transferee corporation and in the tax basis in the corporation where the shareholder is concerned).

To track built-in gains in connection with all carryover basis contributions, the transferee corporation would have to establish an 'adjustment item I' (*Korrekturposten I*) in its tax balance sheet, which tracks the balance between the fair market value of the assets and the carryover basis value assigned to the assets by the corporation. If the contributed assets include shares in other corporations, any built-in gains on such shares would be tracked in a new 'adjustment item II' (*Korrekturposten II*). Both items would be reduced by an amount of one seventh for each year following the tax-effective contribution year.

To address concerns that the ECJ could deem a general anti-abuse period (for example, seven years) to be a violation of EU law, German tax authorities have completely overhauled the system of retroactively triggering capital gains for transactions that violate minimum holding periods. The proposed system is based on Germany's current system that applies to EU share-for-share exchange contributions (that is, a retroactive triggering event for the selling shareholder only if a sale occurs within a seven-year period post contribution).

If the contributing shareholder sells shares in the transferee corporation within seven years following the tax-effective contribution year, with full retroactivity, the transferee corporation would generally recognise additional tax basis in the contributed assets in an amount equivalent to the remaining balance of its adjustment item I. The shareholder would receive additional tax basis in his or her shares in an amount equivalent to the remaining balance of adjustment item I and would be taxed on the net gain. After seven years, there would effectively be no retroactive adjustment.

If the transferee corporation sells shares that have been contributed by the shareholder within seven years following the tax-effective contribution year, the transferee corporation would, with full retroactivity, recognise additional tax basis in the contributed shares in an amount equivalent to the remaining balance of its adjustment item II. The shareholder would receive additional tax basis in his or her shares in an amount equivalent to the remaining balance of adjustment item II, and would be taxed on the net contribution gain. After seven years, there would be no retroactive adjustment.

XII. Taxes

238. Corporate tax: general

Any corporation organised under German law, including a GmbH, is obliged to pay corporate (income) tax in Germany. Only those corporations which are engaged in non-profit activities may apply for a full or partial tax exemption for the non-profit activities in question. All revenues the GmbH generates on a global basis are subject to corporate tax unless a double taxation treaty (*Doppelbesteuerungsabkommen*) provides otherwise. The corporate tax is to be declared on a yearly basis. The managing directors of a GmbH must file a tax return at the end of each business year in the calendar year following thereafter. The tax authorities will then issue an assessment notice.

During the ongoing business year, any corporation, and therefore also a GmbH, may be obliged to make advance payments for corporate tax (*Körperschaftsteuer-Vorauszahlung*), which are based on the corporate tax assessment notice for the previous business year. The advance payments are to be made on fixed dates in each calendar quarter. These advance payments may be reduced or increased if the GmbH or the tax authorities indicate that the expected tax basis will be reduced or increased during the ongoing business year. The advance payments will then be deducted from the actual corporation tax as determined in the yearly tax assessment notice. The corporate tax rate is currently 15%. The corporate tax is due irrespective of whether the annual profits are retained in the company or distributed amongst the shareholders. Furthermore, a solidarity surcharge of 5.5% also applies to the tax rate. Effectively, the corporate income tax burden (including the additional solidarity surcharge thereon) is thus 15.83%.

The shareholders of a GmbH, being individuals and residential German taxpayers, are obliged to pay income tax on the profits distributed to them in their capacity as shareholders of the GmbH. As individuals, however, they do not need to pay the full income tax rate on the distributed profits. Rather, only 40% of the gross dividend will be taken into account as a tax basis for calculating the income tax of the individual shareholder (so-called partial-income system – *Teileinkünfteverfahren*). If the GmbH shareholder is a German corporation, the dividend payments will be 95% tax exempt. The same rules apply with regard to capital gains resulting from a disposition of shares and held as non-current assets (unless the shares have been depreciated to a lower going concern value or certain other disqualifying measures have been taken in the past).

The tax rules for non-residential shareholders are distinct from those described here and will be dealt with in the section on withholding taxation with respect to foreign shareholding entities.

From a practical point of view, it is important to know that most corporations are subject to regular tax field audits (eg, every four years) with respect to their corporate (and also usually trade tax and value added tax, and sometimes even other forms of) tax liabilities. These tax field audits often lead to an adjustment of the previously issued (preliminary) tax assessments and may trigger a significant additional tax burden and interest hereon (6% pa). This might be changed, since it is considered to be an infringement of German constitutional law.

In many cases, a German GmbH enters into a fiscal unit (*Organschaft*) with another tax subject to form a consolidated tax group. The fiscal unit leads to a consolidation/pooling of current profits and losses of the pool members, thus pooling the overall tax payable by the German parent company. Fiscal units may serve to optimise the corporate and potentially also the trade tax and a value added tax burden. It should be noted that the prerequisites for a value added tax fiscal unit are different to a fiscal unit for corporate tax purposes. The fiscal unit for corporate tax purposes requires entering into a profit and loss pooling agreement, whereas a VAT fiscal unit requires not only a financial, but also an economic and organisational integration of the members.

Following recent decisions pronounced by the European Court of Justice, the possibility of cross-border fiscal units has become highly controversial in Germany.

Finally, and this is of particular relevance for larger GmbHs which are members of international groups, Germany has strict transfer pricing rules with regard to the documentation of cross-border intra-group transactions. Insufficient documentation may give rise to additional taxes and penalty payments.

239. Corporate tax: limitation on interest deduction

In 2008, the German legislature introduced a new interest deduction limitation tax rule ('interest barrier rule') regarding interest expenses for German taxpayers, such as for instance a GmbH.

These interest deduction rules apply to all debt financing (including bank financing). Under them, interest expenses are tax-deductible, provided that the total interest expenses do not exceed the total interest earned in the same fiscal year (interest balance). The deduction of interest expenses exceeding the interest balance amount is restricted to 30% of the EBITDA.

However, the law provides for several exceptions by which the borrower (subject to arm's-length conditions) may deduct more or even all of its/his or her overall interest expenses.

First of all, the interest barrier rule is not applicable in so far as the annual net interest expenses balance per company amounts to less than €3 million.

Furthermore, the law stipulates an escape clause for companies that are members of a consolidated group. Under this exception, the interest barrier rule is not applicable in so far as an 'equity ratio' comparison test is passed and no harmful debt financing is in place. This means that the equity ratio per company does not fall below the equity ratio of the consolidated financial statements.

Through certain tax structure measures, the non-deductibility of business expenses in the case of a German GmbH may potentially be avoided. For instance, lease expenses (rather than a debt-financed purchase) are entirely deductible. Such a structure can be achieved, for instance, by way of a 'sale and lease back'. Other strategies aim at relocating interest expenses to subcontractors out of the scope of the interest barrier rule.

Furthermore, it can be an option to generate interest income, thus reducing the net interest expense in respect of the interest barrier rules.

In order to pass the equity ratio test under the escape clause it is advisable to consider improving the equity ratio of the whole group or improving the equity ratio of the German entity affected by the interest barrier rule by means of measures such as the injection of supplemental equity through capital increase and profit retention, or the use of mezzanine instruments.

In summary, there are numerous tax planning strategies by which it is possible to fully or partly avoid the effect of the interest threshold tax rules.

240. Corporate tax: tax losses

Losses incurred during a business year may be carried forward without any time limitation. The subsequent use of such losses, however, is subject to the minimum taxation rules (*Mindestbesteuerung*). This means that unlimited use (by way of off-setting against it) is possible up to an amount of €1 million. For any losses above one million, the use of loss carried forwards is limited to 60% of the profit of the respective business year (ie, thus 40% of the remaining profits must be taxed despite loss carry-forwards).

However, a direct or indirect transfer of shares in an entity may be detrimental to the tax losses where the entity in question is concerned. In 2008, the rules on the forfeiture of tax loss carry-forwards in a German company following a change in ownership of that company were changed. The new rules not only affect corporate, but also trade tax loss carry-forwards and interest carry-forwards under the interest barrier rule (see above). Under the new rules, if more than 50% of the shares in a German company with loss carry-forwards (a 'loss entity') are transferred (to a single buyer or to affiliates of the buyer) within a five-year period, 100% of the current-year losses and loss carry-forwards are forfeited. For transfers of more than 25% but not more than 50% of shares within a five-year period, loss carry-forwards will be forfeited commensurate to the percentage of shares transferred (ie, if 40% of the shares in a GmbH are transferred, 40% of the loss carry-forwards of that GmbH would be forfeited).

Exceptions may apply to certain intra-group restructurings, restructurings of companies in crisis and finally a limitation of the expiring loss carry-forwards commensurate to the amount of hidden reserves of the company.

The European Commission is currently investigating whether the exception for companies in crisis constitutes a state aid measure that would have required prior notification and the approval of the Commission. The Commission is examining whether the exception confers a selective or unequal tax advantage on certain restructurings that cannot be justified under general German tax law principles. The main criticism is that only companies in difficulty may preserve their loss carry-forwards under this new restructuring exception.

Consequently, a decision reached by the Commission that the new exception constitutes state aid could mean that any tax advantage already granted might have to be disallowed, irrespective of any good faith on the part of the taxpayers in complying with domestic German tax laws.

Aside from this, certain tax planning measures may enable relief from a forfeiture of tax loss and interest carry-forwards in a German corporation or group.

In cases where a LossCo has a profitable subsidiary, an option could be an up-stream merger of that profitable entity with the LossCo. The merger should be performed on a tax neutral basis at book value. As a consequence, any taxable income derived from the profitable entity could be offset against current losses and loss carry-forwards of the LossCo.

In contrast, an up-stream merger of a loss-making company with a parent company should be performed at the fair market value. This may lead to a taxable realisation of hidden reserves, for instance from internally generated IP rights.

It should be noted that this type of merger should only be performed if current tax losses are substantial and tax loss carry-forwards do not exceed the threshold of €1 million in order to avoid Germany's minimum taxation rules.

Furthermore, assets that are associated with potential hidden profits and can be amortised over a specific period of time can be sold within a group. The profit realised can be offset against available loss and interest carry-forwards, subject again to the minimum taxation rules.

Finally, a-typical silent partnership structures may be considered as options for even more sophisticated tax planning measures.

241. Withholding taxes on dividends and royalties paid by a GmbH

Generally, Germany imposes withholding taxes on dividends distributed by German corporations (such as a GmbH) to foreign parent companies at the domestic tax rate of 26.38%, irrespective of whether such dividends are exempt from German corporate income tax under a double tax treaty or the EU Parent Subsidiary Directive.

This does not apply if the shareholder is in possession of a withholding tax exemption certificate. In such cases, the distributing GmbH is allowed to treat the dividends as being exempt from German withholding tax. These withholding tax exemption certificates can be obtained upon application from the German Federal Tax Office (*Bundeszentralamt für Steuern*). The application procedure may generally take up to three months.

The withholding tax exemption certificate is granted if the requirements set out in the applicable double tax treaty or the EU Parent Subsidiary Directive are met. This is usually the case if the parent company holds a minimum shareholding over a specific period of time. A withholding taxation at a rate of 15.83% applies to other cross-border payments from the GmbH, for example, royalties. The most important condition for granting a withholding tax exemption certificate (or alternatively a tax refund in cases where the withholding tax has already been paid) is that the prerequisites of the German anti-treaty-shopping rules (or, with respect to the EU directive, anti-directive-shopping rules) are met.

Pursuant to the anti-treaty-shopping rules, a foreign entity will not qualify for tax relief for the GmbH's dividend payments or paid royalty fees as provided for by the EU Parent Subsidiary Directive or the applicable double tax treaty if it is owned by shareholders who would not be entitled to such tax relief if they derived the income directly unless certain requirements are met. The EU Commission initiated EU law infringement proceedings against Germany with respect to these anti-treaty-shopping rules. As a result, Germany has modified its anti-treaty-shopping rules with effect as of 1 January 2012.

Under these modified tax rules, the withholding tax relief for the foreign (shareholder) entity requires that: (i) the GmbH is owned by shareholders that would be entitled to a corresponding benefit under a double tax treaty or an EU directive had they received the income directly; or, alternatively, (ii) if the foreign shareholders' gross receipts in the relevant year are generated from its own business activities.

If the entity fails to meet both of the above requirements, the shareholder is entitled to withholding tax relief only if the following two additional requirements are met:

- Business purpose requirement: there are economic or other non-tax reasons for the involvement of the foreign shareholder entity.
- Substance requirement: the foreign shareholder entity has adequate business substance with respect to its own business purpose of engaging in general commerce. The burden of proof is on the foreign shareholder to demonstrate that there are economic or other relevant (ie, non-tax) reasons and adequate business substance.

Genuine foreign holding companies rarely meet the business purpose requirement, as they do not generally carry out their own business or trading activities but simply hold the shares in the German company. However, the business purpose requirement can also be met if a corporation is involved for legal, political or religious reasons. Mere organisational reasons (ie, integration into a group-wide structure, inheritance planning) are generally not sufficient to meet the business purpose requirement. A legal reason might be the implementation of a stock option plan at the level of the holding company. Also, the execution of managerial functions might generally be a valid business reason.

With respect to the substance requirement, the foreign shareholder entity corporation should employ its own personnel and should maintain a fully furnished office with telephones and email accounts etc. This requirement is not met if the business activity is restricted to the mere administration and holding of the German companies. In particular, the German tax authorities could choose to decline withholding tax relief for a holding corporation which has outsourced all material business activities to third parties. Consequently, most foreign holding companies (ie, without a genuine business activity) as shareholders of a GmbH do not generally meet the commercial activity requirement. However, a circular issued by the German tax authorities provides an exception to this rule, namely, that a holding company will satisfy the commercial activity requirement if it is a 'management holding company'. Management holding companies are companies that engage in the active management of their subsidiaries. The requirement is not deemed satisfied if the management functions are outsourced to law firms or management entities. Also, a pure financing or licensing function is not considered satisfactory. Instead, the management holding company must have at least two subsidiaries and actively influence the business of its subsidiaries. To satisfy this requirement, it is essential that strategic and fundamental decisions with respect to the business of the subsidiaries are made at the level of the management holding company, and that only the day-to-day business takes place at the level of the subsidiary.

If the above requirements are not met, the dividends or, respectively, the royalties paid to the company's direct shareholder are (for tax purposes) considered to be paid to the next indirect shareholder in the corporate chain, that is, the shareholder of the dividend recipient. If this indirect shareholder is entitled to withholding tax relief, these benefits will be available. Otherwise, the German tax authorities will employ a bottom-up approach towards the shareholder chain until either an indirect shareholder is: (i) resident in a non-treaty country, or (ii) qualifies for withholding tax relief, whichever comes first.

In Figure 1, Lux Co is a wholly owned subsidiary of US Co, which holds 100% of the shares in German Co, a GmbH. Assuming that Lux Co has no substance within the meaning of the German anti-treaty-shopping rules, whereas US Co has the requisite substance, the dividends distributed by German Co to Lux Co would be deemed to be paid directly to US Co. Therefore, German withholding tax can be reduced to the extent that the US tax treaty between Germany and the USA provides for withholding tax relief.

When filing for the tax relief, the German tax authorities usually ask a number of very specific questions regarding the group structure, the description of the business activities and the management.

Due to the strict German anti-treaty-shopping rules (even in view of the latest de-regulation), it may be appropriate to consider other means of repatriating profits from a German GmbH other than by

Figure 1. US HoldCo structure

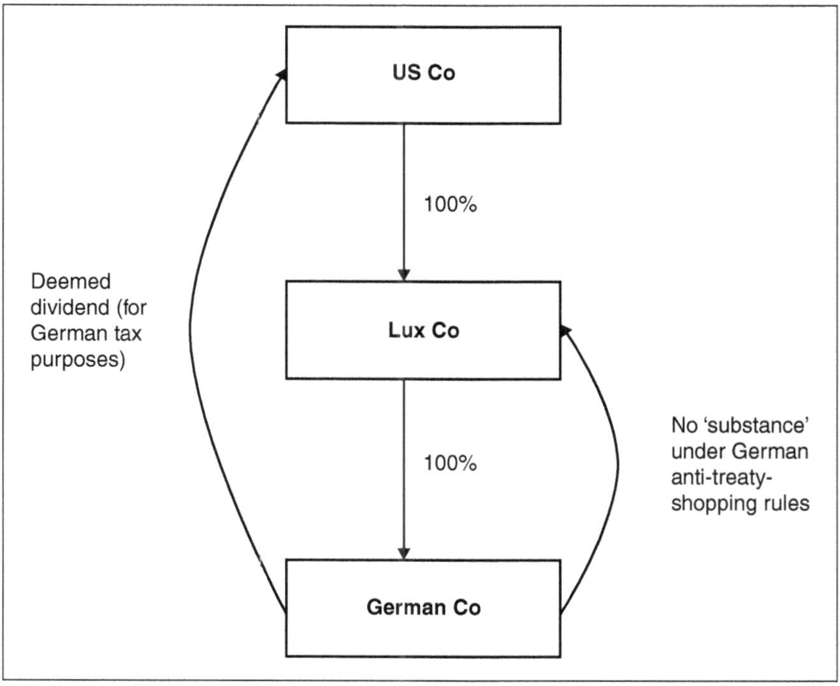

way of dividend distributions. The implementation of a 'silent partnership' structure might serve to withdraw the profit of the German GmbH without triggering German withholding tax. Furthermore, one possible option could be to shift profits accumulated at the level of a German corporation by way of an intra-group sale of the entity at its fair market value. The profit generated by the foreign shareholder from such a sale should be tax exempt in Germany under the rules of most double tax treaties and would thus also not trigger withholding tax.

242. Trade tax

German trade tax is a tax levied by the municipalities and it usually constitutes their most important source of income. By virtue of its legal form, a GmbH is subject to trade tax, irrespective of its business purpose. The tax basis for the trade tax is the revenues generated from the operation of the business as defined by the applicable tax law. The income as calculated for German corporate income tax purposes is modified by certain add-backs and deductions as set out in the German Trade Tax Act (*Gewerbesteuergesetz*). Like the corporate tax laws, the trade tax laws usually prescribe regular advance payments in each calendar year. The trade tax law also prescribes the filing of tax returns. The actual assessment rates (*Hebesätze*) for trade tax are determined by each municipality and may vary from year to year and from municipality to municipality. Effectively, the average trade tax burden for a GmbH is roughly 15%. Smaller communities tend to assess at a lower rate, whereas large cities typically have the highest trade tax rates.

243. Value added tax ('VAT')

Value added tax (*Umsatzsteuer*, 'VAT') is a tax regularly triggered by the supply of goods and services rendered by an entrepreneur (within the meaning of the German VAT laws) in Germany or deemed to have been performed in Germany under German VAT laws. A GmbH or a stock corporation (AG) is usually considered an 'entrepreneur' unless it is a pure asset-managing or -holding entity.

Furthermore, the importing of goods into Germany from a non-EU country and the intra-European acquisition of goods within Germany may trigger German VAT.

Economically, it is the aim of the value added tax system that a tax burden is only borne by the ultimate customer of a product or service, for example, a private consumer or public authorities. If an entrepreneur charges VAT for a product or service supplied to another entrepreneur and the recipient itself uses that product or service him- or herself to provide a service subject to VAT, the receiving entrepreneur may deduct the invoiced VAT as input VAT (*Vorsteuer*) in its VAT declaration.

Currently, the regular VAT rate in Germany is 19%. For certain products or services (such as the sale of food, unless the sale is accompanied by other services, eg, in a restaurant) a reduced rate of 7% applies.[1] It is important to know that significant services are fully exempt from VAT, such as the sale or lease of real estate or most financial or insurance services. The reason for this exemption could be that other taxes apply instead (eg, real estate transfer tax, insurance tax). In some of these VAT-exempt cases, German VAT laws provide for the possibility of opting for an application of VAT. For certain entrepreneurs, opting to apply VAT to the services supplied by them may be beneficial, as only a VAT taxation of their supplied service gives rise to a claim for input VAT deduction with respect to the services received.

Within the European Union, and in view of the necessity of achieving consistent VAT treatment with regard to intra-community supplies of services and goods, the VAT system was already harmonised in 1968. VAT regulations in the EU member states are therefore largely similar. Due to the EU VAT laws, the regular VAT rates in any EU member state may not be lower than 15%. Furthermore, in order to track the VAT liabilities and input VAT claims within the EU, each entrepreneur residing within the EU, or with a permanent establishment in the EU within the meaning of the VAT laws, is given a VAT identification number. For many cross-border intra-community services (and for certain other services or goods provided to entrepreneurs) a reverse charge mechanism has also been introduced. Under the reverse charge procedure, the entrepreneur does not invoice the VAT for the service he or she provides, but the recipient itself is responsible for declaring the VAT for these services. It is important to know that under the reverse charge mechanism, a service is not VAT exempt even if the providing entrepreneur is not allowed to invoice VAT in the situation in question; instead the VAT declaration liability is simply passed on to the receiving entrepreneur.

1 21 February 2005, Value Added Tax Act, s12 – UstG.

244. Real estate transfer tax

A tax which is important in practical terms is the real estate transfer tax (*Grunderwerbsteuer*) triggered by a direct or indirect acquisition or transfer of real property in Germany. A lease right (*Erbbaurecht*) is also treated as real property.

The tax basis for the real estate transfer tax is usually the value of the consideration including additional services agreed between the parties. If the value of the consideration cannot be properly determined or is unacceptable due to its 'symbolic' nature, or in the event that the shares in a company (such as a GmbH) owning real property are transferred, the tax base for the real estate transfer tax will be the value of the real estate calculated according to specific evaluation rules stipulated in the statutory tax laws.[2]

For many years, real estate transfer tax amounted to 3.5% of the tax basis. However, in 2006, the German Federal States were granted the right to determine tax rates autonomously with respect to a transfer of real estate within their territories. Real estate transfer tax rates have therefore either remained at 3.5% (eg, in the state of Bavaria) or have been raised to 5% (eg, in the state of North Rhine-Westphalia; 6.5% in Bavaria).

The real estate transfer tax laws are broadly worded in order to cover any transaction deemed to constitute an indirect transfer of economic ownership in German real estate. For instance, the tax is also triggered when 95% of the shares in a GmbH owning German real estate are transferred to one single shareholder or are concentrated for the first time in the hands of one single shareholder. Furthermore, the tax is imposed on (direct or indirect) transfers of interests in real property-owning partnerships if 95% or more of the interest in that partnership is transferred to a new partner or new partners within a period of five years. Such a change in terms of the partnership interest is seen as if the property was transferred to a new partnership.

There are numerous potential tax structuring models which may be considered in order to avoid or minimise a real estate transfer tax burden in corporate restructurings. For instance, the tax may be avoided by transferring less than 95% of the shares to one shareholder and the remaining shares to an (independent) other

2 *Grunderwerbsteuergesetz* (GrEStG) (German Act on Real Estate Transfer Tax) 2002, s8, para. 2 (FRG); *Bewertungsgesetz* (BewG) (German Act on the Evaluation of Real Estate) 1991, s138, paras. 2, 3 (FRG).

shareholder. Furthermore, a new form of tax exemption has been introduced for certain intra-group restructurings, albeit highly restrictive.

In fact, in some cases foreign (indirect) shareholders of companies owning German real estate are not aware that even indirect share transfers in such entities may entail severe consequences in terms of real estate transfer tax.

245. Other taxes

The GmbH may be subject to specific other taxes depending on the business or transactions it is pursuing or the assets it owns.

There is no general wealth tax currently in place in Germany. However, the municipalities assess property taxes on owned German real estate. Sometimes, in the case of a GmbH which is subject to trade tax, the property tax may be credited against the trade tax.

Germany levies an inheritance and gift tax, potentially triggered through any transfer of goods (or services) without a (fair) consideration. The extent to which a GmbH or its shareholders may itself be subject to this tax is currently unclear, since under corporate tax law the specific rules on 'disguised dividends' and 'disguised contributions' would largely apply to such transactions as well.

One aspect which is highly relevant in practical terms is that a GmbH is liable for the wage taxes to be withheld on the salaries and other benefits in kind (eg, private use of company cars) paid or provided to its employees within Germany. The German tax authorities regularly conduct wage tax audits at German employers' premises (potentially also including a GmbH), focusing on issues such as wage taxes for benefits in kind and wage tax liabilities with respect to (incorrectly titled) 'self'-employed consultants (*Scheinselbständige*).

In Germany, social security contributions withheld by employers from salaries on behalf of their employees are not deemed to be a tax. The social security authorities may, however, conduct social security audits, in particular with respect to statutory pension insurance contributions.

XIII. Group relationships

A. Group relationships based on contract

246. Overview

A GmbH may be affiliated with another company by way of entering into a group agreement (*Unternehmensverträge*). The German Stock Corporation Act provides a list of such possible group agreements,[1] which includes the following:

- domination agreement (*Beherrschungsvertrag*);
- profit and loss transfer agreement (*Gewinnabführungsvertrag*);
- management agreement (*Geschäftsführungsvertrag*) (an entity undertakes to run its business on another entity's account);
- profit pooling agreement (*Gewinngemeinschaftsvertrag*);
- partial profit transfer agreement (*Teilgewinnabführungsvertrag*);
- business lease agreement (*Betriebspachtvertrag*) (an entity leases its complete business to another entity, which runs the business in question on its own account and in its own name against payment of the lease);
- business transfer agreement (*Betriebsüberlassungsvertrag*);
- business management agreement (*Betriebsführungsvertrag*) (agreement not statutorily provided, but generally accepted and often applied in practice; a company receives the management services of another entity which runs the business of the company in the name and on behalf of the company).

Even though these various types of group agreements are listed in the Stock Corporation Act, it is recognised that these types of agreements can also be entered into by two GmbHs or where at least one GmbH is one of the contract partners of the agreement. The specific regulations provided in the Stock Corporation Act for these group agreements[2] also apply to a large extent accordingly when a GmbH is party to such an agreement. There are, however, certain particular requirements in cases where a GmbH is involved.

1 *Aktiengesetz* (AktG) (Stock Corporation Act) 1965, ss291, 292 (FRG).
2 *Aktiengesetz* (AktG) (Stock Corporation Act) 1965, s291 *et seq.* (FRG).

Since domination and profit and loss transfer agreements are by far the most important agreements and are usually entered into at the same time, they shall be dealt with in more detail in the following sections.

247. Domination and profit and loss transfer agreements: general

Under a domination agreement, the dominating company is entitled to give instructions to the management of the dominated company. The management of the dominated entity must comply with these instructions.[3] Under a profit and loss transfer agreement, one entity is obliged to transfer its yearly profits to another entity. If the transferring entity creates any losses, the entity entitled to receive the profits is also obliged to provide compensation for the losses in the other company.[4]

Domination and profit and loss transfer agreements are mainly entered into for tax reasons. By entering into any of these agreements, the entities which are party to these agreements form a tax unit or, alternatively, a fiscal unit (*steuerliche Organschaft*), provided further prerequisites established by the German tax laws are being observed. If this is the case, for corporate and trade tax purposes, both companies must still file tax returns, but are considered one single company with respect to their income. In practice, this means that if one company creates losses whereas the other company operates profitably, the losses of one company may be taken into account to reduce the profits of the other (parent) entity, thus also reducing the tax basis for corporate and trade taxes to which the companies are subject. Usually, the resulting consequences in terms of tax are more favourable because, for instance, no withholding taxes apply to dividends distributed by the subsidiary to the parent entity. In order to be recognised by the tax authorities, such a tax unit and the underlying agreements in connection therewith must exist for a period of at least five (5) consecutive years. If the tax unit is terminated at an earlier point in time, depending on the reason for termination, the tax unit is usually also terminated with retroactive effect and the companies will be treated as if no such tax unit was ever established. This might lead to additional retroactive tax obligations on the part of the companies involved.

3 *Aktiengesetz* (AktG) (Stock Corporation Act) 1965, s308 (FRG).
4 *Aktiengesetz* (AktG) (Stock Corporation Act) 1965, s302 (FRG).

On the basis of European Union law, a profit and loss transfer agreement is not necessarily required for a tax unit for VAT purposes.

248. Domination and profit and loss transfer agreements: conclusion of domination and profit and loss transfer agreements

Both kinds of group relationships require the conclusion of an underlying agreement. The agreement itself is negotiated and signed by the managing directors of the involved companies. The managing directors may not, however, act at their own discretion. They may only sign a group agreement with the consent of the shareholders of the involved entities. This is not only the case where the dominated entity is concerned or the entity is obliged to transfer its profits, but also where the controlling or profit receiving entity is concerned, since entering into such agreements is also associated with obligations for these entities. According to the prevailing, yet disputed opinion, the majority shareholder in the dominated/profit transferring company is not excluded from exercising his or her voting right in the shareholders' resolution granting consent to enter into the group agreement between the company and its majority shareholder. Entering into such an agreement is considered a social act within the company which does not exclude the affected shareholder.

In this context, there is dispute as to which majority is required for a shareholders' resolution within the dominated or profit-transferring entity. According to the prevailing opinion, it is required that such a resolution is passed unanimously, whilst there is also a strong argument in favour of a majority of three quarters of the votes cast being sufficient. Since this question has not yet been finally resolved in the case law, it is advisable to obtain the consent of all the shareholders of the dominated or profit-transferring entity. With regard to the controlling or profit receiving entity, a shareholders' resolution passed with a majority of three quarters of the votes cast is considered sufficient.[5]

The agreement itself must be concluded in writing, but does not need to be notarised. The shareholders' resolution of the dominated or profit-transferring entity by means of which the consent to enter into such an agreement is granted, however, does have to be notarised. The reason for this formal requirement is that by entering

5 *Aktiengesetz* (AktG) (Stock Corporation Act), 1965, s293, para. 2 (FRG) accordingly.

into such a group agreement, the GmbH changes its business purpose. The change of business purpose is only possible based on a change of the articles of association, which in turn requires a notarised shareholders' resolution.[6] Therefore, entering into these group agreements requires a notarised shareholders' resolution. The shareholders' resolution of the controlling or profit-receiving entity, however, does not have to be notarised. Its business purpose will not change by virtue of entering into such an agreement.

To become effective, the control or profit and loss transfer agreement must be filed and registered with the commercial register of the dominated or profit-transferring entity. The public must be informed that the company is party to such a group agreement. The filing must be accompanied by the shareholders' resolutions of both of the entities involved.[7] It is not a prerequisite for the group agreement to become effective that it is also registered with the commercial register of the controlling or profit-receiving entity. Once the group agreement is registered with the commercial register, it becomes legally effective.[8]

The Stock Corporation Act included new provisions in 1995 which set out certain supplementary formal requirements for the conclusion of group agreements in addition to the aforementioned shareholders' resolution and registration with the commercial register. These formal requirements are similar to those applicable in the case of a transformation of the legal form under the German Law Regulating the Transformation of Companies. They call for, for example, the preparation of a report on the group agreement and the audit of the group agreement for both parties by an independent auditor. The auditor must provide a written report on the result of his or her examination, which must be submitted to the respective shareholders' meetings prior to their resolution on the acceptance or denial of the group agreement.[9] It is disputed whether these rules are to be applied accordingly in cases where a GmbH is party to the group agreement. There is only agreement on the fact that the respective procedure does not have to be complied with

---

6 *Gesetz betreffend die Gesellschaft mit beschränkter Haftung* (GmbHG) (Act on Limited Liability Companies), 1892, ss53, 54 (FRG).

7 *Gesetz betreffend die Gesellschaft mit beschränkter Haftung* (GmbHG) (Act on Limited Liability Companies), 1892, s54, para. 1, sentence 1 (FRG); *Aktiengesetz* (AktG) (Stock Corporation Act) 1965, s294, para. 1, sentence 2 (FRG).

8 *Aktiengesetz* (AktG) (Stock Corporation Act) 1965, s295, para. 2 (FRG) accordingly.

9 *Aktiengesetz* (AktG) (Stock Corporation Act) 1965, s293a–f (FRG).

when all the shares of the dominated or profit-transferring entity are held by the other party to the group agreement. The issue has yet to be finally resolved in the jurisprudence. If it is the case that not all shares in the dominated or profit-transferring entity are held by the other entity, it is therefore advisable to observe these formal procedures in order to avoid the group agreement potentially being considered invalid due to formal mistakes.

If the group agreement has been entered into in a manner which does not comply with the requirements outlined above, the agreement will be subject to the regulations pertaining to defective partnerships (*fehlerhafte Gesellschaften*). This usually means that as soon as the agreement has been executed in factual terms, it is considered a valid legal basis for both companies involved and any acts committed thereunder, but may be terminated by each company with effect for the future. However, these principles may not apply if the agreement contains a substantial formal error such as a lack of consent from the shareholders or such like. In such cases, the rules applicable with regard to the protection of the creditors of the company (eg, compensation of losses) shall apply, but not all other provisions which only apply in the relationship between the parties to the group agreement.

249. Control and profit and loss transfer agreements: legal effects; the right to give instructions

If a control agreement is in place, the controlling company is entitled to give the managing directors of the dominated entity detailed instructions regarding how to run the company.[10] Such a right does not exist under a simple profit and loss transfer agreement. In this context, the controlling entity is also entitled to give instructions which are unfavourable to the dominated company as long as the controlling entity is of the opinion that such instruction is favourable to itself.[11] The managing directors of the dominated company may refuse the instruction only when it is obvious that such instruction is not in the best interests of the group.[12] Furthermore, the managing directors of the controlling entity may only give instructions based on the due care and diligence of a prudent business person. If this obligation is violated,

10 *Aktiengesetz* (AktG) (Stock Corporation Act) 1965, s308 (FRG).

11 *Aktiengesetz* (AktG) (Stock Corporation Act) 1965, s308, para. 1, sentence 2 (FRG).

12 *Aktiengesetz* (AktG) (Stock Corporation Act) 1965, s308, para. 2 (FRG).

the managing directors of the controlling entity may be personally liable *vis-à-vis* the controlling entity for any damage caused thereby.[13] The managing directors of the dominated entity must independently assess whether the instructions received are issued under observation of these boundaries. In a GmbH, the right of the controlling entity to give instructions to the managing directors under the control agreement often conflicts with the statutory right of the shareholders of the dominated GmbH to also give instructions to the managing directors.[14] The conflict is solved by giving priority to the instruction rights existing under the control agreement, since the shareholders' consent was required to conclude the control agreement in the first place. The shareholders will nevertheless retain those responsibilities which are mandatorily assigned to the shareholders' meeting of the GmbH (eg, amendment of the articles of association, capital increase or decrease etc).

250. Domination and profit and loss transfer agreements: legal effects; assumption of losses

Under a domination or profit and loss transfer agreement, the dominating company is obliged to assume the annual loss (*Jahresfehlbetrag*) of the dominated entity.[15] This obligation arises by law without any contractual provision being necessary in this regard. The dominating company may not claim that the losses are not based on its instructions or that it has not given any instructions at all. Losses within the context of the regulation means any losses of the dominated entity which would have to be shown in the profit and loss statement if there was no claim for the assumption of losses by the dominating company. The compensation claim becomes due on the effective balance sheet date (*Bilanzstichtag*) of the dominated company. The claim for the compensation of losses becomes subject to the statute of limitations after 10 years from the day in which the registration of the termination of the group agreement was made public.[16]

---

13 *Aktiengesetz* (AktG) (Stock Corporation Act) 1965, s309, paras. 1, 2 (FRG).

14 *Aktiengesetz* (AktG) (Stock Corporation Act) 1965, s308, para. 1 (FRG); *Gesetz betreffend die Gesellschaft mit beschränkter Haftung* (GmbHG) (Act on Limited Liability Companies) 1892, s37 (FRG).

15 *Aktiengesetz* (AktG) (Stock Corporation Act) 1965, s302, para. 1 (FRG) accordingly.

16 *Aktiengesetz* (AktG) (Stock Corporation Act) 1965, s302, para. 4 (FRG) accordingly.

251. Control and profit and loss transfer agreements: legal effects; compensation claims

The Stock Corporation Act provides for adequate compensation claims for the minority shareholders in a dominated or profit-transferring company. Under such agreements, the minority shareholders are first entitled to receive a cash settlement (*Ausgleichszahlung*) relating to the shares they hold in the dominated or profit-transferring company.[17] The amount of the cash compensation is calculated on the basis of the profitability of the company up until entering into the group agreement, taking into account its prospective future earnings. In other words, the minority shareholders should be granted the dividends on their shares as received in the past and as they would – in all likelihood on a sufficiently factual basis – have received in the future if the company had not entered into the control or profit and loss transfer agreement.

Additionally, apart from granting regular profits on the shares, any control and profit and loss transfer agreement must provide that the minority shareholders in the dominated or profit-transferring entity are entitled to sell their shares to the other contract partner in return for an adequate consideration as set out in the group agreement.[18] The shareholders must thus choose whether they wish to receive a yearly fixed dividend and retain their shares, or receive a one-time payment in return for the transfer of their shares. If the dominating or profit-receiving company is itself not subject to a group agreement and does not have a majority shareholder, the consideration to be granted for the transfer of the shares must be in the form of shares of this dominating or profit-receiving company. If the dominating and profit-receiving company is itself subject to a group agreement or has a majority shareholder, the minority shareholders of the dominated or profit-transferring entity must be granted compensation in cash.[19] In both cases (yearly fixed dividend and one-time payment), the adequacy of the consideration is usually evaluated by a third-party auditor nominated by the district court (*Landgericht*) in the district in which the dominated or profit-transferring entity has its place of business.

It is disputed whether these provisions designed to apply to stock corporations also apply in cases where a GmbH is subject to a

17 *Aktiengesetz* (AktG) (Stock Corporation Act) 1965, s304 (FRG).
18 *Aktiengesetz* (AktG) (Stock Corporation Act) 1965, s305 (FRG).
19 *Aktiengesetz* (AktG) (Stock Corporation Act) 1965, s305 (FRG).

group agreement. A corresponding application of these provisions does not appear necessary if it is required that all shareholders of the dominated or profit-transferring entity must give their consent to such a group agreement. If every shareholder must give his or her consent, he or she is sufficiently protected, since the minority shareholders may make their consent contingent upon receiving adequate compensation under the agreement. If one concurs with the opinion that a majority of three quarters of the votes cast in the shareholders' resolution of the dominated or profit-transferring entity is sufficient to enter into a group agreement, the corresponding application of the aforementioned provisions appears to be an adequate means of sufficiently protecting the interests of the minority shareholders. Since, however, according to the prevailing opinion, the consent of any and all shareholders in the dominated or profit-transferring company is required if it wishes to enter into a group agreement (see Section 248), the stronger arguments speak in favour of the non-applicability of the provisions outlined above.

252. Control and profit and loss transfer agreements: legal effects; obligation to transfer profit

The profit-transferring entity under a profit and loss transfer agreement is obliged to transfer its profits to the profit-receiving entity. The maximum profit to be transferred is the annual net income (*Jahresüberschuss*) achieved prior to the transfer of its profits minus any loss carry forwards from the previous year and minus the mandatorily required reserves.[20] A transfer of profits does not occur on the basis of a stand-alone control agreement.

253. Control and profit and loss transfer agreements: legal effects; protection of creditors

Another relevant aspect in relation to control and profit and loss transfer agreements arises in the case of their termination, where, the dominating or profit-receiving company must provide securities to the debtors of the dominated or profit-transferring company if: (i) their claims were established prior to the publication of the registration of the group agreement's termination in the commercial register, and (ii) the creditor demands the provision of such security *vis-à-vis* the dominating or profit-receiving company at the

20 *Aktiengesetz* (AktG) (Stock Corporation Act) 1965, ss300, 301 (FRG) accordingly.

latest six months after the publication in question has been undertaken.[21] The intention behind this provision is to secure the interests of creditors of a dominated company subject to a group agreement and which must transfer its profits or is subject to the instructions of another party. In this regard, until recently it was recognised that when dominated or profit-transferring entities become insolvent or deficient in liquid assets, the creditors of the companies in question may not only claim the provision of securities, but can also directly claim the fulfilment or, respectively, payment of their claims against the dominating or profit-receiving entity.[22] In the meantime, however, the right to a direct claim has been superseded by the legal principle of destructive intervention (*existenzvernichtender Eingriff* – for details see Sections 69 and 262).

254. Control and profit and loss transfer agreements: amendment of group agreements

Any amendment of a group agreement must comply with the same regulations as those which apply when entering into the group agreement. Therefore, all shareholders of the dominated or profit-transferring entity should give their consent to the amendment. The respective shareholders' resolution must be notarised and registered with the commercial register. In the dominating or profit-receiving entity, a qualified majority resolution of three quarters of the votes cast is deemed sufficient.

255. Control and profit and loss transfer agreements: termination of group agreements; statutory reasons

Any group agreement may be terminated at the end of the business year or the contractually agreed accounting period. A termination with retroactive effect is not possible. The termination agreement must be formed in writing.[23]

256. Control and profit and loss transfer agreements: termination of group agreements; termination for cause

Both parties may terminate the group agreement for cause without a notice period.[24] A cause entitling a party to terminate the agreement

---

21 *Aktiengesetz* (AktG) (Stock Corporation Act) 1965, s303, para. 1 (FRG) accordingly.

22 16 September 1995, *Bundesgerichtshof* (German Federal Supreme Court) (II ZR 275/84) – BGH NJW 1986, 188 *et seq*.

23 *Aktiengesetz* (AktG) (Stock Corporation Act) 1965, s296, para. 1 (FRG) accordingly.

24 *Aktiengesetz* (AktG) (Stock Corporation Act) 1965, s297, para. 1 (FRG) accordingly.

is present, in particular, if the other party to the agreement will presumably not be able to fulfil its obligations under the group agreement (eg, to compensate for losses).[25] As a general principle of law, any party may terminate the group agreement for cause if a continuation of the agreement is unacceptable to the terminating party. The courts will take into account any circumstances in the particular case at hand. The termination must be declared in writing.

257. Control and profit and loss transfer agreements: termination of group agreements; ordinary termination

An ordinary termination of a group agreement by way of giving advance notice is not provided for under statutory law. Nevertheless, it is recognised that the parties may agree on provisions in the agreement regarding the ordinary termination thereof. According to the prevailing opinion, a right is not recognised whereby it is possible to terminate the agreement by way of ordinary termination if such a provision is not explicitly provided in the agreement. The parties are of course free at any time to agree on a termination of the agreement by way of a cancellation agreement.

258. Control and profit and loss transfer agreements: termination of group agreements; expiration

Furthermore, a group agreement will automatically be terminated if it was concluded for a limited term and its term expires. In this context, note that group agreements must regularly have a term of at least five years in order to be recognised by the tax authorities (for details see Section 247).

259. Control and profit and loss transfer agreements: termination of group agreements; requirements for shareholders' resolutions

The termination of a group agreement or the conclusion of a prospective termination agreement is effected by the managing directors of the parties to the group agreement. In this regard it is disputed amongst legal scholars whether a shareholders' resolution on the part of the involved companies is required in the event of a termination in order to internally authorise the managing directors

---

25 *Aktiengesetz* (AktG) (Stock Corporation Act) 1965, s297, para. 1, sentence 2 (FRG) accordingly.

to terminate the group agreement, and if so, which majority requirements this should be based on. As regards the dominated or profit-transferring entity, according to the prevailing opinion, it is necessary for a corresponding shareholders' resolution to be passed in this respect. However, there are also those who argue that a shareholder's resolution is not required, as is the case if a group agreement is terminated in situations where a stock corporation is the dominated company. Amongst those who do consider the passing of a shareholders' resolution to be a requirement, there is furthermore considerable disagreement as to what the majority requirements should be for such a resolution. Some scholars demand that the resolution be passed by all shareholders, that is, that the same standard applies as would have been the case when entering into the group agreement. Others consider a majority of three quarters of the votes cast or even a simple majority to be sufficient. There is also disagreement as to whether or not the resolution requires notarisation. Given these considerable uncertainties, in practice it is therefore advisable to obtain the consent of all shareholders of the dominated or profit-transferring GmbH and to have the shareholders' resolution notarised. In any case, the shareholders who are entitled to receive any kind of compensation under the group agreement must give their consent to a respective shareholders' resolution or, alternatively, must pass a special resolution to this effect.[26]

With regard to the dominating or profit-receiving company, there is also no clear line as to whether or not a shareholders' resolution is required and what majority is required in this respect. Therefore, the same majority requirements as those which apply in connection with entering into the agreement (majority of three quarters of the votes cast) should be applied in practice. The respective resolution of the dominating company does not have to be notarised.

The termination of the group agreement must be registered with the commercial register, stating the reason for the termination and the point in time at which the group agreement was terminated.[27] The registration only has a declaratory effect, that is, it is not required in order for the termination to become valid.

---

26 *Aktiengesetz* (AktG) (Stock Corporation Act) 1965, s296, para. 2, s297, para. 2 (FRG).

27 *Aktiengesetz* (AktG) (Stock Corporation Act) 1965, s298 (FRG).

B. Relationships not based on agreement

260. General

Group relationships may also be created and enforced outside of particular group agreements as outlined above. The typical situation which gives rise to a factual group of this kind (*faktischer Konzern*) is when a shareholder holds the majority of the shares in another company without these companies entering into a formal group agreement. The majority or sole shareholder in the dominated company then exercises its/his or her powers within the shareholders' meeting of the subordinated company, or simply as a matter of fact outside of such meetings. Under German law, a distinction is drawn between two different kinds of factual groups. One type is the simple factual group (*einfacher faktischer Konzern*), which is characterised by the fact that the individual measures by which the controlling shareholder influences the dominated company and their resulting specific (negative) consequences may be distinguished individually. If the various measures taken by the company *vis-à-vis* the dominated company can no longer be individually distinguished in terms of their legal and economic consequences, that is, the influence over the dominated company of the dominating company reaches a certain level of density, then such a group relationship is qualified as a qualified factual group (*qualifiziert faktischer Konzern*). The legal consequences associated with these two types of factual group relationships are quite different and will be outlined briefly in the following sections.

261. Simple factual group

The German Stock Corporation Act prescribes certain basic regulations which apply to a simple factual group relationship where a stock corporation is the dominated company.[28] As a general rule, the controlling shareholder is not entitled to inflict any disadvantages upon the dominated company. If it does so nevertheless, it is obliged to grant compensation for the specific disadvantage caused by the controlling shareholder based on its influence in the dominated company. It is, however, generally recognised that these regulations will not apply in a factual relationship wherein the dominated company is a GmbH, since these regulations are too specifically tailored to stock corporations. In addition, the German Act

28 *Aktiengesetz* (AktG) (Stock Corporation Act), 1965, s311 *et seq.* (FRG).

on Limited Liability Companies (section 37 GmbHG) grants a general right to give instructions to the managing directors. This general right to give instructions does not exist in a stock corporation under German law, but only in the case of a control agreement. A general compensation provision for any instruction having a (potentially) negative effect on the GmbH would to a large extent expose the shareholders exercising their instruction right to the possibility of a compensation claim. This is clearly not the intention behind the law.

Rather, the protection of both the dominated company and its minority shareholders is ensured by way of the general duty of loyalty each shareholder has towards the company itself and towards his or her fellow shareholders. The duty of loyalty generally necessitates that business opportunities are exploited for the benefit of the GmbH and that shareholders do not enter into competition with the GmbH. Moreover, a shareholder may not harm the GmbH by his or her behaviour and must pursue and promote the business purpose of the GmbH. Finally, in exercising their rights, shareholders must duly take into account the basic interests of the other shareholders and may not misuse their controlling position to the detriment of other shareholders. A violation of such duties gives rise to a damage claim on the part of the dominated company against the controlling shareholder. Additionally, shareholders' resolutions passed by the majority shareholder in violation of its/his or her duty of loyalty may be challenged by the minority shareholders. The interests of the creditors of the GmbH are also protected indirectly by these mechanisms.

262. Qualified factual group

In a qualified factual group relationship where the individual measures leading to a disadvantage for the dominated entity can no longer be distinguished (which, in practice, would regularly be the case), in principle the controlling shareholder is free to manage the dominated GmbH as it sees fit for its purposes. The provisions regarding group agreements or relating to the simple factual group in the case of a stock corporation as the dominated entity do not apply, not even analogously. Nevertheless, this does not mean that measures may be taken by the controlling shareholder in the GmbH to an unlimited extent. The boundaries with regard to these measures are dictated according to what are defined as acts of interference which lead to the destruction of the economic basis of the GmbH (*existenzvernichtender Eingriff*). In order to qualify as this kind of destructive interference on the part of the controlling shareholder, it is required that a single shareholder, or various shareholders acting in unison, deprive the dominated company of its assets by way of manifest or disguised transfer of assets, or other acts of interference with regard to the assets of the company. As a result of such measures, the dominated GmbH will no longer be able to fulfil its liabilities and is thus no longer able to continue to pursue its business purpose. In other words, the behaviour of the majority shareholder(s) does not take into account the specific purpose of the stated share capital and of the other assets of the GmbH. Their purpose is the satisfaction of the liabilities towards the creditors. Due to the plundering of its assets, the GmbH is pushed towards insolvency and liquidation. Where an intervention is qualified as an intervention which destroys the economic basis of the GmbH, the liability of the controlling shareholder(s) goes beyond the liability required for the maintenance of the stated share capital. The liability also applies if the stated share capital of the GmbH is not affected.

Up until 2007, a destructive intervention (see Section 69) led to a piercing of the corporate veil, with the creditors of the GmbH being entitled to claim damages from the shareholders directly based on the misuse of the legal structure of the GmbH. In 2007, however, the German Federal Supreme Court ruled that a destructive intervention would no longer lead to a piercing of the corporate veil. Instead, it now (only) leads to an internal liability on the part of the shareholders towards the GmbH.[29] The claim of the GmbH towards the interfering shareholder is based on tort law (section 826 German Civil Code). The rule has been confirmed in various subsequent decisions which have since been pronounced.[30] A prerequisite for such a claim is that the shareholder intends to strip the company of its assets with the consequence that the GmbH is no longer able to fulfil its obligations towards its creditors. The creditors of the GmbH may seize the claim of the GmbH towards its shareholder and afterwards pursue the claim directly against the respective shareholder. In contrast to the case where the old law

29 16 July 2007, *Bundesgerichtshof* (German Federal Supreme Court) (II ZR 3/04) – BGHZ 173, 246 *et seq.*

30 For example, 28 April 2008, *Bundesgerichtshof* (German Federal Supreme Court) (II ZR 264/06); 9 February 2009, *Bundesgerichtshof* (German Federal Supreme Court) (II ZR 292/07).

was concerned, this requires that the claim is judicially attached by way of a court proceeding and does not give rise to a direct claim against the shareholder.

Aside from the liability arising from destructive interference, the liability of a shareholder towards its GmbH based on the violation of the regulations pertaining to the maintenance of the stated share capital[31] remains unaffected.[32]

31 *Gesetz betreffend die Gesellschaft mit beschränkter Haftung* (GmbHG) (Act on Limited Liability Companies), 1892, ss30, 31 (FRG).

32 For further details on the maintenance of the share capital see Section 163 *et seq.*

XIV. Liquidation

263. Grounds for liquidation

The Act on Limited Liability Companies lists various grounds which lead to the liquidation of a GmbH by law. These grounds are as follows:

- Expiration of the time period of the GmbH provided in the articles of association.
- A shareholders' resolution to this effect requiring three quarters of the votes cast, if the articles of association do not provide otherwise.
- A court decision or decision of an authority to this effect. A court may render such a decision if it has become impossible to achieve the purpose of the company, or for cause if the cause in question relates to the situation of the GmbH.[1] The motion for cancellation (*Auflösungsklage*) is to be addressed against the GmbH and may be filed by shareholders whose shares in the company amount to at least 10% of the stated share capital.[2]
- Additionally, a GmbH may be liquidated by a court or an authority if it represents a threat to public well-being by way of the shareholders passing illegal resolutions or the managing directors acting illegally with the knowledge of the shareholders.[3] In both of the aforementioned cases, the courts and the authorities must assess whether an exclusion of one or several shareholders is an alternative solution to the problems of the company and whether the GmbH may therefore persist. If the company is liquidated due to it representing a threat to public well-being, the shareholders are not entitled to compensation.[4]

1 *Gesetz betreffend die Gesellschaft mit beschränkter Haftung* (GmbHG) (Act on Limited Liability Companies), 1892, s61, para. 1 (FRG).

2 *Gesetz betreffend die Gesellschaft mit beschränkter Haftung* (GmbHG) (Act on Limited Liability Companies), 1892, s61, para. 2 (FRG).

3 *Gesetz betreffend die Gesellschaft mit beschränkter Haftung* (GmbHG) (Act on Limited Liability Companies), 1892, s62, para. 1 (FRG).

4 *Gesetz betreffend die Gesellschaft mit beschränkter Haftung* (GmbHG) (Act on Limited Liability Companies), 1892, s62, para. 1 (FRG).

- The opening of insolvency proceedings if the insolvency proceedings are not terminated or an insolvency plan is adopted.
- An unappealable court decision by which the opening of insolvency proceedings has been dismissed due to a lack of assets.
- An unappealable decision of the registration court (*Registergericht*) determining that a necessary element of the articles of association is lacking.
- The termination of the company due to a lack of assets.[5]

The articles of association may provide for additional grounds leading to the liquidation of the GmbH.[6] Such reasons could include for instance the achievement of a certain (business) purpose or a certain shareholder reaching a certain age or leaving the company etc. If the articles of association stipulate certain grounds entitling the shareholders to terminate or liquidate the GmbH, it must be carefully examined whether the fulfilment of these conditions should lead to the liquidation of the GmbH as a whole or if only the respective shareholder fulfilling the condition should have the right/obligation to leave the GmbH.

If the grounds leading to a liquidation of the GmbH are eliminated, the shareholders may resolve to continue to operate the not yet fully liquidated company. However, the shareholders may not yet have begun to distribute the assets of the company amongst the shareholders. Otherwise, the rules regarding the raising and maintenance of the stated share capital may be circumvented.[7]

264. Shareholders' resolution

If the liquidation of a GmbH is based on a shareholders' resolution,[8] this resolution requires a majority of three quarters of the votes cast. The articles of association may provide for a different majority. The resolution does not in itself require notarisation. If, however, the shareholders' resolution is combined with other resolutions which

---

5 *Gesetz betreffend die Gesellschaft mit beschränkter Haftung* (GmbHG) (Act on Limited Liability Companies) 1892, s60, para. 1, nos. 1–7 (FRG).

6 *Gesetz betreffend die Gesellschaft mit beschränkter Haftung* (GmbHG) (Act on Limited Liability Companies) 1892, s60, para. 2 (FRG).

7 *Aktiengesetz* (AktG) (Stock Corporation Act), 1965, s274, para. 1 (FRG) accordingly.

8 *Gesetz betreffend die Gesellschaft mit beschränkter Haftung* (GmbHG) (Act on Limited Liability Companies) 1892, s60, para. 1, no. 2 (FRG).

do call for the notarial form, the resolution to liquidate the company must also be notarised. The resolution has real and immediate effect, that is, the registration with the commercial register (see Section 265) only has a declaratory effect.[9] The resolution to liquidate the GmbH does not require particular grounds. However, it can be contested by minority shareholders and will be declared void if the majority shareholders are misusing their voting rights whilst acting in bad faith and thereby breaching their duties of loyalty towards the minority shareholders. This could for example be the case if the only or main purpose of the liquidation is to squeeze out the minority shareholder and a newly founded company of the majority shareholder operating in the same business area assumes the assets and customers of the liquidated GmbH.[10]

265. Registration and publication of liquidation

The liquidation of the company must be registered with the commercial register.[11] The registration only has a declaratory effect. The registration of the liquidation must be published in the company's designated publications (*Gesellschaftsblätter*) (ie, at least in the Electronic Federal Gazette – *elektronischer Bundesanzeiger*) by the liquidators, wherein the creditors of the company are to be requested to contact the GmbH.[12] The opening of the liquidation proceeding itself does not alter the inner organisation of the company.[13] The GmbH maintains its legal identity but changes its business purpose from an ongoing company to liquidation. This means, in particular, that the shareholders maintain their full capacity to amend the articles of association and may give instructions to the managing directors who are now typically acting as liquidators (see next section).

266. Persons responsible for liquidation (liquidators)

By law, the managing directors of a GmbH are also its liquidators, unless the articles of association or a shareholders' resolution

---

9 *Gesetz betreffend die Gesellschaft mit beschränkter Haftung* (GmbHG) (Act on Limited Liability Companies) 1892, s65, para. 1 (FRG).

10 1 February 1989, *Bundesgerichtshof* (German Federal Supreme Court) (II ZR 75 / 07) – BGHZ 103, 184 *et seq.*

11 *Gesetz betreffend die Gesellschaft mit beschränkter Haftung* (GmbHG) (Act on Limited Liability Companies), 1892, s65, para. 1 (FRG).

12 *Gesetz betreffend die Gesellschaft mit beschränkter Haftung* (GmbHG) (Act on Limited Liability Companies), 1892, s65, para. 2 (FRG).

13 *Gesetz betreffend die Gesellschaft mit beschränkter Haftung* (GmbHG) (Act on Limited Liability Companies), 1892, s69, para. 1 (FRG).

provide otherwise.[14] Upon the request of shareholders together holding at least 10% of the stated share capital, the court may appoint other liquidators for cause.[15] This will typically be the case if a managing director/liquidator is thought to be biased, in particular if he or she is the majority shareholder at the same time. The liquidators must be registered with the commercial register by the managing directors of the GmbH.[16] Acting on behalf of the company, the liquidators must supplement the name of the company to show that it is in liquidation (usually using the abbreviation 'iL').[17]

The liquidators are liable towards the GmbH, the shareholders and third parties just as the managing directors are liable. This means, in particular, that they must apply the due care and diligence of a prudent business person and must honour the company payments they make after the company has become deficient in liquid assets.[18]

267. Liquidation proceedings

As the first act to be undertaken, the liquidators must establish an opening balance (*Eröffnungsbilanz*) at the beginning of the liquidation along with a report explaining the opening balance sheet. If the liquidation takes longer than a year, a balance sheet must be prepared following the end of each year in which the liquidation is ongoing along with an annual report (*Lagebericht*).[19] If the GmbH is subject to an auditing requirement, the opening balance sheet must also be audited. However, an audit is not required if a court grants relief from such an obligation. This relief will be granted if the situation of the GmbH appears not to necessitate such an audit in view of the interests of the creditors and the company.[20] Although not

14 *Gesetz betreffend die Gesellschaft mit beschränkter Haftung* (GmbHG) (Act on Limited Liability Companies), 1892, s66, para. 1 (FRG).

15 *Gesetz betreffend die Gesellschaft mit beschränkter Haftung* (GmbHG) (Act on Limited Liability Companies), 1892, s66, para. 2 (FRG).

16 *Gesetz betreffend die Gesellschaft mit beschränkter Haftung* (GmbHG) (Act on Limited Liability Companies), 1892, s67, para. 1 (FRG).

17 *Gesetz betreffend die Gesellschaft mit beschränkter Haftung* (GmbHG) (Act on Limited Liability Companies), 1892, s68, para. 2 (FRG).

18 *Gesetz betreffend die Gesellschaft mit beschränkter Haftung* (GmbHG) (Act on Limited Liability Companies), 1892, s71, paras. 4, 43 paras. 1, 64 (FRG).

19 *Gesetz betreffend die Gesellschaft mit beschränkter Haftung* (GmbHG) (Act on Limited Liability Companies), 1892, s71, para. 1 (FRG).

20 *Gesetz betreffend die Gesellschaft mit beschränkter Haftung* (GmbHG) (Act on Limited Liability Companies), 1892, s71, para. 3 (FRG).

prescribed by statutory law, it is largely held that a final liquidation balance sheet should be prepared if the liquidation proceedings have been terminated.

As well as the preparation of the opening (and closing) balance sheet, it is the liquidators' task to terminate the ongoing transactions, to fulfil the obligations and liabilities of the GmbH, to collect the receivables and to liquidate the assets of the GmbH.[21] In this regard, the GmbH is represented by the liquidators both in and out of court. The liquidators may also enter into new transactions in order to terminate ongoing business. If the last creditors have been satisfied or provided with security and if the last receivables have been collected, the remaining assets of the company may be distributed amongst the shareholders according to their participation in the GmbH in so far as the articles of association do not provide otherwise.[22] However, the distribution is only allowed after a period of one year from the date onwards on which the request to the creditors of the company to indicate their claims against the GmbH was published.[23] If the company is aware of a creditor who has not contacted the company, the outstanding amount must be deposited or the creditor must be provided with security.[24]

After the termination of the liquidation, the GmbH ceases to exist. In this regard there is still disagreement as to whether the GmbH ceases to exist when all existing assets have been distributed or upon the formal act of the cancellation in the commercial register. According to the predominant opinion, the GmbH is only considered fully terminated once all of its assets have been distributed and it has been cancelled in the commercial register. In this context, the liquidators are obliged to register the cancellation of the GmbH with the commercial register once the liquidation process has been terminated.

---

21 *Gesetz betreffend die Gesellschaft mit beschränkter Haftung* (GmbHG) (Act on Limited Liability Companies), 1892, s70 (FRG).

22 *Gesetz betreffend die Gesellschaft mit beschränkter Haftung* (GmbHG) (Act on Limited Liability Companies), 1892, ss72, 73, para. 1 (FRG).

23 *Gesetz betreffend die Gesellschaft mit beschränkter Haftung* (GmbHG) (Act on Limited Liability Companies), 1892, s73, para. 1, s65, para. 2 (FRG).

24 *Gesetz betreffend die Gesellschaft mit beschränkter Haftung* (GmbHG) (Act on Limited Liability Companies), 1892, s73, para. 2 (FRG).

XV. Insolvency

268. General

Under German law, there are two situations in which the management of a GmbH must compulsorily[1] file for insolvency: illiquidity (*Zahlungsunfähigkeit*)[2] and over-indebtedness (*Überschuldung*).[3] These filing obligations serve to protect the (potential) creditors of a GmbH. If the GmbH is in a state of crisis, however, the managing director also has more extensive obligations towards the shareholders. For example, if the GmbH incurs a loss in the amount of half of the registered capital, managers must report this to the shareholders and must call a shareholders' meeting.[4] The managing director faces criminal liability if he or she fails to comply with this reporting duty.[5] The following overview applies to all corporations, including GmbHs.

269. Reasons for filing for insolvency: illiquidity and merely delayed payments

A debtor is deemed illiquid if he or she is unable to satisfy his or her payment obligations. As a rule, illiquidity is assumed if the debtor has ceased payments.[6] This total stoppage of payments must be distinguished from merely delayed payments (*Zahlungsstockung*). According to the Federal Supreme Court, a debtor is deemed to have stopped payments – rather than merely delayed them – when the latter fails to pay at least 90% of his or her mature debts by their due date. Stoppage of payments can also be assumed when the debtor fails to provide payment in due time in areas that are crucial for the latter, for example, wages for employees, key contractors and social security contributions.

---

1 *Insolvenzordnung* (InsO) (Insolvency Ordinance), 1994, s15a (FRG).

2 *Insolvenzordnung* (InsO) (Insolvency Ordinance), 1994, s17 (FRG).

3 *Insolvenzordnung* (InsO) (Insolvency Ordinance), 1994, s19 (FRG).

4 *Gesetz betreffend die Gesellschaft mit beschränkter Haftung* (GmbHG) (Act on Limited Liability Companies), 1892, s49, para. 3 (FRG).

5 *Gesetz betreffend die Gesellschaft mit beschränkter Haftung* (GmbHG) (Act on Limited Liability Companies), 1892, s84 (FRG).

6 *Insolvenzordnung* (InsO) (Insolvency Ordinance), 1994, s17, para. 2, sentence 2 (FRG).

Once debtors have stopped undertaking payments, they can only rebut the assumption of illiquidity if they begin to pay all outstanding and due debts. Payment of the most urgent or largest debts does not refute the assumption.

270. Reasons for filing for insolvency: over-indebtedness

The second general reason for opening insolvency proceedings regarding the assets of a debtor is the status of over-indebtedness. Whereas illiquidity may occur both in the case of individuals and legal entities, over-indebtedness may only occur where legal entities are concerned. Over-indebtedness is deemed to exist if the debtor's assets no longer cover the debtor's existing payment obligations, unless it is highly likely, considering the circumstances, that the respective entity (GmbH) will continue to exist (*Fortführungsprognose*).[7] The question as to whether or not the assets cover the existing payment obligations must be determined from a balance sheet perspective. Over-indebtedness thus consists of two elements: first, the insufficiency of assets for covering the debts according to an actual balance sheet of the GmbH and, secondly, the lack of a positive prognosis for the continuance of the enterprise.

One of the key duties of a managing director of a GmbH is to permanently review the financial status of the GmbH to ensure that it is not in a state of over-indebtedness. The going concern assumption plays a key role here. If there is a going concern assumption, the balance sheet should reflect the assets with their going concern value. If there is no going concern assumption, the managing director must prepare a balance sheet in which the break-up value of the assets is reflected (*Überschuldungsstatus*). The break-up value can be determined by posing the question: what would a third party pay on arm's-length conditions for the single asset? If the assets, assessed this way, still cover the debts, the GmbH is not over-indebted. If, however, the assets no longer cover the payment obligations under this assumption, the GmbH is over-indebted.

In a second step, in line with the going concern assumption, it must be shown that there is a likelihood that the GmbH will be able to continue its business for at least two years. The managing

7 *Insolvenzordnung* (InsO) (Insolvency Ordinance), 1994, s19 (FRG). The InsO definition of over-indebtedness has been amended by the German Financial Markets Stabilisation Act (*Finanzmarktstabilisierungsgesetz*) and the amended definition will apply until 31 December 2013.

director bears the burden of proof in this respect. The manager should therefore keep records of how he or she arrived at the conclusion that there are grounds for a going concern assumption. The German courts will not tolerate a mere fantasy construction. Rather, the records must show in a comprehensible and traceable manner why the prognosis was positive. If it is positive, the company is not over-indebted, even if the assets under a break-up assumption do not cover the debts.[8]

271. Reasons for filing for insolvency: imminent illiquidity

Illiquidity and over-indebtedness constitute the two insolvency grounds (*Insolvenzgründe*) for which it is mandatory for the managing director to file for insolvency within the statutory deadline. Besides these two grounds, it is also possible for the debtor alone (ie, the GmbH) to file for insolvency if the GmbH faces imminent illiquidity (*drohende Zahlungsunfähigkeit*). The debtor is deemed to be facing imminent insolvency if it/he or she is likely to be unable to meet existing payment obligations on the date of their maturity.[9] This insolvency ground is secondary in importance to illiquidity and over-indebtedness. From time to time, however, managing directors file for insolvency on this ground because they are not sure whether or not the GmbH is already insolvent, and they wish to avoid personal liability that could arise from filing for insolvency too late.

272. Competent court

Insolvency must be filed with the competent insolvency court. The competent insolvency court is the local court (*Amtsgericht*) located at the seat of a district court (*Landgericht*). The insolvency court has competence with regard to all insolvency cases occurring within the district of the district court (concentration of competence).[10]

273. Filing obligation and filing right

As outlined above, the managing directors are obliged to file for insolvency in the event of liquidity or over-indebtedness.[11] If they

---

8 In the light of the financial crisis, the aim behind the legislation is that of avoiding insolvency in the case of enterprises to which a going concern assumption applies (*positive Fortführungsprognose*) but which currently find themselves in a situation in which their assets do not cover their debts.

9 *Insolvenzordnung* (InsO) (Insolvency Ordinance) 1994, s18 (FRG).

10 *Insolvenzordnung* (InsO) (Insolvency Ordinance) 1994, s2, para.1 (FRG).

11 *Insolvenzordnung* (InsO) (Insolvency Ordinance) 1994, s15a, para. 1 (FRG).

failed to do so, they would be in breach of their duties as prudent business persons and could be held liable by the GmbH. Timely filing carried out by one managing director is generally deemed sufficient. If the opening of the insolvency proceedings is not filed by all managing directors, the grounds for the latter must be outlined in a plausible way (*Glaubhaftmachung*).[12] Furthermore, the directors have the right to file for insolvency in cases of imminent insolvency (see Section 272).

Situations may occur in which the company has no managing director. The latter may, for example, have laid down his or her position or have been removed by the shareholders' meeting. In the event that the GmbH has no managing directors (either in factual or in legal terms, so-called '*Führungslosigkeit*' (lack of management)), the shareholders of the company are then obliged to file for insolvency.[13] However, this obligation on the part of the shareholders does not exist if they are not aware that the GmbH is illiquid, over-indebted or lacking management.

In addition to the above, the creditors of a GmbH have a right to file for the insolvency of the GmbH in the case of illiquidity or over-indebtedness. Collection authorities for social insurance contributions in particular (*Einzugsstellen für Sozialversicherungsbeiträge*) make use of this right. In almost all cases where it is justified when creditors file for insolvency against the GmbH, the managing director has breached the obligation to file for insolvency in a timely manner.

274. Filing deadline

If the GmbH is illiquid or over-indebted, the managing directors must file for insolvency without undue delay, in any case not later than three weeks after the commencement of illiquidity or a state of over-indebtedness.[14]

This three-week period is an absolute deadline. The managing directors may not fully exhaust this deadline in all circumstances. If there is certainty as regards the existence of grounds for insolvency, the managing directors must file for insolvency immediately. They are only allowed to fully exhaust the three-week deadline if there is a chance that the insolvency grounds will cease to apply or in order

12 *Insolvenzordnung* (InsO) (Insolvency Ordinance) 1994, s15, para. 2 (FRG).
13 *Insolvenzordnung* (InsO) (Insolvency Ordinance) 1994, s15a, para. 3 (FRG).
14 *Insolvenzordnung* (InsO) (Insolvency Ordinance) 1994, s15a, para. 1 (FRG).

to further evaluate whether the insolvency grounds exist. In this critical situation, the managing directors may face a significant risk in terms of personal liability. During this situation, they must not cause the GmbH to make any payments. Only those payments are exempted from this prohibition which a prudent business person would have undertaken in the situation in question. The burden of proof lies with the managing director.[15]

Late filing is a crime which the managing directors or – where there is no management – the shareholders of the company can commit both deliberately and negligently.[16] Endeavours relating to company reorganisation neither extend the three-week deadline nor do they provide an excuse for late filing. This is especially important in cases of over-indebtedness because such insolvency grounds are not easy to determine. Thus, once the managing director becomes aware that the GmbH might be in a state of crisis, he or she should very carefully observe the financial state of the GmbH and should consult professional advisers.

275. Commencement of the deadline period for filing

Whereas illiquidity or over-indebtedness commence irrespective of the knowledge or assessment on the part of the managing director, there is disagreement between the German jurisprudence and legal scholars as to when the filing deadline actually commences. The courts and most scholars tend to assert that the filing deadline in any case begins as soon as the managing director gains positive knowledge of the ground/s for insolvency. However, some argue that this might not be sufficient: it could potentially be too late to protect creditors properly and there could be a risk that the managing director might install mechanisms to protect him or her from gaining positive knowledge in this regard. Moreover, the presence of positive knowledge is hard to prove. Thus, it is commonly understood that the managing director must not ignore what is obvious and must consult professionals who should advise him or her as to the state of the company. Managing directors will only be able to avoid criminal and personal liability if they can show that they have provided

15 *Gesetz betreffend die Gesellschaft mit beschränkter Haftung* (GmbHG) (Act on Limited Liability Companies), 1892, s64, sentence 2 (FRG).

16 *Insolvenzordnung* (InsO) (Insolvency Ordinance) 1994, s15a, paras. 4 and 5 (FRG).

external expert advisers with all the relevant facts and information, that the advisers in question have provided them in turn with a professional opinion, that they have critically reviewed this opinion and thereafter shared the understanding that there is no insolvency and/or over-indebtedness. They should document that they have critically reviewed the opinion provided by external advisers. To this end, they may give a presentation before the shareholders' meeting or the supervisory board and explain their assessment of the situation.

276. Consequences of late filing: personal and criminal liability

The consequences of late filing or the failure to file for insolvency are twofold: the managing director (or the shareholders in charge in lieu of the managing director) faces/face holding both criminal and personal liability.

277. Consequences of late-filing: criminal liability

If the managing director deliberately does not file for insolvency, does not file correctly or files late, he or she will be punished by way of imprisonment for a period of up to three years or will face a fine.[17] If the managing director acts negligently, the punishment would be imprisonment for a period of not more than one year or a fine respectively.[18]

278. Consequences of late-filing: personal liability *vis-à-vis* the GmbH

As regards personal liability, the managing director is in the first place liable *vis-à-vis* the GmbH for payments which he or she has given rise to after the insolvency or over-indebtedness commenced. Managing directors can only avoid this liability if the payments in question are equivalent to those which would also have been made by a prudent business person. The director bears the burden of proof.[19]

17 *Insolvenzordnung* (InsO) (Insolvency Ordinance) 1994, s15a, para. 4 (FRG).
18 *Insolvenzordnung* (InsO) (Insolvency Ordinance) 1994, s15a, para. 5 (FRG).
19 For further details see Section 114.

279. Consequences of late-filing: personal liability *vis-à-vis* the creditors of the GmbH

In the second place, the managing director is liable *vis-à-vis* the creditors of the GmbH in the case of late filing. This liability is again twofold and, in each case, based on tort law.[20]

The creditors already existing at the time insolvency had to be filed can file a claim for damages against the managing director for any damages that arise as a result of the late filing. A consequence of late filing is that the GmbH may have more creditors than it would have at the point in time at which the managing director would have been obliged to file for insolvency. Furthermore, if the filing had occurred in time, the director may have spent less money from the company's accounts, as the insolvency administrator would have stepped in earlier. At the end of insolvency proceedings, all insolvency creditors (*Insolvenzgläubiger*) receive the same percentage of their claim. The percentage therefore decreases if the GmbH has new creditors after the due filing date or less money is available for distribution. The old creditors can thus claim the difference between the percentage they would have received if the managing director had filed insolvency in due time and the percentage they ultimately do receive (*Quotenschaden*).

Parties who become creditors of the GmbH after the point in time at which the managing director should have filed for insolvency can demand their entire claims from the managing director. In most cases, and in addition, the managing director will also face holding criminal liability on the grounds of fraud, as he or she would have misled the creditors regarding the ability of the GmbH to pay its debts. If the creditors had been aware of the insolvent state of the GmbH, they would not have entered into business with it.

280. Consequences of late-filing: personal liability for proceeding costs

The court may refuse to open insolvency proceedings because the remaining assets do not cover the costs of the proceedings (*Abweisung mangels Masse*). However, the court may not refuse to open the proceedings if a sufficient advance payment is made. This advance payment can also be made by a creditor. Following

---

20 *Bürgerliches Gesetzbuch* (BGB) (Civil Code) 1900, s823, para. 2 (FRG) in connection with *Insolvenzordnung* (InsO) (Insolvency Ordinance) 1994, s15a (FRG).

an amendment to the Insolvency Ordinance (InsO) in March 2012, creditors can now claim the reimbursement of an advance payment made by them to cover the costs of the proceedings from a person who culpably failed to file for insolvency in breach of his or her duties. This will typically be the managing director. The person who was obliged to file for insolvency bears the burden of proof that the failure to file in due time did not constitute a breach of his or her duties and was not omitted in a culpable way.[21]

281. Consequences of filing: general

The legal consequences of filing for insolvency are far reaching. In most cases, the court takes its first measures in connection therewith within one day after receiving the motion for opening the proceedings.

282. Consequences of filing: automatic submission of files to the prosecution authorities; typical crimes

The act of filing for insolvency triggers a mechanism which takes effect between the insolvency court which must reach a decision on the opening of the proceedings and the public prosecution authorities. The courts must send a copy of the file to the competent prosecutor *ex officio* (*Mitteilung in Zivilsachen*). The typical investigation carried out by the prosecutor addresses the following:

- Non-payment or late payment of social insurance contributions is a crime in Germany.[22] The managing director must ensure that the employee's portion of social insurance contribution (*Arbeitnehmeranteil an der Sozialversicherung einschließlich der Arbeitsförderung*) is paid to the competent collection bodies (*Einzugsstelle*) in due time. This duty is not dispensed with by way of the employer entering into a wages deferral agreement with the employees. There must be an extra (additional) deferral agreement with the collection bodies. Otherwise, the social contributions are due.
- The books of a GmbH are often not kept accurately in a state of crisis. This is also a crime.[23]
- If the GmbH is in crisis, the managing director must also ensure that he or she does not misrepresent the situation *vis-à-vis* the creditors of the GmbH to the effect that they are

21 *Insolvenzordnung* (InsO) (Insolvency Ordinance) 1994, s26, para. 3 (FRG).
22 *Strafgesetzbuch* (StGB) (Penalty Code) 1998, s266a (FRG).
23 *Strafgesetzbuch* (StGB) (Penalty Code) 1998, ss283, 283b (FRG).

likely to be paid in full and in a timely fashion. If the managing director fails to do this, he or she may be accused of fraud (see Section 279).

- In a state of insolvency, the managing director must ensure that he or she does not fraudulently prefer one creditor over another. This kind of fraudulent preference also constitutes a crime.[24]

If the prosecutor gains knowledge of facts which reasonably indicate that a crime has been committed in the context of the (delayed) filing and opening of the insolvency proceedings, the latter will open criminal proceedings *ex officio*.

283. Consequences of filing: preliminary insolvency administrator

The moment insolvency has been filed, the insolvency court has the right (and the obligation) to take all measures necessary to prevent a (further) reduction of the assets of the GmbH to the detriment of its creditors prior to the issuing of the final decision of the court on whether or not it will open the insolvency proceedings. As one of the first measures, the insolvency court usually appoints a preliminary insolvency administrator (*vorläufiger Insolvenzverwalter*).[25] It can invest the administrator with a wide range of authorities. If the court comes to the conclusion that the management is intact and competent enough to lead the company out of the crisis, the preliminary administrator can play the role of a mere adviser and prepare the report for the final decision on the opening of insolvency proceedings in the background. If the court concludes, however, that the GmbH must be protected from the management in favour of the creditors, it can invest the administrator with full powers. This authority supersedes most of the powers of the managing director, and the GmbH will thereupon only be represented by the preliminary administrator.

284. Consequences of filing: opening of proceedings, appointment of insolvency administrator

The opening of insolvency proceedings requires that a decision to this effect is issued by the insolvency court (*Eröffnungsbeschluß*).[26] Upon the opening of the insolvency proceedings, almost all the

24 *Strafgesetzbuch* (StGB) (Penalty Code) 1998, s283c (FRG).

25 *Insolvenzordnung* (InsO) (Insolvency Ordinance) 1994, s21 (FRG).

26 *Insolvenzordnung* (InsO) (Insolvency Ordinance) 1994, s27 (FRG).

powers of the managing directors are vested in the insolvency administrator by law. The power to dispose of the assets of the GmbH then lies solely with the insolvency administrator.[27]

The opening of the insolvency proceedings also entails the liquidation of the company (*Auflösung*).[28] This means that the purpose of the company changes from the purpose as laid down in the articles of association to the purpose of terminating the company. Notification of the opening of the insolvency proceedings is given in the commercial register (*Insolvenzvermerk*). If restructuring measures initiated by the insolvency administrator fail, the assets must be sold, and the money must be distributed amongst the creditors of the company pursuant to a statutory procedure. Subsequent to this procedure, the company will be deleted from the commercial register and as a consequence will cease to exist. The management will often remain in charge during restructuring measures. This depends on the chances of the revitalisation of the company and upon the insolvency administrator.

285. Consequences of filing: dismissal of opening of insolvency proceedings due to lack of assets

When the insolvency court comes to the conclusion that the GmbH does not dispose of sufficient assets to even cover the costs of the insolvency proceedings, it may refuse to open them. In such cases, the GmbH will immediately be liquidated without an insolvency administrator being appointed and without any attempts to restructure the company.[29]

286. Filing alternatives

In a crisis closely approaching insolvency in the case of a GmbH, there are basically two alternatives to filing for insolvency.

First, the illiquidity or over-indebtedness can be reversed. The shareholders may contribute fresh money into the GmbH. If they do not wish to do this, there are several other mechanisms for achieving such a reversal. For example, the due date of claims *vis-à-vis* the company can be altered by way of a postponement agreement between the company and the respective creditor. Over-indebtedness is more

---

27 *Insolvenzordnung* (InsO) (Insolvency Ordinance) 1994, s80 (FRG).

28 *Gesetz betreffend die Gesellschaft mit beschränkter Haftung* (GmbHG) (Act on Limited Liability Companies) 1892, s60, para. 1, no. 4 (FRG).

29 *Gesetz betreffend die Gesellschaft mit beschränkter Haftung* (GmbHG) (Act on Limited Liability Companies) 1892, s60, para. 1, no. 5 (FRG).

difficult to reverse. In view of the aforementioned consequences associated with late filing, the managing directors should in any case consult expert advisers with experience in dealing with insolvency law issues.

If attempts to reverse insolvency and/or over-indebtedness should fail, one possible option would be to commence a statutory dissolving procedure (*Auflösung*). This, however, requires settlement with the creditors of the company[30] which might not be attainable.

287. Typical claims asserted by insolvency administrators

There are typically two kinds of claim which insolvency administrators will generally seek to establish a basis for once insolvency proceedings have been opened: disguised contributions in kind (*verdeckte Sacheinlage*)[31] and payments back and forth (*Hin- und Herzahlen*).[32] In both cases, the contributions towards the stated share capital might not have been properly made by the shareholders. The shareholders would then be obliged to pay in their contribution anew/for the first time. This would give rise to a claim on the part of the company against its shareholder/s. The insolvency administrator would demand payment in this regard on behalf of the company.

288. Typical claims asserted by insolvency administrators: disguised contribution in kind

Shareholders can fund the company or effect a capital increase by contributing an asset to the company in the place of cash. However, the asset must at least cover the amount that is stipulated in the founding documents or the resolution on the capital increase, respectively. For example, if the shareholders agree in the articles to establish the GmbH with a registered capital of €100,000 and they wish to transfer, for example, IP rights, real estate or claims to the company in order to fulfil this obligation, the shareholders must ensure that the respective asset has a value of at least the stated amount and does not negatively deviate therefrom. A similar situation is given if there is a capital increase: the value of the asset

---

30 *Gesetz betreffend die Gesellschaft mit beschränkter Haftung* (GmbHG) (Act on Limited Liability Companies) 1892, s70 (FRG).

31 *Gesetz betreffend die Gesellschaft mit beschränkter Haftung* (GmbHG) (Act on Limited Liability Companies) 1892, s19, para. 4 (FRG).

32 *Gesetz betreffend die Gesellschaft mit beschränkter Haftung* (GmbHG) (Act on Limited Liability Companies) 1892, s19, para. 5 (FRG).

must at least match the promised increase. The justification in this regard must be outlined and prepared by an accountant, and it must be disclosed.

As regards the disguised contribution in kind, the situation is as follows: if a contribution in cash must be considered – from an economic perspective – as a contribution in kind, and there is a respective agreement that the shareholder wishes to contribute an asset to the company rather than the promised cash, this contribution will not release the shareholder from his or her obligation to contribute in cash. The value of the contribution in kind will, however, be deducted from the shareholder's obligation to pay in his or her contribution in cash.[33] In practice, the typical scenario as regards disguised contributions in kind is as follows: the shareholder has granted a loan to the company in the past. Now, he or she decides to increase the registered capital of the company by way of a contribution in cash. The company then passes a shareholder's resolution that, ostensibly, appears to relate to a proper capital increase by means of a contribution in cash. Thereafter, the shareholder pays in the money he or she promised to contribute in the shareholder's resolution to increase the registered capital. Soon after, the company pays the loan back to the shareholder. The actual contribution in such a case would, then, not be the cash paid in, but the claim for repayment of the loan. In such cases, the company retains its claim against the shareholder to pay in the contribution in cash. The insolvency administrator will demand a second payment from the shareholder and may sue him or her accordingly. The Federal Supreme Court has consistently ruled in such cases that there is an assumption that the shareholder wished to contribute an asset rather than the promised cash if both the payment of the contribution and the repayment of the loan take place in quick succession.[34] This close temporal context can be assumed if the payments in both directions occur within a time period of six to eight months. If the shareholder cannot rebut this assumption, the only way to avoid a ruling being pronounced against him or her would be the ability to show that the claim for the repayment

33 *Gesetz betreffend die Gesellschaft mit beschränkter Haftung* (GmbHG) (Act on Limited Liability Companies) 1892, s19, para. 4 (FRG). For further details on the concept of disguised contributions in kind see Section 161.

34 16 September 2002, *Bundesgerichtshof* (German Federal Supreme Court) (II ZR 1/00) – BGHZ 152, 37 *et seq.*

of the loan was covered by the assets of the company (*werthaltiger Darlehensrückzahlungsanspruch*).[35]

289. Typical claims asserted by insolvency administrators; back-and-forth payment

The shareholder might also be obliged to pay back his or her contribution a second time in connection with a back-and-forth payment (*Hin- und Herzahlen*).[36] In such a scenario, the shareholder and the GmbH agree prior to the effecting of the contribution that the company will provide to the shareholder a service in return which, from an economic point of view, equals the repayment of the contribution of the shareholder, but cannot be qualified as a disguised contribution in kind. If such an agreement exists, the shareholder is only freed from the obligation to pay the contribution (anew) if the repayment of the contribution to the shareholder is covered by a fully recoverable repayment claim (*vollwertiger Rückzahlungsanspruch*), which is due at any time or which may become due at any time upon immediate termination by the GmbH. An agreement to this effect must be disclosed to the respective court maintaining the commercial register. This kind of agreement typically exists between the GmbH and its shareholder in connection with a cash pool.

290. Consequences for cash pooling systems

The shareholders must pay particular attention in this regard if there is a cash pooling system between the company and its subsidiaries. If a group operates a cash pool on a zero-balancing basis and the parent is the entity operating the cash pool, technically it grants a loan to the subsidiary which is in need of cash. In the context of a capital increase, this can mean that the subsidiary pays a loan back to the parent company within the time frame mentioned above. In connection with a disguised contribution in kind, the courts would then assume that the parent company wished to contribute its claim for repayment, rather than cash. The only solution in this situation would be to follow the steps outlined above (back-and-forth payment) which are designed to help the parent company in this situation. However, there is still a risk. The repayment claim may

---

35 *Gesetz betreffend die Gesellschaft mit beschränkter Haftung* (GmbHG) (Act on Limited Liability Companies) 1892, s19, para. 4 (FRG).

36 *Gesetz betreffend die Gesellschaft mit beschränkter Haftung* (GmbHG) (Act on Limited Liability Companies) 1892, s19, para. 5 (FRG). For further details see also Section 162.

not be fully recoverable at any time, or the involved parties may fail to disclose the arrangement to the respective court maintaining the commercial register. They might have their reasons for this (non-disclosure of a cash pooling system) or they may simply forget to do so. The surest way to avoid this situation is to pay the contribution in cash into an account of the subsidiary that is excluded from the cash pool. This might be impractical. However, the Federal Supreme Court does appear to demand this from the shareholders of GmbHs that are part of a cash pooling system.[37]

291. Reform of the Insolvency Ordinance: general

With effect as of March 2012, the Insolvency Ordinance was amended quite significantly in several areas. The following provides an overview of the most relevant changes to the law in so far as they have not yet been outlined above.

292. Reform of the Insolvency Ordinance: preliminary board of creditors

The motion to open insolvency proceedings must now be much more detailed than it had to be in the past. It must contain an overview of the creditors (from the highest claims to the lowest claims and including claims of the tax authorities and the social security systems) and it must disclose which creditors are unsecured and which are secured.[38] This should serve to place the court in a position to appoint a preliminary board of creditors (*vorläufiger Gläubigerausschuss*).

The preliminary board of creditors should play a key role in the decision-making process regarding who the court appoints as insolvency administrator.[39] In the past, neither the creditors nor the GmbH could exert any influence on this crucial decision. The court's decision was barely contestable. Complaints were often made that the court appointed insolvency administrators who did not understand the business of the company or were generally unsuitable due to other circumstances. Now, the court, prior to nominating an insolvency administrator, must hear the preliminary board of creditors regarding the qualifications and the person of the administrator.

37 20 July 2009, *Bundesgerichtshof* (German Federal Supreme Court) (II ZR 273/07) – BGHZ 182, 103 *et seq*. For details see also Section 161.

38 *Insolvenzordnung* (InsO) (Insolvency Ordinance) 1994, s13 (FRG).

39 *Insolvenzordnung* (InsO) (Insolvency Ordinance) 1994, ss22a, 56a (FRG).

The court may not dismiss any administrator proposed by the preliminary board of creditors unanimously unless the proposed person is not suitable for the task. Thus, the amendment of the Insolvency Ordinance in this respect is profoundly significant. The concern is, however, that the biggest creditors, that is, mostly banks, will determine who the insolvency administrator is to be. This might prove detrimental to the interests of smaller creditors.

293. Reform of the Insolvency Ordinance: coercive debt to equity swap; other corporate measures

The insolvency proceedings may – at least to a certain extent – deviate from the insolvency proceedings as envisaged in the insolvency ordinance if an insolvency plan (*Insolvenzplan*) is established.[40] The plan must be submitted to the insolvency court either by the insolvency administrator or by the debtor and it must be approved by the creditors. The board of creditors may advise the administrator while establishing the plan along with the works council and the debtor itself. The insolvency plan may now provide that the claims of the creditors against the company are mandatorily swapped into shares in the company (coercive debt to equity swap).

In addition, the insolvency plan may set out every measure that is possible under corporate law, in particular the mandatory transfer of shares outside of the debt-equity swap. This allows for a significant change in the shareholder structure in an insolvent company if the creditors consider this an appropriate measure. Change in control clauses in existing contracts of the GmbH are waived by law; the contractors of the GmbH cannot terminate the contracts with the GmbH due to the changes in terms of the shareholder structure on the basis of this debt-to-equity swap provided for in the insolvency plan.[41]

294. Reform of the Insolvency Ordinance: reform of insolvency plan law

The legislation pertaining to the insolvency plan has been fundamentally reformed with the aim of facilitating restructuring measures. Creditors will now be able to install a trustee (*Sachwalter*) under certain conditions, rather than having the court appoint an insolvency administrator. This basically allows the current

---

40 *Insolvenzordnung* (InsO) (Insolvency Ordinance) 1994, s217 (FRG).

41 *Insolvenzordnung* (InsO) (Insolvency Ordinance) 1994, s225a (FRG).

administration of the company to retain control, albeit under the control of the trustee. If insolvency proceedings are opened due to over-indebtedness or impending insolvency, the GmbH may motion for protection against foreclosure (protective shield – *Schutzschirmverfahren*). The court can grant this protection in order to allow the GmbH to work out a detailed insolvency plan within a period of up to three months.[42] The prerequisites for this measure, however, are in particular that it is not to the detriment of the creditors and that the intended restructuring of the company is not obviously futile.

42 *Insolvenzordnung* (InsO) (Insolvency Ordinance) 1994, s270 *et seq.* (FRG).

XVI. GmbH & Co. KG

A. Overview

295. General

The GmbH & Co. KG is by its nature not a limited liability company under the German Act on Limited Liability Companies (GmbHG), but a limited partnership (*Kommanditgesellschaft* – KG) under the German Commercial Code (*Handelsgesetzbuch* – HGB). Nevertheless, as can be seen from the company's trade name, the GmbH is an essential part of this limited partnership. It is a mixture of a company with limited liability (the GmbH) and a limited partnership (the KG). The aim behind this form of company is to combine the advantages of both kinds of legal entity.

Despite giving rise to controversy when it first appeared at the beginning of the 20th century, the GmbH & Co. KG has become one of the most important and widely recognised legal entities within Germany. From a statistical point of view, the GmbH & Co. KG is now the third most popular legal entity in Germany with about 200,000 existing companies of this type.[1] Even though a GmbH & Co. KG is subject to the regulations prescribed for limited partnerships under the German Commercial Code, its basic principles and in particular the role of the GmbH in such an entity will be briefly outlined in the following pages.

296. Types of partners

A limited partnership under German law has two different kinds of partners: general partners (*Komplementäre* or *persönlich haftende Gesellschafter*) and limited partners (*Kommanditisten*). A KG must have at least one general partner and one limited partner. There is no limit regarding the number of general or limited partners where the company has more than one of each category.

The general partners are jointly and severally liable with all their assets for all the liabilities of the limited partnership,[2] whereas the

1 Binz/Sorg, *Die GmbH & Co. KG*, 12th edition (2018), s1, Rn. 39.
2 *Handelsgesetzbuch* (HGB) (German Commercial Code) 1897, s161, para. 1, 128 (FRG).

limited partners are only liable pursuant to the amount of liability they have assumed in the articles of association of the KG.[3]

Furthermore, the general partners are the only partners who are entitled by law to manage and represent the KG,[4] whereas the limited partners are by law excluded from acting as managers and representatives on behalf of the company.[5]

297. Types of partnerships

A GmbH & Co. KG may have various structures as regards the participations held in the company and the purpose it is created for.

The structure most commonly chosen is one in which the shareholders of the GmbH and the limited partners of the KG are identical and hold the same percentages of shares in the GmbH and in the KG (a so-called genuine (*echte*) GmbH & Co.). One variation of this form of genuine GmbH & Co. is the so-called One-person GmbH & Co. KG. In this case, the sole shareholder of the GmbH is at the same time the sole limited partner. This structure has been recognised by the courts.

Alternatively, it is possible to establish a GmbH & Co. KG wherein the shareholders of the GmbH and the limited partners of the KG are either different persons and/or their shareholdings in the entities are different. This may be the case if certain shareholders are not meant to have any influence on the management or representation of the company (for more details see Section 303). Another permissible construction is one wherein one GmbH acts as general partner in several different GmbH & Co. KGs (a so-called star-like (*sternförmige*) GmbH & Co. KG). Another situation which can be found frequently is where the KG itself is sole shareholder in the GmbH, meaning in its general partner. This so-called '*Einheits GmbH & Co.*' (Unitary GmbH & Co), where the limited partners have contributed their shares in the GmbH into the KG, has also been accepted by the courts. However, according to the German Commercial Code it is not acceptable that the contribution of the limited partners (*Kommanditeinlage*) is effected via shares in the general partner, unless there is at least one natural person who is unlimitedly liable towards the creditors of the company.[6] In other words,

3 *Handelsgesetzbuch* (HGB) (German Commercial Code) 1897, s171 (FRG).
4 *Handelsgesetzbuch* (HGB) (German Commercial Code) 1897, s161, paras. 2, 116, 125 (FRG).
5 *Handelsgesetzbuch* (HGB) (German Commercial Code) 1897, ss164, 170 (FRG).
6 *Handelsgesetzbuch* (HGB) (German Commercial Code) 1897, s172, para. 6 (FRG).

the contributions of the limited partners in such a situation would have to be made in the form of assets other than the shares in the general partner (ie, additional assets). The advantage of this kind of *Einheits-GmbH & Co.* is, in the first place, that the articles of association of both the GmbH and the KG can be kept simple. Secondly, a transfer of the whole GmbH & Co. KG is simpler since a transfer of the shares of the limited partners is sufficient for this purpose (for more details see Section 306).

298. The GmbH & Co. KG and the *Publikumsgesellschaft* (publicly owned company)

Aside from the types of shareholdings in a GmbH & Co. KG listed above, a distinction is usually also drawn between the 'regular' type of GmbH & Co. KG and the so-called '*Publikumsgesellschaft*' (publicly owned company). From a legal point of view, a *Publikumsgesellschaft* is a partnership, typically in the form of a GmbH & Co. KG, although this is not a legal requirement. The purpose of the company is to collect equity from an indeterminate number of limited partners based on a standard partnership agreement which the limited partners must sign. The participation of the limited partners is thus purely financial in nature. Since *Publikumsgesellschaften* therefore (in economic terms) closely approximate a corporation, a set of particular applicable rules have been developed within the jurisprudence in their regard. The general rules applying to limited partnerships will be outlined below, wherein the particular regulations applicable to the *Publikumsgesellschaft* will be addressed at the end of this chapter.

299. Advantages of a GmbH & Co. KG: limitation of liability and flexible structure

Even though a GmbH offers a lot of flexibility in terms of being able to adapt the internal structures of the company to the needs of the shareholders,[7] the German Commercial Code allows an even greater degree of discretion when it comes to limited partnerships.[8] To give some examples here: the articles of association of the limited partnership do not have to be filed with the commercial register,[9] and

---

7 *Gesetz betreffend die Gesellschaft mit beschränkter Haftung* (GmbHG) (Act on Limited Liability Companies), 1892, s45, para. 2 (FRG).

8 *Handelsgesetzbuch* (HGB) (German Commercial Code) 1897, s109 (FRG).

9 *Handelsgesetzbuch* (HGB) (German Commercial Code) 1897, s161, paras. 2, 106 (FRG).

the rules pertaining to the distribution and extraction of profits (*Entnahmerecht*) can be drafted much more flexibly than in the case of a GmbH. In addition, and depending on the precise tax situation of the investors involved, the GmbH & Co. KG may also entail certain tax advantages compared with a straightforward GmbH.[10]

299a. Advantages of a GmbH & Co. KG: avoidance of co-determination

Under the One Third Employee Participation Act (*Drittelbeteiligungsgesetz*), companies which regularly employ more than 500 (but below 2,000) employees, must mandatorily establish a supervisory board. The employees of such companies are entitled to elect one third of the members of the supervisory board. This applies to a simple GmbH as outlined under Section 141 *et seq*. The One Third Employee Participation Act, however, does not cover limited partnerships, and therefore also not a GmbH & Co. KG. Thus, if co-determination is to be avoided, it is possible to either convert an existing GmbH into a GmbH & Co. KG under the German Law Regulating the Transformation of Companies or to establish the entity as a GmbH & Co. KG from the outset.

The situation is different under the Co-Determination Act (*Mitbestimmungsgesetz*). The Co-Determination Act provides that entities which generally employ more than 2,000 employees must mandatorily establish a supervisory board wherein half of the members are elected by the employees (parity). The Co-Determination Act provides for a special regulation on limited partnerships,[11] namely that if a GmbH (or also an AG) is the general partner of a KG, and the majority of the limited partners holds the majority of the shares or of the votes of the general partner, the employees of the limited partnership are considered to be employees of the general partner, that is, the GmbH. The GmbH then becomes co-determined according to the principles set out under Section 148 *et seq*. As outlined above, this is a typical structure for a GmbH & Co. KG, so that it is often the case that a supervisory board must be established within the GmbH if the GmbH & Co. KG has more than 2,000 employees. However, an exception applies here if the GmbH

---

10 For details see Binz/Sorg, *Die GmbH & Co. KG*, 12th edition (2018), ss16 *et seq*.

11 *Gesetz über die Mitbestimmung der Arbeitnehmer* (MitbestG) (Co-Determination Act) 1976, s4 (FRG).

itself employs more than 500 employees, whereby it is thus itself subject to the One Third Employee Participation Act.

299b. Advantages of a GmbH & Co. KG: third-party management

Under the German Commercial Code, a limited partnership is managed and represented by its general partners, and its general partners only.[12] The general partner in a GmbH & Co. KG is, however, the GmbH. A GmbH does not necessarily have to be run by its shareholders acting as directors. The GmbH may be run by an external third party based on a service agreement with the company.[13] Since the GmbH may engage a non-shareholder as its managing director, in his or her capacity as the director of the GmbH, the third party in question also represents the KG. The GmbH & Co. KG may thus establish third party management.

B. General rules pertaining to a GmbH & Co. KG

300. Establishment

Like any other legal entity, a GmbH & Co. KG necessitates the establishment of articles of association. The articles of association are to be negotiated between the intended shareholders of the company, that is, between the limited and the general partners. The articles of association of a limited partnership – unlike those of a GmbH – do not have to be notarised. The same applies to the articles of association of a GmbH & Co. KG. With respect to the establishment of the GmbH as general partner, the general rules as set forth under Sections 4, 5 *et seq.* apply. This means, in particular, that the articles of the GmbH must be notarised.

The GmbH & Co. KG must be registered with the commercial register.[14] The application must contain the first and family name, date of birth and domicile of each shareholder, the trading name of the company, its place of business, its domestic business address and the power of representation of the shareholders. In addition, the application must contain the names of the limited partners and the amount of their subscription (*Kommanditeinlage*).[15] The shareholders must also file certain amendments to the articles such

---

12 *Handelsgesetzbuch* (HGB) (German Commercial Code) 1897, ss164, 170, 114, 125, 126 (FRG).

13 For details see Section 98 *et seq.*

14 *Handelsgesetzbuch* (HGB) (German Commercial Code) 1897, ss160, 161, para. 2, 106 (FRG).

15 *Handelsgesetzbuch* (HGB) (German Commercial Code) 1897, s162, para. 1 (FRG).

as changes in terms of the company's trading name, its place of business, domestic business address, the admission of a new shareholder or a change in terms of the power of representation of a shareholder.[16] If the contribution of a limited partner is increased or reduced, this increase must also be registered with the Commercial Register.[17]

301. Liability towards third parties

When discussing the liability of a GmbH & Co. KG towards third parties, a distinction must be drawn between four potential types of liability.

301a. Liability towards third parties: liability of a GmbH & Co. KG

The company itself is unlimitedly liable with its total assets for third party liabilities, irrespective of their legal grounds, unless the law or contractual provisions stipulate otherwise. It should be noted that in the case of both a limited partnership and a general partnership (*offene Handelsgesellschaft* – OHG), there is no stated capital, nor is this required.

301b. Liability towards third parties: liability of the general partners

General partners in a KG are personally, unlimitedly, jointly and severally liable for any and all obligations of the GmbH & Co. KG towards its creditors.[18] The creditors of the limited partnership are entitled to directly claim payment from the general partners without first having to claim payment from the limited partnership. Since a limited partnership does not have any stated share capital, the liability of the general partners towards the creditors is unlimited. In the GmbH & Co. KG, however, the general partner is a GmbH. The liability of a GmbH as a general partner in a KG is no different from that of a straightforward GmbH. Thus the liability of the general partner is limited to the assets owned by the GmbH. If the GmbH as the general partner for instance does not have more assets than its minimum stated share capital of €25,000, the liability of the GmbH will be limited to this amount. The shareholders of the GmbH itself may not be personally held liable, or only under very exceptional circumstances (for details see

---

16 *Handelsgesetzbuch* (HGB) (German Commercial Code) 1897, s161, paras. 2, 107 (FRG).

17 *Handelsgesetzbuch* (HGB) (German Commercial Code) 1897, s175 (FRG).

18 *Handelsgesetzbuch* (HGB) (German Commercial Code) 1897, s161, paras. 2, 128 (FRG).

Section 65 *et seq*). Ultimately, the structure of a corporation as a general partner results in the limitation of liability of the GmbH & Co. KG to the assets of the GmbH and of the KG (including the contributions of the limited partners). This contradicts the primary understanding of partnerships under German law, namely that at least one natural person is unlimitedly liable for the obligations of the partnership. This factual limitation of liability by using the structure of the GmbH & Co. KG, has, however, been accepted by law and the courts for over a century now.

301c. Liability towards third parties: liability of the limited partners

The liability of the limited partners towards third parties is limited to the amount of the contribution they subscribed for under the articles of association. The amount of their contribution must be registered with the commercial register.[19] As long as the contribution has not yet been fully paid in to the KG, the creditors of the KG may claim direct payment from the limited partner to the extent of the amount of contribution subscribed for in the articles. If the contribution subscribed for has been paid in in full by the limited partner, he or she may no longer be held directly liable by the creditors of the company personally, but only indirectly by way of his or her contribution paid in to the KG. [20] The personal liability of the limited partner, however, revives if and to the extent the contribution paid in is repaid in whole or in part to the limited partner.[21] In exceptional cases, however, the limited partner may be held unlimitedly and personally liable for the obligations of the KG. This occurs if the company has commenced its business operations with the consent of the respective limited partner prior to the registration of the KG with the commercial register.[22]

The liability of the limited partner towards third parties and as shown in the commercial register (*Hafteinlage*) must be distinguished from the amount the limited partner is obliged to contribute to the KG under the articles of association (*Pflichteinlage*). If the *Pflichteinlage* is higher than the *Hafteinlage*, this means that the limited partner participates in the losses of the company with a higher amount than the sum indicated in the commercial register.

19 *Handelsgesetzbuch* (HGB) (German Commercial Code) 1897, s162, para. 1 (FRG).
20 *Handelsgesetzbuch* (HGB) (German Commercial Code) 1897, s71, para. 1 (FRG).
21 *Handelsgesetzbuch* (HGB) (German Commercial Code) 1897, s172, para. 4 (FRG).
22 *Handelsgesetzbuch* (HGB) (German Commercial Code) 1897, s176, para. 1 (FRG).

The creditors of the company, however, are not entitled to claim direct payment from the limited partner in the amount of the difference between the *Hafteinlage* and the *Pflichteinlage*. It is only the KG which has the right to claim this additional payment from the limited partner, if the limited partner has also not paid in the difference between the *Hafteinlage* and the *Pflichteinlage* in full. Towards third parties, the limited partner is in any case only liable up to the amount of the *Hafteinlage*, if this amount has not (yet) been fully paid in.[23]

302. Liability towards third parties: liability of the managing directors of a GmbH

Regarding the liability of the directors of the general partner (*Komplementär*), the same principles as those set forth under Section 112 *et seq.* apply. For particular requirements/details as regards applicability within a GmbH & Co. KG, see Section 304 below.

303. Management and representation

According to section 164 of the German Commercial Code, the limited partners are excluded by law from managing the company. The same applies to the representation of the company (section 170, German Commercial Code). In this regard, the law stipulates that it is the general partner who is responsible for managing and representing the company.[24] This principle reflects the idea that the shareholder or partner who is personally and unlimitedly liable for the obligations of the company should also be entitled to run the company. The aforementioned provisions regarding the exclusion of the limited partners from the management and representation of the GmbH & Co. KG, however, do not prohibit the limited partners from being granted the power to manage the company under the articles of association. It is also possible that the limited partners are granted power of attorney or even proxy to legally represent the company. In this way, they may thus give rise to obligations on the part of the company despite their limited liability. However, the flexibility of the legal nature of the limited partnership allows for such an arrangement. The power of the general partner to manage and represent the company, however, may thereby not be excluded.

---

23 *Handelsgesetzbuch* (HGB) (German Commercial Code) 1897, s172, para. 1 (FRG).

24 *Handelsgesetzbuch* (HGB) (German Commercial Code) 1897, s161, paras. 2, 114, 125, 126 (FRG).

The right to manage and the liability for obligations may not be separated in partnerships under German law.

Since the general partner in a GmbH & Co. KG is the GmbH, the GmbH itself is represented by its managing directors.[25] The directors of the GmbH thus manage the business of the GmbH as well as the business of the KG as its general partner. If, as is typically the case, the sole purpose of the GmbH is to run the business of the KG, the processes of running the business of the GmbH and of the KG are almost identical.

304. Liability of the directors of the GmbH

As outlined above, the directors of the GmbH are by law also representatives of the GmbH & Co. KG. They are liable towards the GmbH in accordance with the principles set forth under Section 112 *et seq*. The German Commercial Code does not stipulate a provision regarding the liability of the director of the GmbH running the business of the GmbH & Co. KG. Typically, the director of the GmbH has entered into a service agreement with the GmbH itself, and only in rare cases with the KG, wherein it is usually only the GmbH which has a right to give instructions to the managing director, but not the KG.[26] The shareholders of the GmbH, though, may also give instructions regarding the business of the KG, since this is also part of the business of the GmbH and is therefore covered by the instruction rights of the shareholders of a GmbH. It is, however, possible that a right to give instructions is granted to the KG or even a limited partner within the articles of association of the KG.

The managing director of a GmbH, whose primary task is the management of the GmbH & Co. KG, may be liable towards the GmbH & Co. KG itself based on a violation of the latter's service agreement with the GmbH in the event that he or she should be in breach of his or her obligations as a prudent business person. The service agreement between the GmbH and the director has a protective effect for third parties (*Vertrag mit Schutzwirkung für Dritte*). The KG may thus have a direct damage claim against the managing director in the event that he or she violates his or her obligations to properly manage the KG. The same applies, of course, if the service agreement is entered into with the KG itself.

---

25 For details see Section 101 *et seq.*

26 *Gesetz betreffend die Gesellschaft mit beschränkter Haftung* (GmbHG) (Act on Limited Liability Companies) 1892, s37, para. 1 (FRG).

305. Shareholders' resolutions

The law on partnerships does not stipulate specific rules on how shareholders' resolutions are to be passed. The partners are therefore free to determine the formal proceedings pertaining to the convening and holding of the shareholders' meeting. Shareholders resolutions which are defective are generally deemed null and void, unless the articles provide otherwise. The German Commercial Code does not distinguish between resolutions which are merely contestable and void resolutions. The principles of the Stock Corporation Act (section 240 *et seq*, German Stock Corporation Act – AktG) do not apply here.

The law stipulates that shareholders' resolutions in a partnership (and therefore also in a GmbH & Co. KG) must be passed unanimously.[27] The articles of association may, however, provide that resolutions may also be passed with the majority of the votes cast.[28] Resolutions which may be passed with a majority of the votes cast are, however, subject to certain restrictions. If the articles of association only provide for a general majority rule, such a rule shall only cover resolutions on ongoing (regular) business matters and ordinary subject matters. In particular, it is not permissible that the articles of association may be amended based on such a simple majority clause, since such an amendment to the articles of association is not considered part of the regular business of a company. The same would apply to changes in terms of the partnership (admission/dismissal of partners).

If the partners wish for resolutions to be passed on matters outside of the ordinary course of business by a majority of the votes cast, these subject matters must be specified in sufficient detail within the articles of association themselves (*Bestimmtheitsgrundsatz*). The reason for this is that the partners must be clearly aware of the cases in which they may be overruled in a shareholders' resolution and how this would affect their situation within the company. Since it is difficult to distinguish what is merely a part of the ordinary course of business and what goes beyond this, it is necessary to use sufficient diligence in specifying the subject matters in regard to which a resolution may be passed by way of a majority resolution.

---

27 *Handelsgesetzbuch* (HGB) (German Commercial Code) 1897, s161, paras. 2, 119, para. 1 (FRG).

28 *Handelsgesetzbuch* (HGB) (German Commercial Code) 1897, s161, paras. 2, 119, para. 2 (FRG).

Irrespective of the specification thereof in the articles of association, there are certain core elements (*Kernbereiche*) associated with the position as a partner. Resolutions relating to these core elements are thus only possible with the consent of the affected shareholder. Core elements are, for example, the amendment of the articles of association (apart from simple changes thereto which may be covered by the majority clause), the granting and revoking of specific partner rights in the company, an increase in existing or additional contributions to the company or encroachments upon the voting and profit rights of a partner. The provision regarding the core elements rule is independent of the majority rule as outlined above. In cases where the consent of a partner is required, this may be granted either in the articles of association or *ad hoc* when the specific resolution is to be passed.

306. Transfer of shares

With regard to the transfer of an interest in the GmbH & Co. KG, it is necessary to distinguish between whether the share of a limited partner in the KG or a share in the general partner (ie, the GmbH) is to be transferred.

Where the transfer of a limited partner's share is concerned, the share may be transferred either to another (general or limited) partner of the company or to a third party. The articles of association may provide for certain restrictions on the transfer, such as the need to obtain consent from the other partners and/or a right of first refusal on the part of the other partners. The transfer of shares in the company is a basic transaction (*Grundlagengeschäft*). It requires the consent of all partners in the company if the articles of association do not provide for a majority vote on the transfer of shares. If the articles of association do provide for a majority requirement, this must be specified in sufficient detail in the articles (*Bestimmtheitsgrundsatz*). The consent to the transfer may either be granted from the outset in the articles of association or *ad hoc* by way of a shareholders' resolution. It is also possible that all shares in the GmbH & Co. KG (eg, the shares of the limited partners and the shares in the general partner) are transferred to a single person. In this case, the KG would collapse, as it is always the case that at least one general and one limited partner are required in this regard. The transfer of shares by limited partners must be registered with the commercial register.[29] As regards the liability of the acquiring party,

29 *Handelsgesetzbuch* (HGB) (German Commercial Code) 1897, s162, para. 3 (FRG).

it must be stipulated in the transfer agreement that the contributions towards the KG already made by the transferor also count for the acquiring party (*Sonderrechtsnachfolge*). This means that the liability of the acquiring party is then excluded, since the contributions made by the transferor are considered as contributions made by the acquiring party. Otherwise, the acquiring party would be personally and unlimitedly liable for the time period between becoming a limited partner and the registration of this fact in the commercial register. When transferring shares in a limited partnership, it should also be ascertained that the company accounts established for the limited partner share under the articles of association (profit account, loan account, etc) are part of the transaction as well. They are not transferred automatically by virtue of law to the buyer.

If the shares in the general partner (GmbH) are to be transferred, the same regulations as those outlined under Section 179 *et seq.* apply. In particular, the transfer of the shares in the GmbH calls for the notarial form. This also applies to the establishment of the obligation to transfer the shares in the GmbH. If only those shares held by a limited partner are meant to be transferred, the transfer thereof does not demand the notarial form. Only when the GmbH & Co. KG is intended to be transferred as a whole (eg, shares in the general partner and the shares held by the limited partners), does the notarial form requirement with regard to the shares in the GmbH typically also cover the transfer of the shares in the KG.[30]

C. *Publikumsgesellschaft* (publicly owned company)

307. Introduction

A *Publikumsgesellschaft* is also referred to as a 'mass KG' (*Massen-KG*). This describes its main characteristic, which is namely to grant an unlimited or very high number of limited partners access to the KG to collect equity. The *Publikumsgesellschaft* is also often chosen by limited partners for tax purposes, since the intention of many mass KGs is to generate losses which are attributed to the limited partners. However, according to the jurisprudence and applicable law a limit has been set with regard to the attribution of such losses to the (limited) partners. The number and economic significance of such *Publikumsgesellschaften* has therefore decreased in recent years.

---

30 *Gesetz betreffend die Gesellschaft mit beschränkter Haftung* (GmbHG) (Act on Limited Liability Companies), 1892, s15, para. 4 (FRG).

308. Establishment and admission

The *Publikums KG* is usually established as a GmbH & Co. KG, even though other forms are legally admissible. With regard to the establishment of a GmbH & Co. KG in the form of a *Publikumsgesellschaft*, the usual requirements as outlined above under Section 300 apply.

Both the admission to a limited partnership and the transfer of a share in a KG require a transfer agreement which is usually fully negotiated between the company and the limited partner wishing to join the company, or the transferor and the transferee of the share in the KG. With a *Publikumsgesellschaft*, things are slightly different. The intention behind the company is that as many limited partners as possible or as many as are required to fulfil its economic purpose join the company. The limited partners usually only have a financial interest in the company and are not interested or allowed to have influence on the management thereof. Thus, admission is made on the basis of standard agreements. Regarding the admission process, the company is usually represented by the general partner (the GmbH) when entering into the admission agreements. In this regard it also acts on behalf of the other partners of the company. The articles may, however, also provide that the KG itself or a trustee may enter into the admission agreement. The occurrence of an error when entering into the admission agreement usually gives the limited partner a right to extraordinarily terminate his or her membership with immediate effect.

The articles of association are also not negotiated with the limited partners and constitute a standard agreement. The courts, however, do at least submit such standard articles to an assessment under the aspect of good faith.[31]

309. Articles of association

As outlined under Section 305, the articles of association of a 'regular' GmbH & Co. KG may only be amended by a majority vote if the subject matters which may be changed in the articles are explicitly and specifically set forth in the articles themselves. This rule does not apply to a *Publikums KG*. It is accepted by the courts that amendments to the articles of association may always be made by a majority vote. That is not only the case if the articles explicitly provide that changes to the articles may be made by way of a majority vote. In some cases it is also recognised that even if the

---

31 *Bürgerliches Gesetzbuch* (BGB) (Civil Code) 1900, s242 (FRG).

articles state the opposite, namely that an amendment of the article requires a unanimous vote, such a clause will not be able to withstand the good faith assessment undertaken by the courts. It has also been acknowledged in the jurisprudence that a clause in the articles in which a capital increase without limits is possible by way of a majority vote is permissible if there is either no obligation for the limited partners to participate in the capital increase in question or when a limited partner who is not willing to participate in the capital increase has the right to terminate his or her membership. The reason behind such rules is that otherwise a *Publikums KG* with a large and in many cases frequently changing number of limited partners would otherwise be unable to operate effectively.

About the authors

Dr Alexander Schröder-Frerkes
Partner, Germany, Bird & Bird LLP
alexander.schroeder-frerkes@twobirds.com

Until 2014, Alexander Schröder-Frerkes served as managing partner for Germany, head of the Global Corporate/M&A Group and member of the Global Management Board of the firm. Prior to joining Bird & Bird, he was a member of the managing board of a well-known major German law firm. From 1993 to 1994 he worked as a foreign associate in the Chicago office of a highly regarded global US-based law firm. Dr Schröder-Frerkes advises international and domestic clients on M&A, private equity and venture capital transactions, MBOs, group valuations, restructuring and reorganisations, as well as joint ventures. He has considerable experience in corporate/M&A transactions, having advised on various major transactions and is highly regarded for his work in this area. The *JUVE Handbook German Commercial Law Firms 2010–2019* acknowledges him as "one of the most recommended lawyers" and *The European Legal 500 Directory* describes him as "impressive" and of "M&A calibre". In addition, Dr Schröder-Frerkes is Chairman of the American Chamber of Commerce (AmCham) for the chapter of North Rhine-Westphalia and member of the board of the Deutsches Rotes Kreuz Niederrhein (Red Cross). Furthermore, he is a member of a number of Advisory Boards of German companies, including Düsseldorf Airport. In 2010 he was awarded the German Federal Cross of Merit (*Bundesverdienstkreuz*) by the former President of the Federal Republic of Germany, Horst Köhler, for his contributions to the German-American relationship.

Dr Armin Göhring
Senior legal counsel, HENSOLDT Holding Germany GmbH
armin.goehring@hensoldt.net

Prior to his time at HENSOLDT, a world-leading manufacturer of sensor solutions and other defence and security electronics, Armin Göhring worked as a corporate M&A lawyer at Bird & Bird LLP and Hengeler Mueller in Düsseldorf. Dr Göhring was admitted to the Düsseldorf bar in 2004 and studied law at the universities of Würzburg and Geneva. Dr Göhring underwent his training as a junior associate at a Bavarian Higher Regional Court and at major international law firms in Frankfurt/Main and Paris. In 2003 he obtained his Doctor of Law degree (University of Würzburg). In 2004, Dr Göhring was awarded a Master of Laws (LLM) by the University of Chicago Law School. In 2015, he was seconded for six months to the legal department of a world-leading aircraft and defence manufacturer in Southern Germany.

About Globe Law and Business

Globe Law and Business was established in 2005, and from the very beginning, we set out to create law books which are sufficiently high level to be of real use to the experienced professional, yet still accessible and easy to navigate. Most of our authors are drawn from Magic Circle and other top commercial firms, both in the UK and internationally.

Our titles are carefully produced, with the utmost attention paid to editorial, design and production processes. We hope this results in high-quality books which are easy to read, and a pleasure to own. All our new books are also available as ebooks, which are compatible with most desktop, laptop and tablet devices. We have recently expanded our portfolio to include a new range of journals and Special Reports, available both digitally and in hard copy format, and produced to the same high standards as our books.

We'd very much like to hear from you with your thoughts and ideas for improving what we offer. Please do feel free to email me at sian@globelawandbusiness.com with your views.

Sian O'Neill
Managing director
Globe Law and Business
www.globelawandbusiness.com

www.ingramcontent.com/pod-product-compliance
Ingram Content Group UK Ltd.
Pitfield, Milton Keynes, MK11 3LW, UK
UKHW021837150926
8656IPUK00004B/33